The Best of The Great Trail, Volume 1

The Best of
The Great Trail

Volume 1

Newfoundland to Southern Ontario
on the Trans Canada Trail

MICHAEL HAYNES

GOOSE LANE

Edited by Alison Hughes.
Cover and interior photographs by Michael Haynes unless otherwise indicated.
Cover image: Celtic Shores Coastal Trail.
Maps prepared by Todd Graphic, www.toddgraphic.ns.ca.
Cover and page design by Julie Scriver.
Printed in China by MCRL Overseas Printing.
10 9 8 7 6 5 4 3 2 1

We acknowledge the generous support of the Government of Canada, the Canada Council for the Arts, and the Government of New Brunswick.

Goose Lane Editions
500 Beaverbrook Court, Suite 330
Fredericton, New Brunswick
CANADA E3B 5X4
www.gooselane.com

Library and Archives Canada Cataloguing in Publication

Haynes, Michael, 1955-, author
    The best of the great trail / Michael Haynes.

Contents: Volume 1. Newfoundland to Southern Ontario on the Trans Canada Trail.
ISBN 978-1-77310-000-5 (v. 1 : softcover)

1. Trans Canada Trail--Guidebooks.
2. Canada--Guidebooks. 3. Guidebooks.
I. Title.

FC38.H39 2018   917.104'7
C2018-901161-0

Contents

Foreword

Not to be hyperbolic, but The Great Trail is a miraculous achievement!

Stretching over 24,000 kilometres and linking 15,000 communities, this Trail showcases the natural beauty, rich history, and enduring spirit of our land and its peoples.

It began as a bold dream in 1992, when Bill Pratt and Dr. Pierre Camu had the visionary idea to create a continuous trail that would connect all of us, from coast to coast to coast.

This simple and brilliant idea inspired countless Canadians to build something incredible for their children and grandchildren. So many volunteers and partners have helped to develop and maintain the Trail. They have generously donated money, everything from $5 to $5 million to make it happen. It has been an enormous nationwide effort inspired by a big, iconic vision.

The Great Trail is a network of trails that is owned, managed, and operated by our partners, each one highlighting that region's unique landscape and history. From the wild Atlantic coastline of Cape Spear to the historic, picturesque town of Niagara-on-the-Lake, this book features many of these sections, just waiting to be discovered.

In New Brunswick, you can explore the Fundy Trail Parkway, a challenging but rewarding hike along jagged cliffs and through mixed forest. There is Le P'tit Train du Nord, a long-distance path through the Laurentians that epitomizes the "joie de vivre" of Quebec. In Toronto, the Waterfront Trail winds between the skyscrapers of downtown and the serenity of Lake Ontario. My own favourite section of The Great Trail runs along the beautiful Niagara River and I love walking it with my dogs. It is good for my physical and mental health.

Now, after twenty-five years, The Great Trail stretches from coast to coast to coast – knowing that makes me euphoric! Of all the things I have done in my life, with the exception of my family, nothing makes me prouder than helping to create The Great Trail. However, this is just the beginning of our journey. Trans Canada Trail, the non-profit organization that supports the Trail's development, will continue to protect and nurture this grand project for generations to come.

I hope that you also take pride in Canada's national trail, as you find it, use it, and treasure it.

Valerie Pringle, Co-Chair
Trans Canada Trail Foundation Board

Michael Haynes at the end of day six on the Traversée de Charlevoix hike.

Why This Book?

No trail project has captured the Canadian public's imagination quite like The Great Trail. From its inception as the Trans Canada Trail (TCT) in the early 1990s, the vision of a connected pathway crossing Canada has both fascinated the average person and dominated the entire trail development community. In addition, almost from the first public introduction of the concept, individuals have been asking where it can be accessed. For more than two decades, public interest in The Great Trail has been significant and enduring, even when those curious are not particularly outdoor enthusiasts.

From its relatively modest, initial proposal to be a 5,000 km (3,100 mi) more-or-less direct path system stretching from the Atlantic to the Pacific Oceans, The Great Trail has expanded to become an intricate and complex web of trail, road, and water sections from east to west and north to south, totalling approximately 24,000 km (14,900 mi). Its route has changed constantly, almost from its very first days, as new communities clamoured to be added and originally intended alignments have been abandoned. Further, with the recent addition of extended road and water linkages to span gaps, The Great Trail has never been identical from one year to the next. With a system so vast and disparate, and with the trail being an amalgam of hundreds of separate community components, it probably never will be.

In order to at least partially satisfy public curiosity about The Great Trail, I wanted to provide a guidebook profiling it. However, both from a theoretical and practical standpoint, attempting to describe the entire and ever-changing route seemed impractical. Besides, and let's be completely honest here, how many of us are prepared to commit five to six years walking, biking, canoeing, or otherwise traversing by muscle power alone the entire 24,000 km (14,900 mi)? Not me! Most of us – although we might have the enthusiasm safely expressed while sitting in our cozy homes or on a particularly enjoyable day hike – have neither the time nor the skills. There are people who travel the entire route of course, but it will never be more than a handful.

If not the entire route, then why not profile a sample? Instead of including everything, such as the 8,500 km (5,280 mi) of The Great Trail that is currently on roads and highways, why not simply pick and recommend some of the trail's finest and most interesting sections?

Choosing the "Best"

Once I had decided that I would review and feature some, but not all, portions of The Great Trail, I had to determine how to select those sections. Several concerns arose immediately. I had not, for example, traversed the entire trail myself. Every year, the announced length of the trail was longer and more varied, and even its original distance was daunting to contemplate. How could I know which sections were worthwhile, let alone superior? How could I choose what to include and what to exclude?

Furthermore, when I was already advanced in my planning, the TCT Foundation began including multiple, long stretches of water routes. Although I do canoe and kayak, my principal forms of recreation are walking and biking. Would I canoe the Lake Superior shoreline? Finally, nearly 8,500 km (5,280 mi) of the designated route of The Great Trail is currently located on roads and often for quite lengthy stretches. While many of these provide access to exceptional scenery – particularly in Northern Canada – few people would define or accept a road as their ideal choice as a "trail."

So I eventually decided that this book would profile neither water routes nor road connections but be restricted to off-road land pathways. Doing so would subtract approximately 15,500 km (9,630 mi) from consideration, routes that were neither desirable – roads – nor connected to the original five core uses: walking, biking, horseback riding, cross-country skiing, and snowmobiling. That still left between 8,000 and 9,000 km (4,970 and 5,590 mi) of trail from which to choose, and this seemed to me a much more manageable figure.

Once I had the type of experience selected, I quickly decided that I wanted to include at least one selection from every province and to attempt to somewhat balance the number of choices I made both between and within each region. I excluded the northern territories, regretfully, because almost the entire length of Great Trail there was found on either roads or rivers. (Maybe in a future Volume 3?) I did not want to select all mountain and coastal sections simply because these might be my personal preferences but to highlight the best and most interesting in every part of the country. As I was to discover, prairie grasslands might at first glance lack the overpowering presence of the Rocky Mountains or the Atlantic Ocean, yet they soon would reveal themselves to be in no way deficient in either beauty or grandeur.

But how does one define the "best"? Might it be the most scenic? The most remote? The longest wilderness hike? The most rugged terrain? Choosing these factors as selection criteria might seem reasonable to experienced outdoors people but what about average or new Canadians, who might not have any experience in the outdoors at all, yet still want to explore The Great Trail? Maybe the "best" for them might be the closest or most accessible. Further, within a few hours' drive of every major Canadian city, there are usually sections of The Great Trail. Indeed, in many communities it passes through the centre of the urban area.

Fortunately, a workable solution was available. When I was the Executive Director of the Nova Scotia Trails Federation—the partner that coordinated provincial development of what would become The Great Trail—I frequently received telephone calls and emails from individuals wanting to know where they could access the Trail and what parts I could recommend. Over the years, I identified those places where I was confident that visitors would enjoy their Atlantic Canada experience. My colleagues in the other provinces received similar requests for recommendations and eventually developed their own informal list of favourites. So, instead of me picking the "best" sections of The Great Trail in other provinces, I contacted the provincial trail coordinators and asked them.

This did not completely relieve me of choosing, however. Although some of my colleagues provided exactly the number of recommendations that I requested—Alberta, for example, furnished the eight trail selections for which I asked—others did not. Quebec suggested twenty-five, and two provincial trail associations hesitated to provide any recommendations until almost the last moment. In one western Canadian province, I only received the final suggestions when I had driven across the country and arrived there.

Interestingly, each association defined "best" slightly differently. Several favoured remote and rugged trails often used only by hikers, which suited my tastes perfectly! Others preferred cycling pathways, sometimes through Canada's largest metropolitan centres; frankly, I probably looked somewhat out of place on these. Still others attempted to provide a representative and varied mixture of experiences spread geographically between urban, suburban, and rural. These I often found quite interesting as I moved from one type to the other and attempted to understand what each revealed about its province. No two provinces seemed to classify "best" in quite the same way.

Eventually, I received recommendations from every provincial trail association. As a result, I changed my original plan from writing one book, comprised of fifty route selections covering the entire Great Trail, to producing a two-volume work that would include sixty sections of The Great Trail, thirty in the east and thirty in the west.

In addition, I had originally planned to limit each route profiled to between 10 km and 25 km (6 mi and 15 mi). This, I thought, would give hikers options ranging from an easy two- to three-hour ramble to an ambitiously long day of hiking. Perhaps unsurprisingly, nearly every provincial association made suggestions exceeding my limit, often recommending much longer routes that they insisted were essential. On the other hand, there were also a few routes that were shorter than I wanted but so scenic that they could not be excluded, though fewer of these. As a result, there is a wide variation in route distances for the trail sections profiled in this book, ranging from an easy 5.5 km (3.4 mi) route to a rather more challenging 102 km (63.4 mi) one.

Is this the very "best" of The Great Trail? That will always be debated, as we all have our favourites. What I can promise is that I have consulted the people building the trail in each province and have used their judgement as the foundation of my eventual selections. When I finished hiking and biking all the sections recommended by the various provincial trail associations – most in both directions – it turned out that I had travelled slightly more than 1,600 km (990 mi) of The Great Trail, including more than eighteen percent of the 8,500 km (5,280 mi) of the off-road land routes. I trust that you will enjoy your exploration of these Great Trails as much as I did mine.

***

Where The Great Trail begins and ends is a matter of continuous debate. Both St. John's, NL, and Victoria, BC, boast a "Kilometre Zero" marker. In order to respect both perspectives, I decided to profile the routes in eastern Canada from east to west, beginning in Newfoundland and ending in southern Ontario. The routes in western Canada – found in *The Best of The Great Trail Volume 2: British Columbia to Northern Ontario on the Trans Canada Trail* – are profiled from west to east.

Trail Signage

The Great Trail is a collection of hundreds of national, provincial, and municipal park trails, along with many others developed and maintained by community volunteer groups. In addition, thousands of kilometres of The Great Trail are currently located either on road or water. Each trail management authority makes its own decision on how many Trail signs it posts in addition to local signs, and some have elected to display none at all.

As of the writing of this text in November 2017, there are three main designs of Great Trail symbols (see page 23). The brown, red, and green, rigid maple-leaf logo with the Trans Canada Trail Sentier Transcanadien wording was the original design and is still found on many trails, especially those that were completed before the mid-2000s.

The second design, a wavy blue, yellow, and green, stylized maple leaf, was introduced after 2010 and is found on more recently developed routes. The third is the new design for The Great Trail and only started appearing on sections in 2016. It will gradually replace the other markers. However, be prepared for any of these three designs, or even – on some routes – none of them at all.

Discovery Panels

Thanks to a generous donation from the Stephen R. Bronfman Foundation, an ambitious program of installing distinctively designed interpretive panels throughout the entire length of the Trail was instituted in the late 1990s. More than two thousand of these bilingual panels were funded and distributed to the various local trail managers for placement where they wished.

Known as discovery panels, these colourful boards include text and photographs or artwork and mostly profile flora and fauna commonly found along a pathway. More occasionally, they detail distinctive geological, historical, and cultural features. I found the discovery panels linked individual trail segments to the national route even more than the trail signage did.

One-hundred-and-seventy different topics are featured on the panels that were designed with the assistance of various Canadian museums. In addition to these standard discovery panels, trail groups were permitted to install their own unique ones, following the official format. They are few in number, and each one is unique, so encountering one makes for a pleasant surprise.

Many trails have their own interpretive boards in addition to discovery panels. When I refer to them in this book, I call them interpretive panels.

Trail Pavilions

Located in every province and territory of Canada are special pavilions that recognize donors. From its inception, individuals could buy a metre/yard of the then TCT and have their names displayed on one of these structures. The pavilions range in size from single-panel displays to large, three-sided edifices, but each is capped with a distinctive steepled, red, metal roof.

Routes in this book where trail pavilions can be found include: Wreckhouse Trail, Celtic Shores Coastal Trail, Lachine Canal, Ottawa River Pathway, Toronto Waterfront, Niagara River Pathway, and Hamilton to Brantford.

Trail Etiquette

With few exceptions, the entire length of The Great Trail is a shared-use pathway, something which requires all users to be aware of and follow basic rules of courtesy to enhance the safety of themselves and everyone else. A detailed code of conduct is usually posted at trailheads, and many other excellent ones can be found online with a simple search.

Generally, follow the rule that "wheels yield to heels." Cyclists should slow when passing oncoming walkers, ringing a bell when overtaking from behind. Both hikers and cyclists yield to horseback riders and should defer to the rider's judgement as horse behaviour can be unpredictable. (Once, while cycling, I had to stop, dismount, and remove my helmet before a horse would sidle past me.)

On some routes in Newfoundland and Nova Scotia, ATVs are permitted. Although they should defer to walkers and cyclists, I found it easier just to stop, stand aside, and let them pass. In addition, most of The Great Trail is a thin ribbon of public right of way, bordered by private land. The easiest way to respect landowners is to stay on the trail and only leave it at designated access points.

How to Use This Book

You can begin your exploration of these routes with the "Trails at a Glance" table. This provides key information on each of the thirty routes in eastern Canada, including the trail name and route distance, the permitted uses, cellphone coverage, whether dogs are allowed, and if there are fees to use the trail. Finally, it lists the pages in this book where a full route description can be found.

Trail names: In most cases, I use the official name of the trail or trails on which all, or most of, the profiled route is found. Rarely does the route encompass the complete length of the named trails. For other routes, I use prominent features such as the names of the communities where they start and finish (e.g., Waubaushene to Midland) or a geographic reference (e.g., Cape Spear) to name the route.

Distance: The one-way trip distance in kilometres and miles, rounded up to the nearest tenth of a kilometre and mile. Double this distance should you intend to undertake the profiled route as a return trip.

Permitted uses: These are the uses either formally permitted or considered likely to occur on the route being profiled. Typically, that means hiking, bicycling (touring and mountain), horseback riding, inline skating, skateboarding, and ATVs or other off-highway vehicles during spring, summer, and the majority of the fall when the trail is not covered by snow. During the late fall, winter, and early spring, those times of the year when the trail is potentially covered by snow, the uses are snowshoeing, cross-country (Nordic) skiing, and snowmobiling or riding other motorized, winter vehicles. Many trails have official opening and closing dates for summer and winter uses, so check the trail website. Any item marked with an asterisk means that the use is not permitted throughout the entire distance but might be encountered along some sections of the profiled route.

Permitted Uses							
Walking	Biking	Horseback Riding	Inline Skating	ATV	Snowshoeing	Cross-country Skiing	Snowmobiling
✔	—	—	—	—	✔	✔*	—

Dogs: The majority of trails in this book, particularly those within national and provincial park properties, have strict rules about dogs. The index shows where there are no dogs permitted, dogs permitted on-leash, and dogs permitted off-leash. Please respect those without dogs and observe these regulations – and always "poop & scoop!" Whenever the rules vary for different sections of a route, I have highlighted the most restrictive rules and marked them with an asterisk (*).

Trail Fees and other charges: Several of the routes are either entirely located in provincial or national parks, or they pass through them. The parks often charge a daily visitor fee as do some of the other trails. For example, the Traversée de la Charlevoix is not a park trail, but there is a fee to use it, and a permit is required.

In some cases, such as the example that follows of Le P'tit Train du Nord, there is a fee associated only with certain uses. Since fees vary from park to park, season to season, and year to year, I have indicated with a dollar sign ($) where fees are required, and users must check ahead to determine the cost. Again, an asterisk beside the dollar sign indicates that fees apply to only a portion of the route or some uses.

In the example of Le P'tit Train du Nord, the profiled route is 43.5 km (27 mi) in length. Walking and biking are allowed throughout the entire trail length, and inline skating is permitted on sections. During the winter, snowshoeing is permitted in some areas but not in others, as are cross-country skiing and snowmobiling. Fees are charged and dogs are not permitted on any portion of the trail. Further details follow, such as where the trail is asphalt surfaced and that only cross-country skiers pay a fee in this case. Walkers, bicyclists, snowshoers, and inline skaters pay no fees to use the trail. Snowmobilers pay for a provincial permit to use all groomed trails.

P'tit Train du Nord	43.5 (27)	W, B, I*	S*, X*, Sm*	N	$*	207

THE TRAILS

Once you have selected a trail, turn to the page indicated. Every route starts with a description of the area and some background about the trail. This includes historical, natural, and geographical information, often in information sidebars, as well as some additional detail on its regulations or restrictions and a trail map. This is followed by:

Distance: the one-way trip distance in kilometres and miles.

Ascent and descent: the total ascent and descent of the profiled route in the direction with which I present it, measured in metres (feet). Reverse these figures if travelling the route in the opposite direction; double them if doing a return trip.

Map: a detailed map for each route, showing its path through the neighbouring terrain and key features identified in the text. These maps indicate nearby communities and main roads, as well as vital topographical information such as elevation and rivers.

Trail conditions: all the types of treadway – trail surface – that are encountered along the route profiled. Many pathways incorporate more than one surface type, such as a paved section when it passes through a community, although some of them often do so only for short distances. The possibilities are: asphalt (paved roadway, concrete sidewalk), crushed stone (gravel or limestone crusher fines), compacted earth (dirt road, former forest roadway), and natural surface (woodland footpath, rock, sand).

Cellphone coverage: indicates yes, no, or partial cellphone coverage on a route at the time when I traversed it. For example, the Traversée de Charlevoix is labelled partial because it has very bad cell reception overall but has numbered signs at many high points where there is cell reception. Please note that the coverage in some provinces, such as Newfoundland and Labrador, varies considerably depending upon the service provider. I used Bell Canada; consult your provider's coverage map if you use a different service.

Hazards: brief cautionary notes in one or two words describing the potential dangers on the trail. Some, such as road crossings, are certain to be met. Others, such as ticks and poison ivy, are known to occur along the route but can be avoided with caution. Still others, such as wildlife or coastal weather, are possible hazards that are location and season specific, the occurrence of which is likely unexpected. The hazards are:

- **cliffs:** When I list "cliffs" as a hazard, it is because that particular trail features a section with at least one high, vertical drop with no guardrails – and where you are usually a long way from help.
- **coastal weather:** On a sunny summer day, a walk alongside the ocean is one of the most relaxing experiences available. However, visit that same coastline when a northern gale is lashing it, and you might think that you are undertaking an Arctic expedition. There is often little to shield you from the full force of nature's power; discomfort is certain, and hypothermia a distinct possibility for those unprepared. Like alpine weather, coastal conditions can change rapidly and unexpectedly. Cyclists and hikers should take precautions.
- **high usage:** On a few of the routes, particularly those passing through Canada's major, metropolitan areas, the sheer number of people using the pathways is a significant hazard. Particular care must be taken by cyclists in these locations because many of the trail users are families, novices,

and others whose behaviour is unpredictable. Where so many people share the trail, reduced speed is the only correct response.

- **hunting:** In some cases, The Great Trail passes through areas where big-game hunting for bear, caribou, deer, or moose is permitted, usually during the fall.
- **isolated areas:** Two of the routes in this volume, the Gaff Topsails and the Traversée de Charlevoix, travel into some of the most remote regions of their provinces, far from any community or assistance. While trail users should always make adequate preparations and notify others of where they are going and when they should be expected to return, these two routes require particular thoughtfulness before undertaking them. Most people rarely venture so far into the backcountry.
- **mosquitoes:** Though some consider mosquitoes and blackflies a hazard, I consider them simply part of the Canadian landscape—unavoidable and inescapable. Expect to encounter them in all but the most urban routes; late spring and early summer are usually when they are at their worst.
- **poison ivy:** These skin-irritating plants are increasingly found along the edges of many trails and fields. Managed trails usually post warning signs, but as both poison ivy and other noxious plants such as giant hogweed are spreading and extending their range, they could be growing anywhere alongside the pathway. The best way to avoid poison? Stay on the path.
- **road crossings:** Most longer trails, particularly those that have been created on former railways, require multiple road crossings. Quite often these are over highways where the speed limits are 80 or 90 kph (50 or 55 mph), and in many cases, road and trail cross each other at a diagonal, making visibility difficult for both the trail user and approaching automobile traffic. Of all the hazards trail users face, this is actually the most certain and truly dangerous.
- **rugged terrain:** The majority of the paths profiled in this book are wide, level, and surfaced with crushed stone. Others, however, wander over the landscape regardless of hills, rocks, rivers, or any other obstacle. When I thought that the terrain was of more than average challenge, I've mentioned it.
- **ticks:** These are small eight-legged spider-related animals—not insects—that attach themselves to mammals and gorge on their blood. Unfed ticks are small, not much larger than a sesame seed, and they move around on the ground, grass, and bushes, waiting to attach themselves to any animal that brushes past. Although a tick bite is usually painless and causes only skin irritation and swelling, a small percentage of ticks carry serious diseases, including Lyme Disease. DEET on clothes is effective at repelling ticks, but other measures are also prudent. For more information on ticks, visit http://ncc-ccn.gc.ca/posts/tick-safety-in-the-capital and for

information about Lyme Disease visit www.phac-aspc.gc.ca/id-mi/tick-info-eng.php. Black-legged ticks are extending their range through much of southern Canada, so consult a provincial website for local up-to-date information.

- **wildlife:** Wildlife encounters tend to be what most people fear when hiking or biking on trails. Stories of bear attacks, though extremely rare, are usually gruesome and captivating. But in addition to bears, the wrong interaction with any wild animal can result in injury or death. For example, in 2013 in Belarus, a man was killed by a beaver! Nor are wild animals found only in the wilderness. Even in urban areas in Canada, coyotes, raccoons, and skunks can be found, so caution is always advisable. However, for the purposes of this book, I have only listed wildlife as a hazard where more aggressive large species such as bear, bobcat, and wolf are commonly known to roam. In *The Best of The Great Trail Volume 2: British Columbia to Northern Ontario on the Trans Canada Trail*, this list includes mountain lions, badgers, and rattlesnakes.

Permitted uses: a table showing what activities are officially permitted on all or part of the trail when there is snow or no snow.

Finding the trailhead: information on roads to trails, parking areas, and trail signage.

Trailhead: the GPS coordinates of both the start and finish of each profiled route. In addition, the community name most closely associated with each is mentioned next to the coordinates.

Observations: a very brief description of my impressions of each particular route. In almost every instance, I had never hiked or biked the trail before and, in many cases, had not even travelled to that part of the country. Many may find my thoughts on the route interesting and informative.

Route description: a hike or bike through the route. In every case, I describe junctions and landmarks from the perspective of someone following the trail in the direction I have indicated with distance markers. If travelling in the opposite direction, remember to reverse my bearings.

Further information: links for pertinent websites, such as the local trail group, the area's tourism association, associated parks or municipals, or anything else I thought useful.

Sidebars: boxed descriptions of some of the plants, animals, geological features, and human history that you might encounter on the various trails. These are intended to be brief samples to whet your curiosity about the terrain through which you are hiking/biking and to encourage you to learn more.

Trails at a Glance

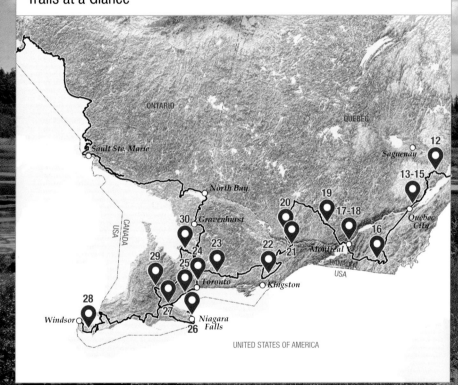

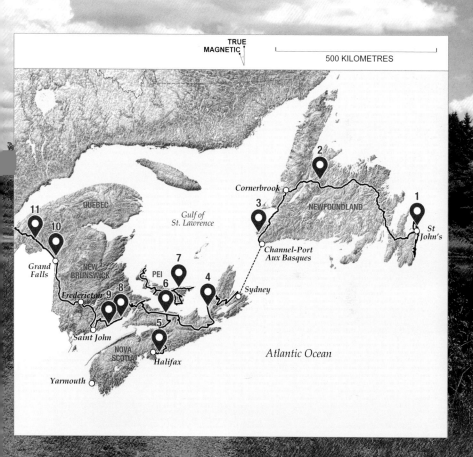

Trails at a Glance

Best of The Great Trail – Eastern Canada						
Trail Name	Length km (mi)	Permitted Uses (no snow)	Permitted Uses (snow)	Dogs	Fees	Page
Uses (no snow): W = Walk, B = Bike, A = ATV, H = Horseback Riding, I = Inline Skating Uses (snow): S = Snowshoe/Walk, X = Cross-Country Ski, Sm = Snowmobile * = Permitted on some sections of the route, but not all						
Newfoundland and Labrador						
1. Cape Spear	17 (10.5)	W	S	L*	N/A	27
2. Gaff Topsails	100.9 (62.7)	W, B, H, A	S, X, Sm	O	N/A	36
3. Wreckhouse Trail	23.8 (14.8)	W, B, H, A	S, X, Sm	O	N/A	47
Nova Scotia						
4. Celtic Shores Coastal Trail	90 (56)	W, B, H, A	S, X, Sm	L	N/A	58
5. Salt Marsh – Atlantic View	9.8 (6.1)	W, B, H	X	L	N/A	71
6. Tatamagouche	13.2 (8.2)	W, B, H, A	S, X, Sm	L*	N/A	78
Prince Edward Island						
7. Mount Stewart to St. Peters Bay	26.5 (16.5)	W, B	Sm	L*	N/A	89
New Brunswick						
8. Fundy National Park	18.9 (11.7)	W	S, X*	L	$	99
9. Fundy Trail	10.5 (6.5)	W, B	S, X	L	$	109
10. Grand Falls to Florenceville	82.2 (51.1)	W, B, H	S*, X*, Sm	L*	N/A	116
Quebec						
11. Petit Témis	28.2 (17.5)	W, B, I*	Sm	L	N/A	131
12. Traversée de Charlevoix	92.3 (57.4)	W, B*	X	N	$	139
13. Sentier des Caps de Charlevoix	8.8 (5.5)	W	S, X*	L	$	161
14. Sentier Mestachibo	13.1 (8.1)	W	S	L	N/A	169

15. Parcours des Anses	13 (8.1)	W, B, I	S, X	L	N/A	177
16. Eastman–Mont Orford	15.3 (9.5)	W, B	S, X	N*	$*	184
17. Canal de Chambly	18.8 (11.7)	W, B	S, X	L	N/A	192
18. Lachine Canal	21.8 (13.6)	W, B	S, X	L	N/A	199
19. Le P'tit Train du Nord	43.5 (27)	W, B, I*	S*, X*, Sm*	N	$*	207
20. Wakefield–Gatineau Park	10.5 (6.5)	W, B*	S*, X*	L*	N/A	216
Southern Ontario						
21. Ottawa River Pathway–West	25.6 (16)	W, B, I*	S, X	L	N/A	226
22. Cataraqui Trail	36.8 (23)	W, B, H	S, X, Sm	O	$*	237
23. Kawartha Trans Canada Trail	21.1 (13.1)	W, B, H*, I*	S, X, Sm*	L	N/A	246
24. Uxbridge Township	10.7 (6.6)	W, B, H	S, X	L	N/A	253
25. Toronto Waterfront	19.4 (12.1)	W, B, I	S, X	L	N/A	260
26. Niagara River Pathway	55.4 (34.4)	W, B, I*	S, X	L	N/A	268
27. Hamilton to Brantford	39.1 (24.3)	W, B, H*	S, X	L	N/A	281
28. Chrysler Canada Greenway	35.8 (22.2)	W, B, H*	S, X	L	N/A	291
29. Kissing Bridge Trailway	16.4 (10.2)	W, B	S, X	L	N/A	298
30. Waubaushene to Midland	22.8 (14.2)	W, B, I	S, X, Sm*	L	N/A	309

Legend for trail signage and map symbols

Signage for The Trans Canada Trail/The Great Trail:

original   c. 2010   c. 2016

Trail amenities:

 Bridge   Information   Rustic cabin

 Camping   Outhouse   Services (gas, $, etc.)

 Drinking water   Parking   Washroom

3. Wreckhouse Trail

NEWFOUNDLAND

1. Cape Spear

Everyone has their favourites, and one of mine is unquestionably the East Coast Trail (ECT) on the Avalon Peninsula of Newfoundland. This is a true hiking trail, a wandering footpath wending its way over and around challenging terrain features. What makes it even more remarkable is that it begins in St. John's, the largest city in the province, and instantly—instantly—becomes a trek as challenging and remote as anything on the Appalachian Trail.

The scenery is breathtaking. From the fantastic cragginess of Signal Hill to the lonely perch of Cape Spear, located on the easternmost point of North America and a National Historic Site of Canada, there is scarcely a moment when your gaze is not captured by panoramas of surpassing beauty. Can you detect that I liked it? Then go see for yourself; you won't be disappointed. One note—dogs are permitted off-leash on the East Coast Trail until you enter Cape Spear National Historic Site, after which they must be leashed.

1. Cape Spear Trail

TRUE
MAGNETIC

Contour Interval: 20M

2 KILOMETRES

Elevation

240

0

Metres

Signal Hill

St. John's

P

Cahil Point

St. John's Harbour

Fort Amherst Road

0.0

Beaver Pond

St. John's Bay

2

Duck Pond

4.6

5.9

Freshwater Bay

Freshwater Bay Pond

Spriggs Point

7.5

1

Deadman's Bay

Blackhead Point

Cape Spear

Cape Bay

Blackhead

P

11.4

Blackhead Road

15.0

17.0

CAPE SPEAR NATIONAL HISTORIC SITE

300
Metres
0
Kilometres   2   4   6   8   10   12   14   16   17

1. Cape Spear

Distance: 17 km (10.5 mi) – one way
Ascent: 672 m (2,205 ft)
Descent: 602 m (1,975 ft)

Trail conditions: asphalt, crushed stone, natural surface
Cellphone coverage: partial
Hazards: cliffs, coastal weather

Permitted Uses							
Walking	Biking	Horseback Riding	Inline Skating	ATV	Snowshoeing	Cross-country Skiing	Snowmobiling
✔	—	—	—	—	✔	—	—

Finding the trailhead: Your walk begins from a parking area on the Fort Amherst Road, overlooking the Prosser's Rock small boat dock and the entrance to St. John's Harbour at The Narrows. A large sign cautions that there is no parking beyond this spot.

Trailhead: 47°33'52.7" N, 52°41'16.9" W (Start – St. John's)
47°31'12" N, 52°37'24.7" W (Finish – Cape Spear)

Observations: I hiked this with Adrian Tanner, a founding Board Member of the East Coast Trail Association, before the group had formally agreed to associate with The Great Trail. We had an enjoyable scramble up and down the rugged terrain, but I had to abandon Adrian at the start of the ominously named "Deadman's Bay" section before we finished. However, he was there to meet me when I arrived at Cape Spear, having been given a lift by a kindly local.

I found this to be a surprisingly challenging ramble and was pleased that we had parked a car at either end. I could not have managed the return walk on the same day. Yet I would not have missed it, and this is one of the few routes in this book that I would drop everything to hike again.

Route description: From the parking area, walk up the road. Signal Hill looms over The Narrows on its opposite side, and there is a large rock face on your right. You pass a few houses and a barrier at 375 m/yd before reaching the official start of the East Coast Trail (ECT) at 500 m/yd. There are a number of directional and distance signs here. One says that Cape Spear is 15.3 km (9.5 mi) distant; another one states that Cappahayden is 215 km (133.6 mi) further!

Almost from the instant you cross the little bridge connecting the road to the footpath, the trail climbs. Moreover, the ground is rocky, and the grade is steep. In the next 450 m/yd, you climb more than 100 m (328 ft). The reward, initially, is the superb view back to Signal Hill. By 1 km (0.6 mi), you are almost as high up as the tower of the National Historic Site and have views of the impressive rock formations between it and the Atlantic Ocean.

Although trees surround you when you start the climb, as you ascend, the landscape becomes one of barren rock and low vegetation with scattered clusters of spruce huddling in hollows. One interesting feature as the trail becomes mostly rock surfaced is that the trail markers are mostly at ground level, bolted into the sandstone, siltstone, and conglomerate.

At 1.3 km (0.8 mi), another perspective is gained and a particularly grand one. The trail arrives at a viewing point at the edge of a very steep slope. Signal Hill is still close and the urban area of St. John's is beginning to come into view behind you. Ahead to the left, most of the jagged shoreline that you eventually hike is revealed. Freshwater Bay and Deadman's Bay lie far below, and in the distance, the small bump that is the Cape Spear Lighthouse sits barely visible on the most far-off scrap of land. Pray for a clear day when you hike because this vista must be seen.

The route continues along a barren crest overlooking Freshwater Bay. To the left are the Atlantic Ocean and the serrated coastline, where waves ceaselessly pound. To the right, there are rocky knolls with small ponds scattered in the troughs between them. The trail overlooks several, and at 2.2 km (1.4 mi), it passes a sign naming one as Soldiers Pond.

A small bridge crosses the outflow, after which the trail turns right and climbs a short staircase. Informal paths are found throughout the barrens; the main trail should be easily distinguished among them. Wherever there are trees, there may be white markers fixed to some; these are route indicators.

This delightful walk along the roof of the ridge continues, crossing small wet areas on narrow boardwalks called "puncheons" and having frequent exceptional views. At 4.5 km (2.8 mi), the trail passes a sign for Duck Pond. The path has begun to descend before reaching the pond, but just past, it turns sharply left and within 150 m/yd becomes a plummet.

4.6 km (2.9 mi) After the pleasant amble on the rolling, open barrens, this is unremittingly steep. The trail follows a tapered declivity etched by a tiny creek. It is rough and rock strewn with several boulders interposing and is cloaked by thick vegetation, including some very tall trees. This is by far the most challenging section of this walk and requires patience and care to traverse. In addition, as you descend, you lose cell coverage. There is limited or no cellphone coverage between 4.5 km (2.8 mi) and 11 km (6.9 mi).

East Coast Trail (ECT)

In 1994, a dedicated group of volunteers opened a 25 km (15.5 mi) stretch of hiking trail on the east coast of the Avalon Peninsula. With little government support initially, the newly formed East Coast Trail Association managed to open 220 km (136.7 mi) by 2001, incorporating the visually stunning landscape between St. John's and Cappahayden.

In 2003, the East Coast Trail (ECT) from Cape Spear to Placentia was officially designated as part of the National Hiking Trail. In 2012, *National Geographic* named the ECT one of the ten best adventure destinations in the world. Nor has this ambitious group finished; in 2015, they officially reached 300 km (186.4 mi) of opened pathway, constructed to international standards, and more is planned. In 2016, the ECT welcomed The Great Trail (then Trans Canada Trail) to share the footpath between St. John's and Cape Spear.

The forest hides your gaze from anything other than your immediate surroundings until almost the bottom of the hill. Though still 15 to 20 m/yd above the water, at 5.5 km (3.4 mi), the trail arrives on the bank of Freshwater Bay. Your route is to the right, following the shoreline and gently dropping to sea level by the time it reaches the cobble beach 400 m/yd later.

5.9 km (3.7 mi) The trail turns left and picks its way across the wide, stone beach that separates a pond to the right from the ocean. Although black-and-white posts mark the route, if you look closely, you may also notice that most of the stones in

the path are smooth topped. Volunteers patiently placed them thus to ease the way across this broken terrain, and every winter or after each big storm – which happen with a certain frequency in Newfoundland – these volunteers return and replace the scattered pathway.

In addition to the rocks, there may be some metal scraps littering the beach. According to research on the Hidden Newfoundland website, this rusting detritus is what little remains of the SS *Thetis*, famous for rescuing the seven survivors of the Greely Arctic expedition in 1884. The cobble beach is 400 m/yd across, connecting to the trail where there is a small clearing and an informal campsite. Looking back to the ridge on the far side of Freshwater Bay, the steepness of the slope you descended is evident.

Naturally, the trail climbs again as soon as you quit the beach, but it is much more gradual than the rapid ascent from Fort Amherst. The terrain remains rocky, however. There are areas where it is level, though these are usually boggy and traversed on puncheons. Much of this section is also under forest canopy, so the viewpoint overlooking Freshwater Bay at 7.3 km (4.5 mi) is welcome. However, just 200 m/yd further, a short side trail to Spriggs Point yields far more impressive views, this time in the direction of Deadman's Bay.

7.5 km (4.7 mi) From here, the trail turns right nearly 180˚ and tracks along the clifftop coastline. Marvellous views of the serrated shoreline and nesting sea-birds are numerous, at least until you reach the Peggy's Leg sign at 8.5 km (5.3 mi). Shortly after this, the path begins to descend and moves into stands of densely packed white spruce. There are even places where the vegetation provides an overhead canopy, which is uncommon along the ocean's edge.

The trees bordering the trail are so thickly packed that the ocean can be distinctly heard but not seen through most of your trek around Deadman's Bay. There are a number of small bridges, puncheons, and boardwalks crossing frequent wet areas. At the look-offs at 9.4 km (5.8 mi) and 300 m/yd later, the ocean and coastline are visible, but these are rare breaks in the tree-lined barrier.

The hillside is often quite rocky as well, making walking challenging. At 10 km (6.2 mi), there is a stone walkway crossing a wet area, and there are several locations where stone staircases assist navigating short slopes. You finally emerge from the dense woods at Cliff Point at 10.5 km (6.5 mi) and within another 150 m/yd, you can sight the houses of the community of Blackhead in the distance.

The walk to the village is open on a footpath clearly etched into the coastal mosses and plants. It is also descending, mostly quite gently though with occasional short, steep pitches. Somewhere along here, your cell coverage should return.

⚲ **11.4 km (7.1 mi)** The trail comes into Blackhead where there is a modest ECT trailhead parking area. A directional and distance sign states that the section just completed is called the Deadman's Bay Path. Cross the new small bridge on the far side of the parking lot and then continue straight up the road. There is a directional and distance sign where the pavement ends, 200 m/yd from the beach.

The next section to Cape Spear is named the Blackhead Path. About 50 m/yd further, on gravel now, an arrow directs you left onto a footpath that plunges back into thick brush. This new footpath skirts some private property, making 90° left turns at its corners, and is often bordered by sturdy fences.

At 12.1 km (7.5 mi), the detour comes out of the forest and returns to the coastline where it reconnects with its original track. From here to the top of Blackhead Point, the trail remains in the open, climbing the hillside steadily but not steeply, offering increasingly impressive views of the coastline back towards St. John's. There are many informal side paths on this hillside so watch for the black-and-white posts that mark the main trail.

At 13.3 km (8.3 mi), a sign announces your arrival at the crest of this exposed headland. Some stone foundations are the sole evidence of human habitation. From here, not only are there views of some of the urban area of St. John's beyond Signal Hill, but Signal Hill Lighthouse glows white in the afternoon sun in the other direction.

The trail now descends the open slope facing Signal Hill, which remains in sight for the rest of the walk. The path meanders to skirt frequent wet areas, or it crosses them on plank walkways known as puncheons or on the knotted roots of thickly packed white spruce. Several wooden staircases ease the descent.

At 14.5 km (9 mi), the path crosses over the remains of an old stone fence, after which it arrives alongside the shoreline.

The parking areas and throngs of people usually found at Cape Spear contrast starkly with the solitude enjoyed on the Deadman's Bay Path. Even though you probably encountered a number of walkers on the Blackhead Path, it was few compared to what may be found at Cape Spear on a sunny summer day. After a short stroll over grassy meadows, you'll see the road and trail converge at the entrance to the National Historic Site.

15 km (9.3 mi) The path reaches a narrow bridge crossing a culvert. An ECT sign indicates that you have finished the Blackhead Path. Once over the bridge, you are in Parks Canada property, but that need not be the end of the walk. A distinct track continues to the entrance parking lot and beyond. Follow it as it curves round the Cape close to the shoreline.

This is quite easy walking in comparison to the ECT. At 16 km (10 mi), the track links to a crushed-stone pathway and boardwalk that lead to a viewing platform and in 250 m/yd to the easternmost point in North America – or at least the furthest point safely possible to walk to where a high, chain-link fence prevents scrambling over the tidal rocks to go further.

The path climbs the hill, heading towards the lighthouses. But before it reaches them, it must first pass through the remains of a World War II coastal battery. There are interpretive panels, and short tunnels connect the positions. A staircase climbs to the "new" lighthouse (1955) and the Visitor Centre, where a final staircase climbs to the site of the original lighthouse (1835).

17 km (10.6 mi) At the top of the hill, the views are again impressive. Nothing but the Atlantic Ocean is to the east, but sightings of icebergs, whales, and rare seabirds are all possible. Beyond the lighthouse, the ECT beckons those who wish to continue. However, Parks Canada has wisely positioned its iconic Red Chairs on the hillside, facing west. Sit and enjoy the scenery; this section is completed.

Further Information:
Cape Spear National Historical Site: www.pc.gc.ca/en/lhn-nhs/nl/spear
East Coast Trail Association: www.eastcoasttrail.com
Hidden Newfoundland: http://www.hiddennewfoundland.ca/ss-thetis
Hike Canada/National Hiking Trail: www.nationalhikingtrail.ca
Visiting St. John's: www.stjohns.ca

Moose

One of the largest animals you may encounter in Canada's forests is the largest member of the deer family, the moose. Standing nearly 2 m (6.6 ft) high and weighing as much as 600 kg (1,300 lb), the moose is an imposing sight. Add the bull's antlers, which can be 2 m/yd wide, and a close encounter with a moose can be a heart-pounding experience.

Moose are usually quite timid around humans, but during the fall, rut bulls can become dangerously aggressive. In fact, I am more apprehensive of a moose encounter than I am of meeting an aggressive bear. Moose can be active throughout the day, but your best opportunity to see one is at dusk and dawn when they venture out of the bush.

2. Gaff Topsails

I have known the Executive Director of the Newfoundland T'Railway Association, Terry Morrison, for more than twenty years. And in all that time, there was one section of The Great Trail that he continually recommended: Gaff Topsails. When the railroad was operating, the Gaff Topsails was a legendary place of deep snows, wild winds, and passenger trains stuck in snowdrifts for days and running short on food. On his railroad website, David J. Gagnon quotes eminent railroader A.R. Penney, who wrote: "The direct route over the Gaff Topsail was feasible but it was certainly not practicable. The railway should never have been built there." (http://members.kos.net/sdgagnon/nfe.html) The same might now be said by the faint-of-heart about the trail.

With a gap of more than 85 km (52.8 mi) between permanently settled communities, this may be the most remote section of The Great Trail in eastern Canada. The area takes its name from a cluster of hills that arise from an otherwise flat landscape, jutting out of the Newfoundland Central Plateau, a region of bog, wetlands, and barrens. These 60 m to 120 m (197 ft to 393 ft) high protuberances are christened Main Topsail, Mizzen Topsail, Gaff Topsail, and Fore Topsail, the names of sails on ocean-going sailing ships.

This area is starkly beautiful, home to caribou and moose, and completely isolated. While the T'Railway goes up and over the plateau, the Trans-Canada Highway makes a long detour around it, adding 60 km (37.3 mi). The only buildings along the route are occasional cottages and clusters of one-room shacks, grandly labelled "Lodges," which are unoccupied through most of the year.

There are no services of any kind, and the T'Railway through here is used by jeeps and trucks, as well as ATVs. Cyclists might be able to complete this in one day but should be prepared for two and come equipped with several spare tires/tubes. Hikers should pack for a four-to-five-day excursion. Be prepared for changeable and extreme weather, even in summer.

2. Gaff Topsails – West

TRUE
MAGNETIC

Contour Interval: 50M

10 KILOMETRES

Howley
P ⚺ S
0.0

Sandy
Pond

Kitty's Brook

Kitty's
Brook
17.9 25.8

Chain
Lakes 38.9

Gaff
Topsail

The
Main
Brook

Goose
Pond

Quarry

59.0
60.3

Mary
March

Elevation
550

80

Metres

Hinds
Lake

500
Metres
0
Kilometres   20   40   60   80   100

2. Gaff Topsails

Distance: 100.9 km (62.7 mi) –
one way
Ascent: 733 m (2,405 ft)
Descent: 724 m (2,375 ft)

Trail conditions: compacted earth,
loose stone
Cellphone coverage: partial
Hazards: isolated area, wildlife

Permitted Uses							
Walking	Biking	Horseback Riding	Inline Skating	ATV	Snowshoeing	Cross-country Skiing	Snowmobiling
✔	✔	✔	—	✔	✔	✔	✔

Finding the trailhead: This route begins in the tiny — fewer than 250 people — village of Howley, 14 km (8.7 mi) from the Trans-Canada Highway down bumpy paved Highway 401. Howley is the last community before the Newfoundland T'Railway ventures into the wilderness of the Gaff Topsails and is a popular outdoors destination. Though small, lodging, a restaurant, and a grocery store can be found there.

Howley is also famous, or perhaps infamous, as the location where the first moose were released into Newfoundland in 1904. As any Newfoundlander can tell you, moose have adapted to their new home very, very well, and their robust population constitutes a serious hazard for nighttime drivers.

Trailhead: 49°09'58.2" N, 57°07'15.3" W (Start — Howley)
48°58'37.8" N, 56°02'11.1" W (Finish — Badger)

Observations: I biked this over two very tough days. During my time on the trail, I saw no other hikers or bikers and only a few ATVs. These always kindly stopped and asked me the same question: "Do you know where the h**l you are?" And with good reason; this part of the Newfoundland T'Railway is extremely remote, and there is no place to exit should you encounter problems. Walkers and cyclists do not usually travel here.

Most of the treadway is rocky and rutted, making biking slow and bouncy. Unfortunately, when the trail is not full of potholes, it is covered by heavy gravel, reducing your speed and vastly increasing the workload. I was pleased to have experienced this remote and visually striking part of Newfoundland, but very glad to finish it.

Route description: You begin your trek at a small park, which is dedicated to the original moose release. The T'Railway in this area is more like a road than a pathway, and in fact, you must drive on it to reach the parking area. Shaded beneath some birches are a few interpretive panels, picnic tables, benches, and garbage cans.

Head left; the trail passes through the community, next to a small pond, and across Highway 401 about 500 m/yd from the start. For the next 400 m/yd, the path is crowded by thick, bordering vegetation, but as soon as it crosses 11th Avenue, it widens into a track clearly heavily used by motorized traffic. In fact, this first section is a road used by commercial logging.

Now almost arrow straight, the trail moves into a region of wetland and peat bogs. The ground on either side is generally low, and ponds are common. There are many potholes, and these are filled with water, making cycling a bit of an obstacle course. In other places, heavy ballast—the large loose gravel used on railbeds—reduces speed to a crawl. At several points, it appears as if the entire trail is sinking into the bog. To the east, your objective beckons, a line of hills high above the trees bordering the pathway.

This area is austerely appealing but uniform and repetitive, interrupted only by Goose Brook at 6.4 km (4 mi), which is crossed by a 25 m/yd bridge. Other than the trail, a powerline, side trails, and roads, there are no signs of human structures, and the trail is straight for extended stretches with only minor elevation changes.

This begins to change at 11.9 km (7.4 mi) when you sight the first building since leaving Howley. I saw only three small cottages, each on a low wooded hill, although there is a sign that proclaims the area to be "Cumbyville." From here, the trail narrows and begins to climb in earnest. Higher ground borders the path, and there are even spots where the T'Railway becomes a creek bed. The trail also curves more often as it picks its way through the hillier terrain.

⦿ **17.9 km (11.1 mi)** A sign announces that you have arrived in Kitty's Brook, although I did not see the first cabin until 400 m/yd further. About the same time, the large body of water with the same name should be visible to the left. At 18.6 km (11.6 mi), there is a cluster of small cabins with cleared land around each. A few were even occupied when I passed through, and there was cell coverage from 16 km (10 mi) to 30 km (18.6 mi).

About 400 m/yd from these buildings, a large track branches off the T'Railway, and the main trail narrows considerably and becomes much rougher after this. It was so rutted and rocky that I walked my bike in some sections. The brook and trail parallel each other, and the boisterous brook seems quite loud in the otherwise silent forest.

At 22.2 km (13.8 mi), the trail crosses Kitty's Brook on a steel truss bridge, from which there are excellent views, and 150 m/yd later, another major track branches left. About 150 m/yd after that is a distinctive cottage, built around a former CN caboose. This tidy little lodge boasts two flag poles and a satellite dish. This is not the only rail car converted into a hunting cabin; there are two more about 1 km (0.6 mi) later.

When you cross the small bridge at 24.8 km (15.4 mi), notice the TCT markers affixed to it. These are some of the few signs found on the route, other than the locality indicators and some large yellow signs indicating distance. These are not entirely accurate but are fairly close.

Kitty's Brook on the right is more often heard than seen but is crossed again on a steel bridge at 25.8 km (16 mi). Just before reaching it, there is a metal pipe on the left, signed "spring water." It is cool and refreshing and I used it to refill all my bottles. Brook and trail remain close, though as you climb the rushing waters become calmer and begin moving more sedately. The fairly narrow ravine also begins to open up, particularly to the left, and the tops of nearby hills are bare of trees.

At an unsigned junction at 29.8 km (18.5 mi), where both branches appear equally well-used, keep left. As you climb, views of ponds – the Chain Lakes – are visible to the left. From an informal camping site and viewing platform at 30.9 km (19.2 mi), there are wonderful views of both the lakes and the surrounding hills.

Almost exactly 2 km (1.2 mi) later, a side trail to the left leads onto a barren hillside. If you can manage the diversion, climbing to the crest for the view is worthwhile. Expect the temperature to be considerably cooler than at Howley and windy as well. Just 250 m/yd beyond this point, a sign states you have reached Pond Crossing.

Not surprisingly, there are small pools at first with a cluster of twenty to thirty shacks about 400 m/yd from the sign. The trail passes between them, entering a fanciful area of ponds, bogs, and low rolling barren hills on which only a few scattered trees cling. Pond Crossing is more than 300 m/yd in elevation higher than Howley – and still not yet the highest point of the trek.

Small bridges span tiny, but lively, brooks and wet areas while the trail picks its way between hills and water. High hills no longer dominate the horizon, only the thick brush. Although this changes at 37.8 km (23.5 mi) when the trail turns sharply right, and the imposing bulk of Gaff Topsail towers above the surrounding ground.

Around 450 m/yd further, a sign affixed to a tree says "Welcome to the Gaff." However, first there are more ponds, and the cluster of cabins is not reached until crossing another small bridge.

38.9 km (24.2 mi) The trail arrives in the middle of the hunting and cottage centre of Gaff Topsail, an unpretentious cluster of mostly one-room shacks. Workers and their families once lived here year round to keep the railway functioning in

Newfoundland T'Railway

The railroad across Newfoundland was completed in 1898 and operated until 1988, after which the rails were removed and the 906 km (563 mi) line was abandoned. In 1997, the 883 km (549 mi) of the main line between Port aux Basques on the west coast and St. John's on the east coast were proclaimed as the Newfoundland T'Railway Provincial Park.

The volunteer-run T'Railway Association intends to develop the entire corridor as a multi-use, recreational trail. However, it has only been able to make improvements as funds have become available, and as a result, the condition of the pathway varies considerably. Near urban areas, the T'Railway is used mainly by pedestrians and cyclists, and usually is surfaced in crushed stone and supplemented with amenities such as benches, rest areas, and viewing platforms. In remote areas such as the Gaff Topsails, ATVs and snowmobiles are virtually the only users. The bridges are safe and decked, but you can expect the treadway to be rutted, potholed, and if surfaced usually covered with large gravel that is challenging to bike on.

winter. Today it is deserted for most of the year and houses seasonal hunters and fishers. There is no electricity and there are no stores; the only land access is the T'Railway.

The trail then works its way around the rocky promontory known as Gaff Topsail, which stands more than 100 m (328 ft) higher than the terrain around it. The T'Railway comes quite close to its base, and at 40.8 km (25.4 mi) there is a side trail (footpath) that ascends to its summit, another potential exploration for those still energetic. (Not me, I am afraid.)

The next section is among some of the most exposed of the entire route. There are few trees, and the nearby ground is low and seemingly all bog or brook, especially when crossing the bridge over Wolf Brook at 43.5 km (27 mi). To the left, the dome of the Main Topsail perches on the far horizon, while ahead, the Mizzen Topsail dominates the low landscape.

After "The Gaff," I found it difficult to tell if I was still climbing. At 44.1 km (27.4 mi), a sign on the right announces "Summit, Mile 328, Elev. 1554," but even after this, I thought that the trail continued to climb at least to the next cluster of houses at 46.3 km (28 mi). "House" is too grand a term for these tiny, one-room shacks though many boast ostentatious names such as Hunter's Choice Lodge, Maple Flint Lodge, and Saint Nick's. The trail makes a sharp curve left just before

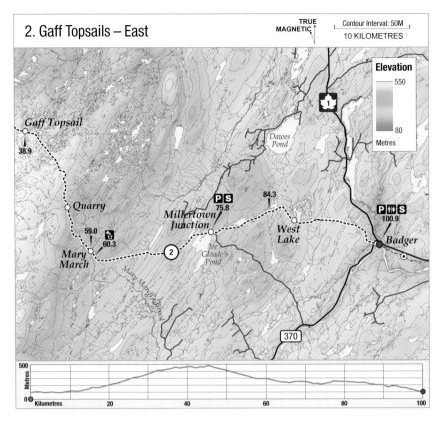

2. Gaff Topsails – East

TRUE
MAGNETIC

Contour Interval: 50M

10 KILOMETRES

Elevation

550

80

Metres

Gaff Topsail

38.9

Dawes
Pond

Quarry

P **S**
75.8

84.3

Millertown
Junction

West
Lake

P **S**
100.9

59.0

60.3

Joe
Gloade's
Pond

Badger

Mary
March

Mary Marc... Brook

370

500

Metres

0

Kilometres   20   40   60   80   100

the buildings, then afterwards enters a lengthy right turn, and an entirely new panorama opens up.

The trail distinctly descends now and works along a ridge as it drops. To the left and ahead is a wide vista of ponds and bogs, interspersed with ranks of trees and bordered by distant ridges of bulging hills. The highest prominence visible to the left is Misery Hill. The area is awe-inspiring both for its visual beauty and also for the remarkable quiet. It was so extraordinarily quiet, in fact, that I found myself holding my breath so as not to break it.

Several ATV tracks branch right, heading up a low ridge with seemingly the only dry ground nearby. The main trail continues to descend, crossing the steel Quarry Brook Bridge #2 at 50.9 km (31.7 mi) and Quarry Brook Bridge #1 less than 1 km (0.6 mi) later. Interestingly, both bridges are exactly 16.46 m/yd long.

Quarry, another cluster of ramshackle hunting shacks, is just past the halfway point of the trek. A former CN bunk car, now displaying a chimney and porch, is particularly quaint. On the left is the excavation that gave this place its name. The descent continues down the ridge slope with grand views of the taiga-like landscape.

As the elevation lowers, the trees sheltered by the ridge are taller and more densely packed. Even larch is found, supplementing the white and black spruce populating the bogs edges. At times, you'll have no view; then the trail enters an area where the bogs creep up to both sides of the rail embankment, and a wide vista opens up. There are many tiny streams draining to the lower lands on the left, but these are crossed on culverts. The next steel bridge is found on West Creek, at 58 km (36 mi). There is no cellphone signal from 55 km (34.2 mi) to 81.5 km (50.7 mi).

59 km (36.7 mi) The trail crosses Mary March Brook, a wide stream fed by all the small brooks passed while descending the long ridge. This is another through truss, one of only two in this section of the T'Railway. (The other was at Kitty's Brook.) Once across, there is a short climb with the pathway enclosed by a thick tree border.

After a fairly long, straight ascent, it curves left at 60.3 km (37.5 mi); there is a sign for a spring on the right about 10 m/yd from the main track. Shortly afterwards, another collection of derelict cabins lines the T'Railway for several hundred metres/yards. Along the way, there is a prominent sidetrack branching right.

At 61.9 km (38.5 mi), the trail makes a slight adjustment left and settles into the longest straightaway on the entire Newfoundland T'Railway. It also descends again into a river valley, so that the track extends onward towards the horizon like a prairie road. It ends at 67.2 km (41.8 mi) when it turns slightly right and crosses Patrick's Brook. As it descends, the tree border gives way to bogs near brook level.

Sadly, at this point in my travel I was overtaken by a storm with high winds, lashing rain, and visibility of maybe 10-20 m/yd. As a result, I noticed little of the next several kilometres, except that it was mostly downhill and that there were several side trails and numerous isolated cabins. By 72.5 km (45 mi), the cabins began to have identifying numbers affixed, and they began to increase in frequency. There were more side roads, more cottages, and the treadway actually was easier to ride because SUVs and trucks had swept most of the large ballast to the side. You might see some small lakes to the left. About 74.8 km (46.5 mi), a large lake appeared on the right through the mist.

75.8 km (47 mi) You arrive at the entrance to the Junction Lodge at Millertown Junction and in the middle of a number of buildings sitting on the shore of Joe Gloade's Pond. This is another small resort community but is populated year round and is connected to the remainder of the province by Highway 371 (dirt). Although there are no stores, there are several larger lodges where accommodations can be arranged and meals obtained.

Because the branch line to Buchans is separated from the main rail line here, and ATVs and other vehicles use the road and rail line indiscriminately, there are several potentially confusing side tracks in this little community. However, there are two main junctions, and each has a blue direction/distance marker. Badger is indicated as 27 km (16.8 mi) distant.

The next section was probably the most difficult. Once across Highway 401, at 76.8 km (47.8 mi), the trail was surfaced with large, loose gravel. My bicycle's forward progress was slowed almost to a walk, and several times I skidded when I encountered deeper piles. It was tough sledding. To add to the challenge, the route climbs almost 50 m (164 ft) from Millertown Junction to the high ridge cresting at Skull Hill. It dominates the right, while on the left, the trail passes Constance Lake and parallels a small brook for a considerable distance, providing a good opportunity to replenish water bottles. (Remember to filter/purify.)

84.3 km (52.4 mi) The trail arrives at a signed junction and a large gravel pit, which is likely the source of the fresh ballast covering the T'Railway. Keep straight; the good news is that the trail becomes much more rideable a short distance beyond the junction. By the time it reaches the bridge at Skull Hill Brook, 1.3 km (0.8 mi) later, it is much better.

At the next major junction, 87.5 km (54.4 mi), keep straight. Soon afterwards, the gravel ballast disappears and potholes return – most of them filled with water and as wide as the trail. From here until Badger, side tracks are so frequent that I do not mention them. Similarly, cottages are found near almost every lake or stream. Most are quite humble, but some – such as one beside Skull Pond – are newer and look similar to year-round residences.

Lake Bond is on the left when you cross the culvert over its brook at 89.8 km (55.8 mi). A rather prominent, rusted car sits beside the trail at 92.7 km (57.6 mi), and another gravel pit is less than 1 km (0.6 mi) further. The terrain alternates between bands of thick forest and open expanses of bog. When the trail passes through one of the last areas of extensive bog, around 95 km (59 mi), a range of hills comes into view directly ahead.

As the trail continues to descend, forested areas increase in frequency and size, restricting your view. About 96 km (60 mi), a powerline crosses the trail, after which there is more gravel covering the treadway for a short distance. Through the gaps, you might even notice some old rails peeking through. Yellow, distance signs reappear. (The first that I noticed was the km 4 marker.) By 97.5 km (60.6 mi), there are hardwoods among the trees lining the trail. Side trails increase in number, and by 98.8 km (61.4 mi), the buildings of Badger come into view. It crosses Memorial Drive, the first paved surface since Howley, at 100.2 km (62.3 mi). To the left is the large new building housing the fire department and municipal government.

For the remaining 700 m/yd, the T'Railway runs between Sunset Drive to the left and Church Street to the right with backyards abutting the trail. There is even a parallel walking path to the right, separated from the T'Railway by a fence.

100.9 km (62.7 mi) When you reach the next paved road crossing at Main Street, your trek ends. There are businesses nearby, and it is only 200 m/yd to the Trans-Canada Highway, where there are restaurants and a motel. Only 50 m/yd further along the trail is the bridge crossing the Exploits River – but I suspect you are ready to stop here.

Further Information:

Newfoundland T'Railway Council: www.trailway.ca
Newfoundland and Labrador Tourism: www.newfoundlandlabrador.com

3. Wreckhouse Trail

In Newfoundland and Labrador, the majority of The Great Trail is located on the former route of the Newfoundland Railway. Now named the T'Railway, this extends 883 km (549 mi) and connects St. John's on the east coast to the western terminus in Channel-Port aux Basques, where there is a ferry connection to mainland Canada.

The section of the T'Railway near Channel-Port aux Basques has been named the Wreckhouse Trail in honour of a particularly dangerous area of barrens where trains were regularly blown off the narrow-gauge railway. Even today when the winds are at their peak, large trucks can be tipped, and that section of the Trans-Canada Highway is closed.

I was exceptionally eager to ride the Wreckhouse Trail before I arrived, then subsequently disheartened at the rough condition of the T'Railway. Many of the potholes, filled with water, cannot be skirted because of the thick vegetation and are too deep to bike through. Nevertheless, I absolutely recommend this route to those unfazed by a mere "bumpy" ride, because the scenery is magnificent. For natural coastal beauty, this genuinely is one of the best on The Great Trail.

3. Wreckhouse Trail

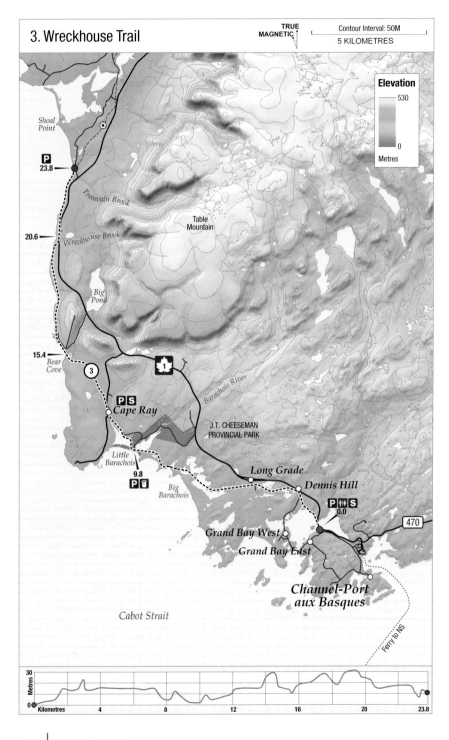

TRUE
MAGNETIC

Contour Interval: 50M
5 KILOMETRES

Elevation
530
0
Metres

Shoal
Point

P
23.8

Trainvain Brook

Table
Mountain

20.6

Wreckhouse Brook

Big
Pond

15.4

Bear
Cove

3

Barachois River

P S
Cape Ray

J.T. CHEESEMAN
PROVINCIAL PARK

1

Little
Barachois

9.8
P

Big
Barachois

Long Grade

Dennis Hill

P
0.0
S

470

Grand Bay West

Grand Bay East

Channel-Port
aux Basques

Cabot Strait

Ferry to NS

30
Metres
0
Kilometres   4   8   12   16   20   23.8

3. Wreckhouse Trail

Distance: 23.8 km (14.8 mi) – one way
Ascent: 145 m (476 ft)
Descent: 136 m (446 ft)

Trail conditions: asphalt, compacted earth, sand
Cellphone coverage: yes
Hazards: coastal weather, road crossings, wildlife

Permitted Uses							
Walking	Biking	Horseback Riding	Inline Skating	ATV	Snowshoeing	Cross-country Skiing	Snowmobiling
✔	✔	✔	—	✔	✔	✔	✔

Finding the trailhead: Begin this trip at the Railway Heritage Centre, about 3 km (1.9 mi) from the Marine Atlantic Ferry Terminal. The centre is conveniently located near a number of businesses, including a hotel and Tim Hortons. From the parking area, a gravel path leads the 150 m/yd past a collection of old railway cars and benches to a trailhead kiosk where there are interpretive panels and maps of the entire Newfoundland T'Railway. There is another sign that announces this is also the starting point for the Newfoundland section of the International Appalachian Trail.

Trailhead: 47°35'27.4" N, 59°09'48.4" W (Start — Channel-Port aux Basques) 47°43'57.6" N, 59°17'51.2" W (Finish — MacDougalls Gulch)

Observations: After a promising start at a well-defined trailhead, I almost abandoned this route several times in the first 5 km (3.1 mi). The T'Railway quickly became a poorly surfaced track, littered with water-filled potholes and encroaching vegetation. However, the scenery was frequently exceptional, sufficiently so that it made issues with the condition of the trail less important. I found this to be the most mentally challenging piece of trail in eastern Canada, but once I understood that this is best done riding a mountain bike and with a willingness to get wet and muddy, I was fine.

The T'Railway, for a number of reasons, seems primitive to those accustomed to the crushed-stone surface on the rail trails of Quebec and southern Ontario. Walkers and cyclists are uncommon on the T'Railway in this area. The only traffic I saw on the T'Railway, except for a pickup truck and a camper van, were quite a few side-by-side ATVs. Add heavy, motorized usage to extremely limited

Human Weathervane

Newfoundland is known for its wild weather, but even by its standards the gales of Wreckhouse are legendary. Southeast winds, funneled through the narrow gullies of the Long Range Mountains, blast across the flat barren land at more than 200 kph (125 mph). Trains were regularly blown off the tracks.

In 1939, desperately searching for any reliable method of predicting the winds, the railway company hired a local trapper, Lauchie MacDougall, who claimed the ability to "smell' their approach. Whenever he thought a blow was approaching, he telephoned the railway agent in Port aux Basques, and the trains were delayed.

In 1950, a new CN railway dispatcher thought the method horribly unscientific and ignored Lauchie's warning. The wind at Wreckhouse lifted three loaded freight cars like feathers and dashed them into the ocean. Lauchie kept his job, and the railway heeded his advice until his death in 1965.

funding for development and maintenance and it is entirely understandable why the trail experience is different.

By the end of this route, after traversing the Wreckhouse Barrens and its outstanding scenery, I had made the transition from enthusiast to skeptic and back to fan. It is tough but worthwhile.

Route Description: The very first thing that you do is cross the longest bridge on this route, the 50 m/yd plus Grand Bay steel beam. Once across, the trail surface is broken asphalt – quite bumpy. On the left is the gorgeous basin of Grand Bay with houses perched on the barren lands surrounding it. Alders grow thickly on both sides of the trail, their bushy branches narrowing the trail considerably.

At 820 m/yd, there is a small viewing platform and bench overlooking a tiny cove and another one 550 m/yd further. At 1.5 km (0.9 mi), the asphalt ends, and 200 m/yd later, there is an awkward double road crossing over Dennis Road and Grand Bay Road West at a diagonal. Be cautious of traffic. The trail then drops to low ground, where the Trans-Canada Highway is to the right and a trucking business to the left.

From this point, the trail surface is the remains of the former railbed; most of the ballast has been removed leaving the compacted earth of the base. However, this has degraded with use from a smooth, level track into a series of deep, wide, water-filled potholes. For the next several hundred metres/yards, the trail goes from one puddle to the next in repetitive undulation. Because of the thick alders bordering the trail, most cannot be avoided.

At 2.1 km (1.3 mi), there is an interesting little causeway crossing Dennis Pond that has almost been worn away to water level. After this, there is more heavy ballast – large gravel – on the treadway. There are fewer potholes, but the gravel is difficult to bike through. It can also be challenging for walkers. Yet the surrounding area of bogs and tarns is quite lovely and hints at the fierce climate of this desolate area. Unfortunately, ATVs grind through the bog, churning the paths into a soupy morass.

There is another viewing platform with a bench at 3.2 km (2 mi), and Edna's Road is crossed 1 km (0.6 mi) later. Once across this road, the T'Railway settles into a long, descending straightaway, where the adjacent peat bogs drain onto the trail at the low spot, 800 m/yd from Edna's Road. Through this section there are no houses – and lots of puddles.

At 5.4 km (3.4 mi), on another short causeway, coastal dunes are visible to the left, but they hide the ocean beyond. At 6.2 km (3.9 mi), you reach the viewing platform with the best vista. It is on a small rise above the fairly long causeway crossing Big Barachois, and on the horizon, you can see the barren slopes of the Long Range Mountains for the first time. There is another viewing spot 900 m/yd further, but the view is rather more modest. Only another 250 m/yd later, you should see the ocean for the first time, visible through breaks in the dune wall. At 8 km (5 mi), there is a tiny bridge spanning the outflow of a small pond; to your left lies a lovely, small, sand-and-gravel beach.

Beyond the bridge, the T'Railway has been almost washed away by the encroaching ocean. Massive boulders have been placed to protect the treadway, but even so, expect this to be one of the roughest spots on this route. From here, the trail curves behind Windsor Point, then reconnects to the ocean at another small beach. Many houses are visible, and for some of these, the T'Railway is their driveway.

9.8 km (6.1 mi) After crossing another small causeway, a sign announces your arrival in J.T. Cheeseman Provincial Park, which is both a picnic ground and camping area. As soon as you reach the park sign, the treadway becomes soft sand: it is impossible to bike, so walk. On the left are high dunes and on the far side an inviting white-sand beach. The Cape Ray Lighthouse should be visible – unless it's foggy.

There is a picnic/parking area with outhouses about 200 m/yd further, a good place for a snack and access to the park's wonderful beach, usually buffeted by lively waves. The trail runs behind the high dunes with a viewing platform on higher ground to the right. About 300 m/yd further, a boardwalk branches right, heading to the campground.

The trail curves right, edging the water but turning away from the barrier beach. At 11 km (6.8 mi), houses appear ahead, and within 200 m/yd, there is a road with homes beside the trail to the right; this is the community of Cape Ray. There is very little tree cover beside the trail here, and the houses are quite close. At 11.6 km (7.2 mi), the trail crosses the paved road, and 500 m/yd later crosses Highway 408. If you need refreshments, there is a store to the left. Ahead, the leading edge of the Long Range Mountains appears much closer.

Abandoned Railroads

Railroads were the superhighways of the late 19th and early 20th centuries, often the only practical method to move goods and people over land before the invention of the automobile. Every community vied for a railway connection; having a railway station meant prosperity and growth while being passed by meant decline and economic stagnation.

By the end of World War II, however, railroads were unmistakably in decline, and all but the most profitable routes were abandoned. Yet their role in transportation is not over, for in the past two decades, thousands of kilometres of rail lines have been converted to recreational trails for walking, cycling, and cross-country skiing.

For the next 1 km (0.6 mi), the trail is straight. At first there are houses nearby to the right, but road and trail soon separate, leaving only a powerline to parallel the track. As the T'Railway moves inland, the ocean is no longer visible, but the mountains to the right appear closer and much more impressive.

This is a difficult section, pitted with potholes and very rough, but at 13.3 km (8.3 mi) the potholes (mostly) end. Except for the striking mountains nearby, there is little to view. To the left, it is a sea of spruce and higher ground hides the ocean. At 14.1 km (8.8 mi), there is a small pond on the right, after which the trail makes a long turn left and begins to descend. About 500 m/yd later, the ocean once again comes into view, shortly after which a major ATV track crosses the T'Railway.

📍**15.4 km (9.6 mi)** You arrive at the bridge crossing Bear Cove Brook, a beautiful location. The ocean is a stone's throw to the left with a tempting cobble beach; to the right is a small pond bounded by steep-sided hills, including a nearby knoll with a communication tower on top and a road running straight up it. (I imagine the views are fantastic, but I did not look.)

Once across the bridge and up the far side are several abandoned concrete structures slightly above the trail and to the right and one occupied residence. At 16 km (10 mi), a gravel road connects to the trail and splits left 450 m/yd later to provide vehicle access to Red Rock Point. On the right, perhaps 100 m/yd later, is a gravel pit.

What follows is perhaps the most scenic portion of this route. The T'Railway heads onto the Wreckhouse Barrens, an open area nearly devoid of tree cover and often close to the water's edge, where there is a low cliff. To the right, the Long Range Mountains rise nearly 500 m (1,640 ft) above the coastal strip and appear like a fortress wall denying entry further inland.

Ahead in the far distance, the prominent peak of Cape Anguille, the most western point on the Newfoundland peninsula, extends into the cobalt-blue Gulf of St. Lawrence. The trail works its way across these open barrens, staying near the ocean. By 18.5 km (11.5 mi), the Trans-Canada Highway is quite close to the trail and remains so for the remainder of the route.

📍**20.6 km (12.8 mi)** The trail curves right where it crosses Wreckhouse Brook and arrives at a tunnel beneath the highway. This provides access to a large parking area beside Wreckhouse Pond with impressive views of the nearby mountains. The trail now parallels the highway and is quite close for a short distance. The traffic noises from this busy road are distracting. However, the nearby scenery is dramatic and exquisite, and the two tracks soon diverge with the T'Railway returning to the shoreline.

By 21.9 km (13.6 mi), houses come into view on the coastline ahead, and the trail curves right, following the coastline into a shallow cove. The rocks of this

section appear to be replaced by a sand beach. The trail drops down to cross MacDougall's Brook at 23.3 km (14.5 mi).

23.8 km (14.8 mi) The trail crosses a small dirt road amid a cluster of small residences. (I could find no name for either the community or the road.) The Trans-Canada Highway is less than 500 m/yd to the right. The beach extends on the left and is rarely busy, so a pleasant place to relax before the return trek. The T'Railway continues, of course, but moves inland to follow the Codroy Valley. For ocean scenery, go no further, and retrace your route back to Port aux Basques.

Further Information:

Channel-Port aux Basques Railway Heritage Centre: www.portauxbasques.ca/tourism/railway_heritage_center.php

Channel-Port aux Basques Tourism: www.portauxbasques.ca/tourism

International Appalachian Trail: www.iat-sia.org

4. Celtic Shores Coastal Trail

4. Celtic Shores Coastal Trail

One of the longest off-road sections of The Great Trail in Nova Scotia is the 90 km (56 mi) stretch from the Canso Causeway to Inverness along the west coast of Cape Breton Island. The Celtic Shores Coastal Trail is one of the best maintained and signed routes in Atlantic Canada and deserves its growing reputation for quality. Five community organizations combined to develop and manage the former rail line, which has been surfaced with crushed stone and is open to a wide variety of uses.

This route can be most easily used by bicycles and motorized vehicles. Motorized and non-motorized uses seem to coexist quite well with the majority of ATV users adhering to the posted 30 kph (18.6 mph) speed limit. As camping is not permitted along the trail route, users must stay at a B & B or campground, which limits the overnight options. Although cyclists can probably complete the full route in one day, I recommend that hikers commit five days to undertake it, as follows:

- Day 1: Canso Causeway to Creignish, 11.1 km (6.9 mi)
- Day 2: Creignish to Judique, 17.1 km (10.6 mi)
- Day 3: Judique to Port Hood, 16 km (10 mi)
- Day 4: Port Hood to Mabou, 20.1 km (12.5 mi)
- Day 5: Mabou to Inverness, 25.7 km (16 mi)

4. Celtic Shores Coastal Trail – South

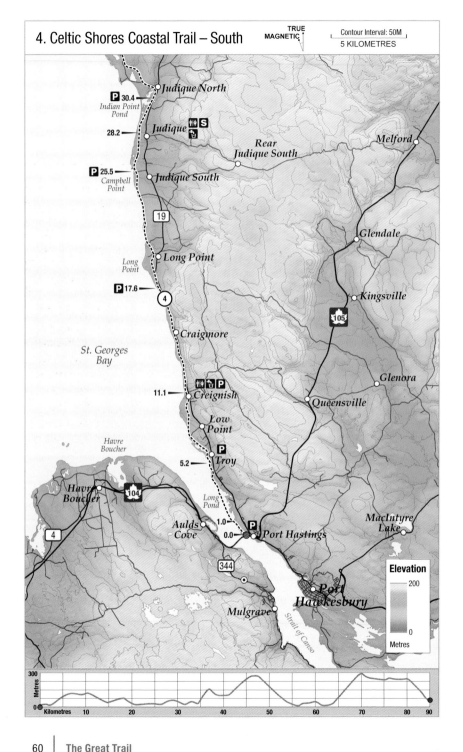

TRUE
MAGNETIC

Contour Interval: 50M
5 KILOMETRES

Judique North

P 30.4
Indian Point
Pond

28.2 — Judique

Rear
Judique South

Melford

P 25.5
Campbell
Point — Judique South

19

Long
Point — Long Point

Glendale

P 17.6 — 4

Kingsville

Craigmore

105

St. Georges
Bay

Glenora

11.1 — Creignish

Low
Point

Queensville

Havre
Boucher

P — Troy
5.2

Havre
Boucher

104

Long
Pond

1.0
Aulds
Cove   0.0

P
Port Hastings

MacIntyre
Lake

4

344

Port
Hawkesbury

Mulgrave

Strait of Canso

Elevation
200

0
Metres

4. Celtic Shores Coastal Trail

Distance: 90 km (56 mi) – one way
Ascent: 408 m (1,338 ft)
Descent: 363 m (1,191 ft)

Trail conditions: crushed stone, natural surface
Cellphone coverage: yes
Hazards: coastal weather, road crossings, wildlife

Permitted Uses							
Walking	Biking	Horseback Riding	Inline Skating	ATV	Snowshoeing	Cross-country Skiing	Snowmobiling
✔	✔	✔	—	✔	✔	✔	✔

Finding the trailhead: The Celtic Shores Coastal Trail begins on the Cape Breton side of the Canso Causeway, where two trailhead pavilions sit at the end of a parking lot located on the left immediately after crossing the steel swing bridge. One of these is a Trans Canada Trail kiosk; the other was built by the local trail community and is crammed full of interesting interpretive information, including a map. From here the path's route is not obvious, for it seems to be part of the lawn for the Coast Guard Station. However, if you walk past the trailhead pavilions and keep near the base of the steep slope on your right, there are additional directional signs. The Troy Station Trailhead at 5.2 km (3.2 mi) is the usual starting point for cyclists.

Trailhead: 45°38'52.7" N, 61°24'44.2" W (Start — Canso Causeway)
45°41'25.8" N, 61°26'30.6" W (Cycling Start — Troy Station)
46°13'51.6" N, 61°18'35.9" W (Finish — Inverness)

Observations: This trail was easy to ride and pleasant, thanks to the excellent condition of its treadway. I finished it in three days although I could have done so more quickly, doing the walking portion from the Canso Causeway along Ghost Beach, cycling from there to Port Hood, and cycling again from Port Hood to Inverness.

Each section provided a different experience. The nearly 40 km (25 mi) to Port Hood follows the Strait of Canso, so coastal views are common. Then the trail turns inland, and the remainder of the trip to Inverness follows rivers and passes near lakes. The exposed strip of land of Ghost Beach is an enjoyable walk but dangerously exposed in a storm, so it cannot be biked, making the first 4.1 km (2.5) mi a separate and unique adventure.

Route description: After crossing the lawn, the narrow track is squeezed between the hillside and the station's buildings and runs alongside a chain-link fence topped with barbed wire – not particularly scenic. Fortunately, after 600 m/yd, the station ends and the trail comes out into an open, grassy field.

Close on the left are the concrete piers of the Canso Canal with superb views of Aulds Cove, the Canso Causeway, and the large quarry at Cape Porcupine on the opposite side of the Strait of Canso. Directly ahead lies Ghost Beach, a long, low, curving spit of land with water on either side that is connected to the mainland by a bridge at 1 km (0.6 mi). This impressive steel structure crosses the fast-moving outflow of the large Long Pond.

For the next 2.6 km (1.6 mi), the route follows windswept Ghost Beach, which is barely 50 m/yd wide at its thickest, and at times narrows to barely 10 m/yd. Although the former railbed was intended for cycling, storm surges have washed away nearly any trace of a managed path. This is rough walking and impossible cycling.

On a calm day, Ghost Beach is exceptionally scenic; Long Pond is busy with ducks, geese, and mergansers, while eagles frequently perch near the mouth of Mill Brook. When stormy, the ocean is steel grey, and winds funnel down the strait, lashing waves onto the seaward-facing rocks and drenching hikers with sheets of spray. Even the birds hide with only the gulls bobbing on the surging ocean.

The final few hundred metres/yards of the beach are rocky cobble, often covered in seaweed after storms, reconnecting to the mainland at 3.6 km (2.2 mi). There are houses near at hand, but before you reach them, you encounter the track of the former rail line. For the next 950 m/yd, the path remains unimproved, sometimes sandy, sometimes rocky, but distinct. At 4.7 km (2.9 mi), it reaches a small bridge, beyond which the trail is surfaced with crushed stone. About 450 m/yd beyond that, the first distance marker, a large, blue sign with white lettering, reads "km 5."

📍**5.2 km (3.2 mi)** The Troy Station Trailhead, the usual starting point for cyclists, is quite elaborate with regulatory signage, interpretive panels, benches, tables, and a kiosk with information and a map. A fence separates the parking area from the trail, and the shelter overlooks the ocean.

From here, the trail is easy riding, following the well-surfaced path as it proceeds through a mostly forested section, punctuated by infrequent private road crossings. At these, there are usually yield signs facing the path, and when the trail crosses a public road, there is typically a barricade to prevent cars and trucks from accessing the track. Every 1 km (0.6 mi), there is a distance marker, enabling you to keep track of your progress.

Initially, the route remains close to the Strait of Canso. About 1 km (0.6 mi) from the Troy Station Trailhead, the path is evenly surfaced with asphalt, a

Bald Eagle

Wherever you are in Atlantic Canada, closely watch the large birds flying nearby. The chances are quite good that you may sight a bald eagle gliding past or perched in a spruce and looking for prey. With a wingspan reaching 2 m to 2.5 m (6.6 ft to 8.2 ft) and its distinctive white head, this majestic bird is unmistakable in flight, slowly riding the air currents with as little wing movement as possible.

Once killed indiscriminately as a pest, it is now illegal to kill or injure an eagle anywhere in Canada. Their numbers have increased rapidly in recent years as they are no longer hunted. These massive raptors are enormously popular with visitors.

covering that lasts for nearly 2.4 km (1.5 mi). Once the trail leaves the shoreline at 7.1 km (4.4 mi), it remains veiled by forest for a considerable distance. Though it does have some straight sections, it often curves pleasantly.

By 10.3 km (6.4 mi), it is clear that the highway and pathway are converging, and several houses are visible above and inland. About 300 m/yd further, the path reaches an area where there is cleared ground on both sides and a small community.

11.1 km (6.9 mi) A side trail leads uphill a short distance to the Creignish Recreational Centre, where there are washrooms and drinking water available. Its parking lot also acts as a trailhead, and there is a map kiosk beside the side trail. Highway 19 is only about 50 m/yd from the trail, and the trailhead sign provides directions and distance to lodging, gasoline, restaurants, grocery stores, and a variety of other services.

The pathway continues as before, sitting slightly higher than the ocean and usually a trifle lower than Highway 19. About 1 km (0.6 mi) from Creignish, there is a bench with an interpretive panel next to it. Otherwise, the trail emerges occasionally from among the trees, sometimes quite close to the road, other times slightly further away. Private road crossings are common.

At 15.5 km (9.6 mi), there are a barn and pastures to the left with horses. The deep marks left in the crushed stone by their hooves are evidence of their trail use and should be visible on both sides of the farm's entrance road. At 17 km (10.6 mi), the trail passes near a derelict house, after which there are magnificent views to the west where Cape George is the highest point on the horizon.

17.6 km (10.9 mi) A side trail to the right leads uphill to Christy's Lookoff, which is a parking area and trailhead on Highway 19. In the parking area are benches and interpretive panels, and—as advertised—a fine view of St. Georges Bay. On the trail is a directional sign, which informs you that it is still 73 km (45.4 mi) to Inverness.

From here to the next trailhead are the best views of the ocean, excepting Ghost Beach of course. After running mostly through forest and crossing numerous private drives, at 20.9 km (13 mi) the trail moves completely away from any vegetation, bisecting a large property with a house on the right and tennis courts to the left. After that, the trail follows the top of a steep embankment above the water with a farm to landward.

At 23.8 km (14.8 mi), tiny St. Michael's Pioneer Cemetery is marked by an interpretive panel with a bench facing the water. Just 250 m/yd beyond that, the trail crosses Walkers Cove Road, where there is another directional and distance sign. The trail returns into woodland here, including a rare area where there is an overhead canopy of branches. At 25 km (15.5 mi), a sign informs you that a small bridge spans Campbells Brook.

25.5 km (15.8 mi) About 500 m/yd from the bridge, the trail crosses Baxters Cove Road, where there is another parking area. About 200 m/yd past the road, there is a picnic area on the left overlooking the harbour area. It has tables and an interpretive panel. The next few kilometres are interesting, as the path track is closer to sea level, and there are more ponds and marshes bordering it, and it crosses a few small bridges.

At 28.2 km (17.5 mi), just before the sign for Og Brook, there is a side trail to the community of Judique. This is 700 m/yd from the main path but has the only stores available until Port Hood. To the left, 200 m/yd away, is a gorgeous ocean beach. A picnic table sits near the brook; on the far side, another side trail leads to Judique.

There is an excellent view of the beach dunes and Barachois Pond from the bridge at Livingstones Pond, 600 m/yd further, and at 29.3 km (18.2 mi), a sign labels the adjacent clearing as being Judique Station, but no building remains.

There is an odd diversion at 30.1 km (18.7 mi) where the trail makes an abrupt curve off the original track of the rail line. An adjacent landowner overenthusiastically built his yard on the abandoned track before it was designated a trail. The local community group built around it rather than destroy the new lawn.

This unusual chicane with its sharp turns through the trees is short, and within 100 m/yd, the trail emerges into a meadow. To the left is a gorgeous estuary known as Indian Point Pond; ahead lies a short bridge, the km 30 marker, and a trailhead area next to Highway 19.

📍**30.4 km (19 mi)** You arrive at the Michaels Landing Trailhead where there are benches, shelters, interpretive panels, a historical plaque, a trailhead kiosk, and a map. Sixteen kilometres (9.9 mi) remain to Port Hood.

The long Judique Interval Bridge is reached at 31.5 km (19.6 mi), and there is a pleasant rest area with bench and panel at Allen Ian's Pond, 36 km (22.4 mi). In between, the trail crosses the paved Shore Road two times. After the pond, Shore Road is crossed one more time, as is Joe Effie Road (gravel), before reaching the attractive bridge and causeway crossing Little Judique Pond at 38.6 km (24 mi). There is a picnic table at the head of the bridge and an interpretive panel.

Once across Little Judique Pond, the trail climbs noticeably and curves around Captains Brook, which is to the right and below. When the trail crosses Railway Station Road (gravel) at 40.5 km (25.2 mi), the land to the right is cultivated and lower. Shore Road is encountered one final time at 41.8 km (26 mi) and soon traffic noises on the right make it clear that you are approaching a community. For a short distance, trail and highway run nearly parallel until the trail crosses Highway 19 at a very awkward diagonal at 43.3 km (27 mi).

Across the road, the trail passes close to a number of houses and over several driveways. There are even signed side trails to campgrounds and the Nova Scotia Liquor Commission. There is one final stretch of forested trail before it reaches the Port Hood Station trailhead, which is on a hill with a lovely view of Port Hood Beach and Island. There are benches, tables, interpretive panels, and a directional sign to local services.

📍**44.3 km (27.5 mi)** As soon as it leaves Port Hood Station, the trail turns sharply away from the ocean and, other than a few houses, passes no more of the community. After 400 m/yd, there are amenity signs where it crosses Sharon Drive and again at Dunmore Road, 46.2 km (28.7 mi). The area is thickly forested with mostly hardwood trees that are not particularly tall.

Over the next several kilometres, the trail curves multiple times, all the while slowly climbing more than 45 m (147.6 ft) higher than Port Hood Station. It crests shortly before reaching Beaton Road (gravel) at 51.5 km (32 mi), then begins a long, mostly level curve to the left. It reaches Upper Southwest Mabou Road 850 m/yd later, and an interpretive panel is positioned just before it. An amenities sign indicates that there is a golf course – should you feel the urge – just 3 km (1.9 mi) to the right.

The grade changes to downhill, dropping quite briskly. Off to the right, through breaks in the vegetation, you can see that the track is much higher than

4. Celtic Shores Coastal Trail – North

TRUE MAGNETIC

Contour Interval: 50M
5 KILOMETRES

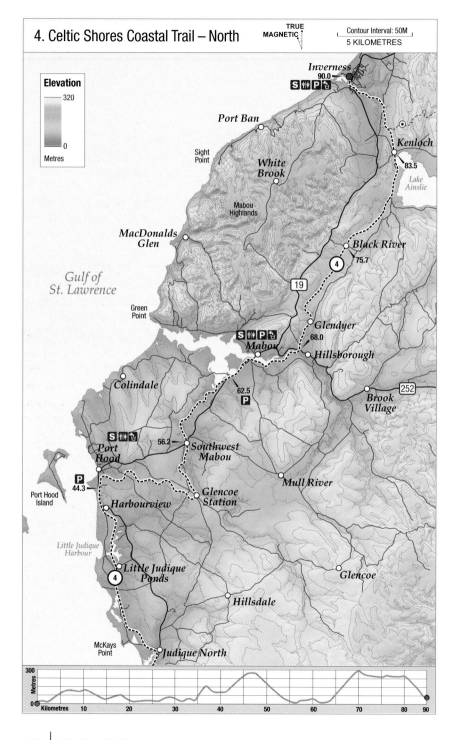

Elevation

320

0

Metres

Inverness
90.0

Port Ban

Kenloch
83.5

Lake Ainslie

Sight Point

White Brook

Mabou Highlands

MacDonalds Glen

Black River
75.7

4

19

Gulf of St. Lawrence

Green Point

Glendyer
68.0

Mabou

Hillsborough

Colindale

62.5
P

Brook Village

252

56.2

Southwest Mabou

Port Hood

Mull River

P
44.3

Port Hood Island

Glencoe Station

Harbourview

Little Judique Harbour

4

Little Judique Ponds

Glencoe

Hillsdale

McKays Point

Judique North

300
Metres
0
Kilometres 10   20   30   40   50   60   70   80   90

the ground to the right. You might see the Southwest Mabou River at least 50 m (164 ft) below. The trail continues its weaving descent, crossing Mabou Road at 53.7 km (33.4 mi) and again 1.1 km (0.7 mi) later. About 300 m/yd after the second crossing, there are clear views of the river valley, and it is apparent that the trail sits atop a cliff high above the river. An interpretive panel talks about the farms below and how they benefitted from the railroad.

As you emerge from the trees near the km 55 marker, there are cultivated fields on both sides of the trail. Unusually, a barrier gate that crosses the path 800 m/yd later is nowhere near a road, but you might encounter farm equipment either crossing or driving along the trail for the next 400m/yd.

56.2 km (34.9 mi) The trail reaches an exceptionally dangerous road crossing here at Highway 19. This is a 90 kph (55 mph) highway, and visibility is limited for drivers in both directions. Stop, dismount if cycling, and dash across when certain it is clear.

My favourite section of this entire route comes next, as the trail runs alongside the Southwest Mabou and Mabou Rivers. A directional and distance sign on the far side of Highway 19, where there is room for parking but no official trailhead, indicates that Mabou is 8 km (5 mi) and Inverness 34 km (21.1 mi) away.

The trail immediately passes through a deep cut in the hillside, then makes a sudden drop – and climb soon after – where a bridge was removed and not replaced. About 700 m/yd from the road, a signed snowmobile trail branches left, and 400 m/yd later, the trail crosses a small bridge. Now almost level with the water, the trail turns right and runs at the base of sheer hillsides through a narrow valley alongside the river. The trail crosses the river at 59.4 km (37 mi) on a steel truss bridge in a narrow gap between two rock faces; it is quite impressive.

Here the rougher ground is left behind, and the trail enters into a wider area, where the river broadens, and there are some small fields and ponds. Path and river remain close but not in quite so constricted a space. At 60.9 km (37.8 mi), a bench facing the river offers decent views of the looming Mabou Highlands.

About 450 m/yd further, the path turns into a wooded area and climbs away from the water. There is another bench and interpretive panel at 62.3 km (38.7 mi) before the trail reaches houses and Highway 19.

62.5 km (38.8 mi) The path crosses the Little Mabou Road and arrives at a delightful trailhead, which overlooks both the highlands and a large cove. A picnic shelter, trailhead kiosk, bench, parking area, and map are all found here.

From here to Mabou, the trail remains near both road and buildings. It even makes a minor detour around the new fire hall, which was built right on the former railbed. At 64.4 km (39.8 mi), it again crosses Highway 19. However, this is a 50 kph (30 mph) zone, and several businesses are nearby. To access the village of Mabou and all its services, turn left and cross the bridge.

The trail continues along the bank of the broad Mabou River and is enchanting from here to Glendyer Brook, 3.7 km (2.3 mi) away. The views across the river of the village and the Mabou Highlands are extraordinarily picturesque. Bald eagles are almost always sighted. There are bridges, ponds, panels, and many viewing areas. It must be experienced.

68 km (42.3 mi) After crossing the river on a steel truss bridge, the trail reaches Highway 252 at Glendyer Station and changes dramatically. From here, it enters the most remote portion of the entire route and some of the most remote areas travelled thus far. At first, the path and road run parallel with high hillsides to the left, a creek to the right, and a few buildings and small farms ahead in the tapered valley.

The trail also begins to climb again to what is the highest elevation of the entire route. Shortly after crossing the creek, about 69 km (42.9 mi), the path separates from the road, hugging the side of the brook as it climbs. There is little to see but forest as thick vegetation lines the pathway, although a few small bridges cross some tiny creeks and wetlands. This is the only section of this route where cell coverage might not be adequate. As the trail climbs to the high point at 74.4 km (46.2 mi), the narrow valley below gradually broadens into low marshy land, choked with alders.

75.7 km (47 mi) The trail reaches Blackstone Road (gravel) shortly after farms become visible to the left. This lonely looking trail access point has only a directional and distance marker, noting Inverness is 13.5 km (8.4 mi) further.

Forest soon swallows the trail again, and there are long, straight stretches through the flat landscape with numerous small marshes. At 78.6 km (48.8 mi), there is quite a large one, and about 800 m/yd later, there is a small bridge. At 79.3 km (50.3 mi), a longer bridge crosses Saddlers Brook. The low hills of the Mabou Highlands line the left horizon.

The trail remains quite remote all the way to the West Lake Ainslie Road at 81 km (44.4 mi), after which road and trail once again parallel each other for more than 1 km (0.6 mi). Shortly after they separate, the trail reaches the shore of Lake Ainslie, where there is a rest area at 82.9 km (51.5 mi) with tables, benches, an interpretive panel, and lake access. Enjoy the moment, and the view, because the path soon turns away from the large loch, curving left and beginning the final approach to Inverness.

83.5 km (51.9 mi) The trail reaches the road between Strathlorne and Scotsville. There is a small cluster of houses near here, including an old church renovated as a home. The trail runs alongside small Kennedys Brook amid old farmland crawling up the slope of Godfreys Mountain. The ground remains higher to the right as the grade drops, beginning the final descent towards the ocean. Deepdale Road

is crossed at 86.7 km (53.9 mi), and 1 km (0.6 mi) later is the surprisingly large Deepdale Trestle at 111.6 m/yd long and 21.4 m (70.2 ft) high.

As you approach Inverness, there are several side trails for motorized vehicles, including one to a clubhouse on the right. By the km 88 marker, houses are visible to the left and below. At 89.5 km (55.6 mi), the trail reaches Highway 19, which becomes Central Street in Inverness. A sidewalk heads uphill into the community, but the trail continues on the opposite side of the road. It curves right, offering superb views of Inverness Harbour. Benches, interpretive panels, sheltered picnic tables, garbage cans, and public art (sort of) are found in the final few hundred metres/yards.

90 km (55.9 mi) The trail end arrives with little fanfare at Beach Road #1, where it stops suddenly. The former train station, now used by local businesses, is across the narrow street. There is a trailhead kiosk, but nothing that indicates this is an end as well as a start. To the right about 200 m/yd away are the community businesses – including an excellent café. To the left, a boardwalk leads to the ocean, where there are picnic tables, a fine place to relax.

Further Information:
Celtic Shores Coastal Trail: www.celticshores.ca
Destination Cape Breton: www.cbisland.com
Nova Scotia Trails Federation: www.novascotiatrails.com

Coyote

Coyotes are becoming increasingly comfortable living near and among human habitations — and are the most recent wild animal to be elevated by the Department of Natural Resources and Parks Canada from nuisance status to a threat to humans. Rarely exceeding 30 kg (66 lb), coyotes resemble large brownish-grey dogs. They range everywhere and eat almost anything, including plants and berries. However, they prefer snowshoe hare and other small mammals — even cats from homes that edge on forests.

Accustomed to being shot on sight by farmers and hunters, coyotes are quite shy about allowing themselves to be seen. Scat in the middle of the trail with the fur of recent kills mixed through it is usually your only clue they are nearby. Should you sight a coyote, walk away slowly — never turning your back. If it approaches, try to scare the animal away by making noise, swinging sticks, and generally acting aggressive. Never feed it; habituated coyotes almost always end up being destroyed.

5. Salt Marsh – Atlantic View

The Cole Harbour Salt Marsh is one of the most popular coastal walks in Nova Scotia. It is unlike any other route in the province with most of its length running along a slender causeway, ocean water lapping at both sides. This walk is a birder's paradise; herons, shorebirds, ducks, geese, and more than a hundred other species can be viewed from its embankment. Although close to busy suburban districts, virtually no houses can be seen. All the abutting lands are crown owned and protected from urban development. Dawn and sunset are particularly attractive times to walk this remarkable section of The Great Trail.

Lawrencetown Beach, barely a thirty-minute drive from downtown Halifax, is also an extremely popular destination. While enjoyed by families and visitors in July and August for its 1.5 km (0.9 mi) of south-facing, gleaming-golden sand and supervised swimming, Lawrencetown has also become something of a mecca for both local and international surfers. Although its usual 1.5 m (5 ft) waves have been characterized by local surfers as "uninspiring beach peaks," Lawrencetown comes alive with surfers in the winter and spring when the swells are pushed higher by west or northeast winds. Then online surfer slang calls it "one of the heaviest spots around."

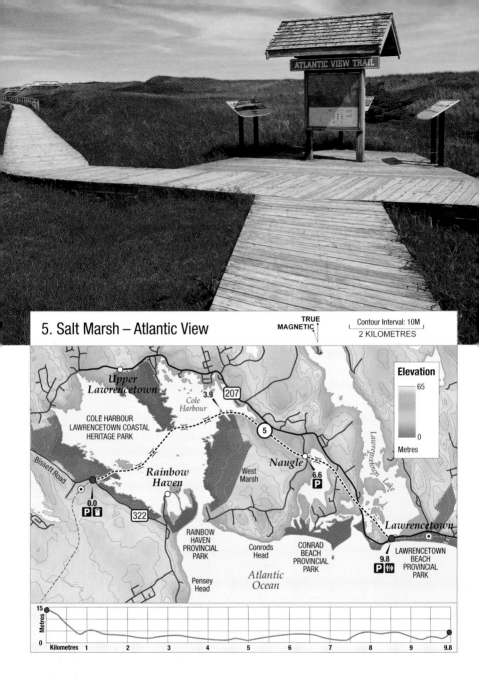

5. Salt Marsh – Atlantic View

TRUE
MAGNETIC

Contour Interval: 10M
2 KILOMETRES

Elevation
65

0
Metres

Upper
Lawrencetown

Cole
Harbour

207

COLE HARBOUR
LAWRENCETOWN COASTAL
HERITAGE PARK

5

Lawrencetown Lake

Bissett Road

Rainbow
Haven

West
Marsh

Naugle

6.6
P

0.0
P

322

RAINBOW
HAVEN
PROVINCIAL
PARK

Conrods
Head

CONRAD
BEACH
PROVINCIAL
PARK

Lawrencetown

9.8
P

LAWRENCETOWN
BEACH
PROVINCIAL
PARK

Pensey
Head

Atlantic
Ocean

15

Metres

0

Kilometres   1   2   3   4   5   6   7   8   9   9.8

5. Salt Marsh – Atlantic View

Distance: 9.8 km (6.1 mi) – one way
Ascent: 47 m (154 ft)
Descent: 57 m (187 ft)

Trail conditions: crushed stone
Cellphone coverage: yes
Hazards: coastal weather, poison ivy, road crossings, wildlife

Permitted Uses							
Walking	Biking	Horseback Riding	Inline Skating	ATV	Snowshoeing	Cross-country Skiing	Snowmobiling
✔	✔	✔	—	—	—	✔	—

Finding the trailhead: The trailhead for the Salt Marsh Trail is located at 806 Bissett Road and has had to be constantly expanded since the trail first opened in 2000. Actually, so many people visit this trail that a nearby second parking area was added, and knowledgeable locals park at more distant lots at the Cole Harbour Heritage Park. The facilities at the start are modest with only garbage cans and a trailhead kiosk.

The trailhead for the Atlantic View Trail at 6.6 km (4.1 mi) is quite elaborate with a large parking area and the trail passing beneath a gateway. In the small park built up around this trailhead, there are covered picnic tables, benches, garbage cans, a viewing platform overlooking the West Marsh, and a large kiosk featuring a map of the trail. There are even some side trails.

Trailhead: 44°39'26.4" N, 63°26'54.7" W (Start — Bissett Road)
44°38'38.9" N, 63°20'52.4" W (Finish — Lawrencetown Beach)

Observations: As I live fairly close to Cole Harbour, I have been able to walk or bike this trail on numerous occasions, in winter as well as summer. It is kept in excellent condition, and there are almost always plenty of other people. My only complaint? It is over too soon, so make sure you linger a while at Lawrencetown Beach.

When I considered this section for inclusion, I cycled on the Atlantic View Trail for several kilometres beyond the beach, continuing as far as the trailhead parking area on Highway 207. There were some quite interesting spots; however, Lawrencetown Beach is such a great destination that it just made sense to finish there. If you have time, definitely extend your trip.

Route description: The path begins unexceptionally; once past the gate, the wide, crushed-stone pathway passes through a thickly forested area, dense white spruce preventing long views. For the first 700 m/yd, it seems to be a woodland walk, pleasant but nothing special. However, within 100 m/yd, the trail emerges from the forest and narrows to a slender finger of elevated land perched above ocean water, lapping on both sides at the Cole Harbour Salt Marsh. For the next 3 km (1.9 mi) plus, the trail remains a slender causeway, punctuated only by four bridges and occasional small islands.

The first of these is less than 200 m/yd away along a short side footpath. Rosemary's Way faces nearby Glasgow Island and provides a bench for sitting and watching the several species of diving birds that frequent the narrow passage. After another 200 m/yd, you reach a second tiny island, where there is a large information pavilion, outhouses, and a covered picnic table, as well as the km 1 marker.

The Bald Eagle Bridge sits barely 100 m/yd away after a bronze plaque, which identifies the salt marsh as the Peter McNab Kuhn Conservation Area. On the far side of the bridge is a trail interpretive panel next to another bench.

The route continues over the exposed and often wind-whipped causeway to the tip of Flying Point about 1.4 km (0.9 mi) later. Wild roses grow thickly on both sides of the trail, and extensive grassy areas are exposed in the shallow salt marsh at low tide. You cross over the Canada Goose Bridge and past another interpretive panel, entitled "Wild about roses."

After Flying Point, the trail curves right and crosses two more bridges: Ready Aye Ready bridge, commemorating the contributions of the Canadian Forces Naval Construction Troop (Atlantic) that built it, and the G. Fraser Conrad Brothers bridge, named for the man who donated equipment to rebuild all four bridges after they were destroyed by Hurricane Juan in 2003. Note the large protective stones now placed on both sides of the causeway.

3.9 km (2.4 mi) The trail reconnects to the mainland and enters a wooded area, the point where many walkers turn back. However, it is less than halfway to Lawrencetown Beach, so keep going. Although thickly wooded, glimpses of open water are possible to the left for the next 800 m/yd. However, for much of this section few views are available, and by 4.5 km (2.8 mi), the trail has settled into a long, straight stretch with the occasional bench.

When you reach the km 6 marker, where the path has begun curving very gently to the left, only 500 m/yd remain of the Salt Marsh Trail. Quite suddenly, the path reaches a gate at the West Lawrencetown Road where it is diverted away from the former railbed.

6.6 km (4.1 mi) The main path makes a short semi-circular detour through the Atlantic View trailhead park before returning to the former railbed. Almost

The Blueberry Express

Many rail trains, particularly on the branch lines, earned a nickname. In Ontario, the Kingston to Pembroke was referred to locally as the Kick & Push; the passenger train in Queens County, PEI, received the label Gaelic Express. The passenger train that lumbered through the rough terrain between Upper Musquodoboit and Dartmouth — and over the Cole Harbour Salt Marsh — was known as the Blueberry Express.

Work finally began on the long-wished-for railroad for eastern Nova Scotia in 1912, with the first passenger trains beginning in 1915. Although originally planned to continue to the town of Guysborough, track was only laid as far as Dean, less than halfway. However, between then and 1960 for passengers, and until 1982 for freight, as many as fourteen trains a day made the round trip to Dartmouth. Over the years, the line deteriorated, and its freight business increasingly transferred to road transport. Canadian National Railway applied as early as 1975 to abandon the route but was not able to do so for a number of years.

Opinion is divided on how the line earned its nickname. Some say it was because of the many baskets of blueberries transported to market in Halifax/Dartmouth. Others are certain that it was because the train was so slow and made so many extended stops that passengers would leave it to pick the many blueberries growing alongside the tracks.

immediately after, it crosses a much shorter causeway, this time over a small body of open water named the West Marsh. There is a charming-looking horse farm on the drumlin to the right.

At 7.5 km (4.7 mi), the trail crosses the quiet Conrad Road where Lawrencetown Pizza and Grocery – including ice cream – is only a few hundred metres/yards to the left. The route is fairly straight and flat in this low-lying, wet ground, and the bordering trees are more straggly and shorter, both signs of proximity to the ocean. About 600 m/yd from Conrad Road, there is a covered picnic table overlooking a small pond, and at 8.5 km (5.3 mi), the trail crosses busy Highway 207 at an odd angle; be extra cautious here. Fortunately, the trees have completely given way to windswept grasses, so visibility should be good.

The remaining distance is quite lovely. Little more than 100 m/yd from the road, the trail crosses Lawrencetown Lake over a long wooden bridge. With the low ground and few trees, Lawrencetown Beach is actually in sight in the distance. The nearly straight pathway passes between lakes and marshlands with only one low tree-covered hill to the right before arriving once again at Highway 207.

9.8 km (6.1 mi) Across Highway 207, the crushed-stone pathway ends and is replaced by a boardwalk. Cyclists must dismount for this section. Again, the trail crosses the road at a sharp angle, and there is no crosswalk. Once across the road, you are inside Lawrencetown Provincial Park. There is a trailhead kiosk, featuring a map and interpretive information.

This is the formal end of this route, but the white-sand beach is just out of sight over the low dunes. To the left is a public building with washrooms, changing rooms, and picnic tables. The Atlantic View Trail continues on the far side of the beach, should you wish to explore further. If not, Lawrencetown Beach is a wonderful place to relax before you begin your return hike or bike.

Further Information:

Atlantic View Trail Association: www.atlanticviewtrail.com
Cole Harbour Parks & Trails Association: www.chpta.org
Lawrencetown Beach: http://www.novascotia.com/see-do/outdoor-activities/
    lawrencetown-beach-provincial-park/1939
Tourism Nova Scotia: www.novascotia.com

Great Blue Heron

One of the most distinctive and stately birds you might sight is the great blue heron. Standing over 1 m (3.3 ft) high, it is Canada's largest heron and is the most widely distributed across the country. It is usually sighted perched motionless in areas of calm water, its long neck bent, waiting for a fish to venture in range for a lightning-fast strike with its sharp beak, or flying majestically overhead with deep, slow wing beats. Herons are migratory, generally arriving in April and heading south between mid-September and late October. They nest high in trees, which they might abandon if disturbed; never approach their nests.

6. Tatamagouche

The name Tatamagouche is derived from the Mi'kmaq term "Takumegooch," which roughly translated means "meeting of the waters." It's the location where the Waugh and French Rivers run into a sheltered harbour off the Northumberland Strait. Its first European residents were Acadians, who were expelled from their land throughout mainland Nova Scotia (at the time, including New Brunswick) by the British in 1755. The community, like so many in the region in the 19th century, had a shipbuilding phase that lasted into the age of steam.

The railroad, which opened in 1887, ushered in new commercial opportunities such as the opening of the dairy creamery in 1925, which operated until 1992 and produced its own brand of "Tatamagouche Butter." It was during this period, when the Sutherland Steam Mill opened in nearby Denmark, that industry was no longer tied to water for either energy or transportation.

Today, Tatamagouche remains a small but vibrant community. It vaunts its own brewery and chocolatier, and every Saturday hosts a bustling Farmers Market at Creamery Square. Frequent musical, artistic, and other activities are hosted at the Grace Jollymore Joyce Arts Centre, while the Fraser Cultural Centre showcases local, regional, and nationally acclaimed artists.

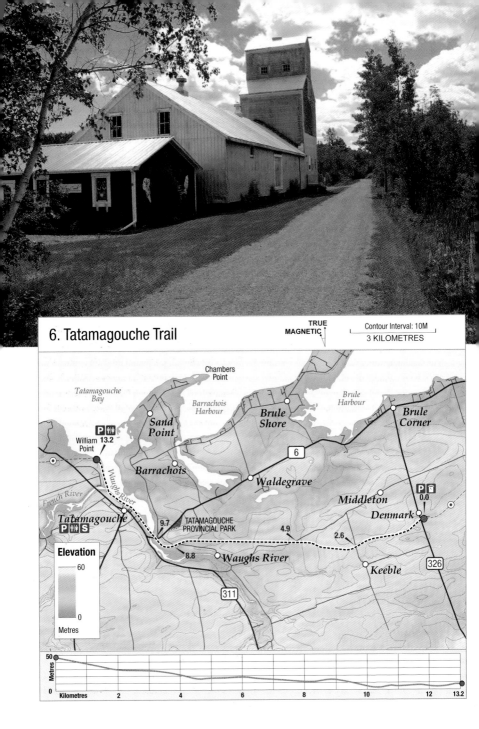

6. Tatamagouche Trail

TRUE
MAGNETIC

Contour Interval: 10M

3 KILOMETRES

Tatamagouche Bay

Chambers Point

Barrachois Harbour

Brule Harbour

Sand Point

Brule Shore

Brule Corner

P 🚻 **13.2**
William Point

Waughs River

Barrachois

6

Waldegrave

French River

Middleton

Denmark

P 🚻
0.0

Tatamagouche
P 🚻 S

9.7

TATAMAGOUCHE
PROVINCIAL PARK

4.9

2.6

326

Elevation

60

0

Metres

8.8 ◇ **Waughs River**

Keeble

311

6. Tatamagouche

Distance: 13.2 km (8.2 mi) – one way
Ascent: 77 m (253 ft)
Descent: 85 m (279 ft)

Trail conditions: compacted earth, crushed stone
Cellphone coverage: yes
Hazards: road crossings, ticks, wildlife

Permitted Uses							
Walking	Biking	Horseback Riding	Inline Skating	ATV	Snowshoeing	Cross-country Skiing	Snowmobiling
✔	✔	✔	—	✔	✔	✔	✔

Finding the trailhead: Start in the Sutherland Steam Mill Museum's parking lot. The Steam Mill was built on this site to take advantage of the transportation mobility provided by the rail line. When the museum is open, they permit you to use their washrooms and get drinking water. Other than a picnic table and garbage can, there are no outside facilities. The trail crosses Highway 326 immediately beside the museum. There are gates on the trail, facing the road where you cross Highway 326, and regulatory signage but no directional information.

Trailhead: 45°42'32.6"N, 63°09'33.2"W (Start — Denmark)
45°43'38.5"N, 63°18'13"W (Finish — Tatamagouche)

Observations: This rail trail is in very good condition with a hard-packed surface and few potholes, so it was very easy to ride on my hybrid "cross" bike. I encountered several ATVs during my trip, but all slowed and moved to the right to pass, showing politeness and good etiquette. I did the same. I quite enjoyed my brief luncheon stop in Tatamagouche and relaxed for a while in Nelson Memorial Park before finishing my ride. This was easy and fun, especially as it is almost all downhill from Denmark to Tatamagouche.

Route description: This area is thinly populated, so most of the trip is out of sight of human habitation. This is nowhere truer than at the start, where the full forest foliage creates a leafy barricade and suffuses everything with a green tinge. Within seconds, you are swallowed up by the thick forest; this is not unattractive but might be a trifle disconcerting at first.

The treadway is in good shape, even though it does not have a crushed-stone surface but rather the compacted earth of the railbed after all the stone ballast was removed. There are remarkably few potholes, so it should be easy for both cyclists and walkers. As with all rail trails, this route is wide at about 3 m/yd and often straight for considerable distances.

The first item of note occurs at 1.2 km (0.7 mi), where the trail crosses Briar Brook. Instead of a bridge, there is a culvert, and the path suddenly dips several metres/yards to cross it. (The train needed to stay level, but hikers and bikers do not.) This is rather uncharacteristic for a rail trail and might catch the unwary by surprise. The forest remains unbroken and constant until 1.8 km (1.1 mi), where a new ATV side trail connects to the right. The treadway is often rougher at such busy points, so be mindful if cycling.

2.6 km (1.6 mi) About 200 m/yd before the trail crosses the wide, unobstructed Wallie Mingo Road, it emerges from its forest shroud to views of cleared fields and houses, particularly to the left where the ground gently slopes down towards Briar Brook. I found the tidy fields and modest houses tranquil and charming, an appealing rural haven. The track immediately re-enters thick forest, so the fleeting vision of houses and fields at the road seems almost imagined. Signs on the far side of the road warn that horses may be encountered on the next section, and though I saw their hoofprints on the trail surface, I did not meet any equestrians.

At 3.5 km (2.2 mi), you reach the first of many swamps and wetlands, and another gravel track connects here. About 150 m/yd further, there is a solitary interpretive panel next to a pond (ominously, the blackfly). A regulatory sign states that the speed limit is 50 kph (30 mph); be aware that ATVs might be travelling that quickly.

Another interpretive panel sits within sight of a lovely farm and barn on the right at 4.1 km (2.5 mi). Although there have been cleared fields before along the trail, this is the first cultivated land. There are glimpses of more, usually to the right, all the way to the next road crossing.

Before that, there is a lovely big swamp containing a beaver lodge about 250 m/yd from the farm. Beavers are usually nocturnal, but I did sight a muskrat cruising about, and a kingfisher was chattering away in the trees.

4.9 km (3 mi) The trail reaches the Upper River John Road, where there are nearby buildings and fields but not services. As usual, there is no directional signage or maps. In addition, the pathway crosses this 80 kph (50 mph) highway at a bad angle where the road curves, reducing visibility. Exercise extreme caution when crossing.

Once again, the track enters a forested area, but from this point, glimpses of fields are more common. When the trail passes a pond at 5.3 km (3.3 mi), there are cultivated fields on its far side. Three hundred metres/yards after that, farm equipment crossings become frequent, one at 5.7 km (3.5 mi) and another 100 m/yd further. The trail is rougher here, as portions were clearly used by the machinery.

At 6.3 km (3.9 mi), a large, flooded forest lies to the left side of the trail. You might notice a sign on a tree far out in the middle of the pond that explains this is a TCT Beaver Pond Conservation Project in cooperation with Ducks Unlimited, but you probably can't read it without binoculars.

Back in the thickly wooded area, only the frequent wetlands create openings alongside the trail. There is quite a large one on the right at 7.6 km (4.7 mi), and the largest one on this route is 200 m/yd further on the same side.

8.8 km (5.5 mi) The trail crosses Jim Sutherland Road (dirt), visible for 200 m/yd before reaching it. Gates line both sides of the trail to restrict vehicle access and to slow trail riders. As with other road crossings, houses and fields are visible near the pathway.

About 150 m/yd after it passes the road, the trail curves right in the most distinct turn thus far. For the first time, the ground on the right is noticeably higher while to the left it falls away. At 9.4 km (5.8 mi), there is a short space where the ground is a few metres below you on both sides.

9.7 km (6 mi) Abruptly, the trail comes out of the trees and arrives at Highway 6, which is usually a quite busy road. The large Lockerby Memorial Cemetery is on a hill to the right, while on the left, you can see the Waughs River and some of Tatamagouche's buildings. Regulatory signage decorates the gate on the opposite side of the road, with the most important information being that the maximum speed is now 20 kph (12.5 mph).

From here, the pathway is surfaced with crushed stone, somewhat improving the ride. Just 200 m/yd from the road, the trail crosses the Waughs River on a steel through-truss bridge with excellent views of the river estuary to the right. The bridge is decked and railed, and there is an interpretive panel crediting the Canadian Military Engineers for their work repairing this structure.

Short Line and Butter Trails

Along Nova Scotia's North Shore, the Trans Canada/Great Trail follows the route of the Intercolonial Railroad's former Oxford Junction to Stellarton "Short Line." This 127 km (78.9 mi) long railroad began operating both freight and passenger service in 1887 and continued running trains until 1986. By 1989, the rails had been removed, and the line waited another decade before beginning its new life as a recreational corridor.

Several groups and municipalities manage this facility, but the 4 km (2.5 mi) within the Village of Tatamagouche are known as the Butter Trail and are maintained by the volunteers of the Tatamagouche Area Trails Association. It is due to their efforts that this is the only section surfaced with crushed stone.

About 400 m/yd beyond the river, the trail arrives next to a very large, open trailhead parking area, clearly utilized for other purposes. Some picnic tables are positioned adjacent to the pathway, and directly ahead is the slightly incongruous sight of a long row of railroad cabooses and a few dining cars, still mounted on rails. This is the Train Station Inn, a unique B&B, with a restaurant in the former railway station and lodging in retired railway cars.

The trail passes alongside many of the rail cars and takes a slight wiggle around them where the former railbed is blocked. Once round this minor diversion, a gleaming-white grain elevator is ahead. Or it once was; now it is home to artisans and shops. A side trail to a nearby restaurant branches left before you reach the elevator.

Just beyond the grain elevator at 10.8 km (6.7 mi), the trail reaches Creamery Square, a complex of new buildings that houses a Farmers Market, a heritage centre, and an arts centre. There are a bike rack, benches, and interpretive panels next to the trail and washrooms in the Creamery complex.

Pine Street, the road access to Creamery Square, crosses the path 50 m/yd from the bike racks. About 100 m/yd to the left are grocery stores, coffee shops, and other businesses. This is the best location to access the community, because beyond Creamery Square, the trail quickly returns to being bordered by thick forest.

The trail runs near water level and quite close to the water's edge, while most of Tatamagouche is built on higher ground. In summer, the thick vegetation hides each from the other. At 11.5 km (7.1 mi), the path passes above a gravel road. To the right is Patterson's Wharf, a community-built rest area overlooking the Waughs River estuary, featuring barbeques – stone fireplaces really – as well as benches and tables.

The trail past this is a lovely forested glide to the long bridge crossing the French River at 12.2 km (7.6 mi). Expansive views into Tatamagouche Bay are possible from its deck, and the large structure of the Tatamagouche Centre can be seen on the bank opposite. The Village of Tatamagouche officially ends at the river. The remaining 1 km (0.6 mi) is enclosed by forest until the final 200 m/yd. Views of the water are possible throughout, and side trails are common in the last 500 m/yd.

13.2 km (8.2 mi) The trail arrives at Nelson Memorial Park, which is both open and forested, and quite large at 19 ha (47 ac). Several buildings sit to your left on top of a long, sloping lawn, including large picnic shelters, some with barbeques. Washrooms can be found there. To the right are more picnic tables, benches, a gazebo, and floral gardens.

The trail curves left and back among the trees, but I recommend stopping near the parking area. On the right, the open view reveals the broad expanse of Tatamagouche Bay. Side paths lead to tables and benches, an ideal lunch location. Stop here, and relish the beauty of the setting, before returning to Denmark and the Sutherland Steam Museum.

Further Information:
Municipality of Colchester County: www.colchester.ca/trans-canada-trail
Sutherland Steam Mill: https://sutherlandsteammill.novascotia.ca/
Village of Tatamagouche: https://villageoftatamagouche.com/tourism/
    what-to-do

PRINCE EDWARD ISLAND

Confederation Trail

The Confederation Trail is the name of a recreational trail system developed on the route of the former Prince Edward Island Railway, which was abandoned in 1989 by Canadian National Railway. The provincial government acquired the right of way in 1994 and by 2000 had developed the main line from Tignish to Elmira, more than 273 km (170 mi).

Additional branch lines have been developed in recent years with the Stratford-Iona section officially opening in late 2014. The Confederation Trail network currently developed exceeds 400 km (248.5 mi) in total length. Surfaced with crushed stone, it is ideal for walking and biking. In winter, it is leased to the snowmobile association.

Prince Edward Island was the first province to complete one hundred percent of their Great Trail route. They are still able to claim that they are one of the few provincial routes almost completely made up of off-road pathway.

7. Mount Stewart to St. Peters Bay

With more than 400 km (248.5 mi) of trail from which to choose, people from PEI might be expected to give several suggestions for their favourite section of the Confederation Trail. However, almost without exception, they answered that it is the section between the communities of Morell and St. Peters Bay. Perhaps this should not be surprising because this is the portion of the trail with the most ocean views.

As an outsider, my view is slightly different. Although I agree that the trail from Morell to St. Peters Bay is exceptionally scenic, I think that it is worthwhile to include the section between Mount Stewart and Morell too. By doing so, it adds a picturesque stretch along the Hillsborough River and includes areas of woodland and farmland that, taken with the ocean views, provide almost a complete sample of everything you might see on PEI – except for beaches.

I feel that I should also state that the trail community of PEI was deeply disappointed that I chose to profile only one section of their trail. I can assure you and them that I made that decision not because no other sections were worthy but because of book limitations. From Mount Stewart to St. Peters Bay should only be your first sample of a wonderful trail system that is part of The Great Trail – the Confederation Trail.

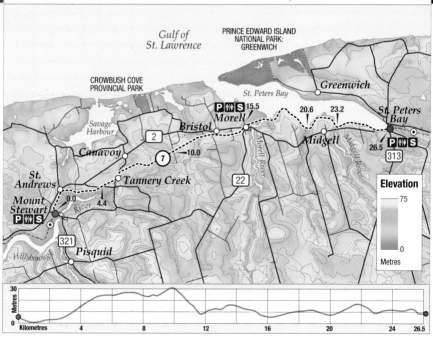

7. Mount Stewart to St. Peters Bay

TRUE
MAGNETIC

Contour Interval: 10M
5 KILOMETRES

7. Mount Stewart to St. Peters Bay

Distance: 26.5 km (16.5 mi) – one way
Ascent: 114 m (374 ft),
Descent: 110 m (360 ft)

Trail conditions: crushed stone
Cellphone coverage: yes
Hazards: road crossings

Permitted Uses							
Walking	Biking	Horseback Riding	Inline Skating	ATV	Snowshoeing	Cross-country Skiing	Snowmobiling
✔	✔	—	—	—	—	—	✔

Finding the trailhead: This route begins in the parking lot of the Hillsborough River Eco-Centre, which sits adjacent to the Confederation Trail. You might wish to visit their bakery before starting or use their washroom. On the grounds are picnic tables, garbage cans, several interpretive panels, and a directional sign, indicating that the community of Morell is 16 km (10 mi) away.

Trailhead: 46°21'59.3"N, 62°52'13.7"W (Start — Mount Stewart)
46°24'53.9"N, 62°34'47.8"W (Finish — St. Peters Bay)

Observations: This ride was finished too quickly. I was treated to a beautiful sunny October day. The trees were just beginning to change colour, and shoals of migratory birds populated the waters and banks of St. Peters Bay. In additional to individuals walking and cycling, many families were enjoying the trail, which provided the day with a relaxed, convivial atmosphere. The excellent treadway allowed for high cycling speeds, and I reached the community of St. Peters Bay seemingly before I finished warming up. My only disappointment was in Morell, where I was told there was a great new chip wagon. The crisp, cool October air seemed perfect for poutine, but they said that they did not use curds, but grated mozzarella. Quel dommage!

Route description: Begin by crossing Highway 22 (Main Street); the main trail and the Cardigan branch trail connect 100 m/yd later. Keep left, passing the km 204 marker 100 m/yd from the junction. The brush bordering the pathway is lush though not terribly high, and wetlands bordering the Hillsborough River soon appear on the right. At 900 m/yd, there is an interpretive panel and 100 m/yd later a short boardwalk to an observation deck overlooking a small pond.

The trail curves right, bordered by extensive wetlands, before crossing St. Andrews Creek at 2.3 km (1.4 mi). From here, there is an excellent view to the right of the Hillsborough River. The first of the distinctive, sheltered picnic tables is reached 250 m/yd later. Nearby are three more interpretive panels and a sign directing you up a side trail to a B&B.

The trail begins climbing gradually with the Hillsborough River visible to the right. About 800 m/yd beyond the shelter is a viewing platform with an interpretive panel about "The Love of Horses." Shortly afterward the fields end, and trees block further river views.

♀4.4 km (2.7 mi) As it continues to climb, the track curves left, crossing the distinctive red soil of PEI on clay-surfaced Highway 323. It remains thickly forested for the next 1.2 km (0.7 mi) until crossing Highway 352, also clay-surfaced. After this, there is a large blueberry field on the left, the first of several you'll encounter.

A very remote section follows, particularly for PEI as it is the most densely populated province in Canada. The next 2.7 km (1.7 mi) are thickly wooded, interspersed with frequent patches of boggy ground and the occasional interpretive panel. By rail trail standards, the climb is quite noticeable; your legs are able to tell.

Just past the km 213 marker, the trail opens up onto fields, and there are even two communication towers nearby. It is 600 m/yd further to the crest where the full extent of the size of the blueberry fields is evident.

♀10 km (6.2 mi) The trail crosses clay-surfaced MacEwan Road, a very modest thoroughfare. Heading downhill now, the trail bisects a sizable blueberry field. About 900 m/yd from the road crossing sits a large rest area, still in the middle of the blueberry field, containing a bench, sheltered table, and three interpretive panels.

After it finally re-enters the forest – lovely hardwoods here – the trail crosses Kenovan Road 400 m/yd later. About 700 m/yd beyond that is MacKinnons Pond, which the trail crosses on a high embankment. The trail remains in dense forest, broken only by the occasional road crossing. Perry Road crosses 250 m/yd from the pond, and Settlement Road is 550 m/yd after that at 12.8 km (8 mi). Both of these are paved, and from both crossings, you can see Highway 2 to the left.

There was a new sign on the trail near Settlement Road, added in the two years between my travels on this section, which provided direction to a nearby B&B. Island Trails wisely is planning to add more signs similar to it. By the time you read this, there likely are many others that I have not mentioned.

Another 1 km (0.6 mi) of thick forest follows before a large beaver pond is reached. This is relatively new, so the drowned trees still rise from the water like ghostly sentinels. An osprey had established a nest not far from the path, and its brood made quite a racket screeching for their meal. This pond continues for 400 m/yd, until it crosses Coffin Road.

The final 1.2 km (0.7 mi) into Morell is a pleasant level ride with houses and lawns progressively replacing the trees bordering the pathway. There are numerous interpretive panels, two about 300 m/yd from Coffin Road, and some others as you near the community.

15.5 km (9.6 mi) The trail reaches Highway 2 in Morell, where the former train station has been converted into an information centre, café, and outdoor activity centre. In the summer and early fall, this can be quite a busy spot, bustling with many walkers and cyclists. Should you wish to explore the community or need something not available at the café, other businesses are nearby.

Across the road, a directional sign states that the community of St. Peters Bay is 12 km (7.5 mi) further. Elmira, the eastern end of the Confederation Trail, is 54 km (33.6 mi) away. Leaving Morell, the path enters a long wooded straightaway after crossing Red Head Road, just 150 m/yd from Highway 2. Within 800 m/yd, unhindered views of the Morell River Estuary are possible on the right. At the km 200 marker, there is yet another interpretive panel. (If you read them all, this significantly enhances but slows your ride.)

About 400 m/yd later, the trail reaches the Morell River Bridge; at 72 m/yd, it is the longest structure on the entire Confederation Trail. To the left is St. Peters Bay, and the land on the far shore belongs to the Greenwich Dunes fragment of Prince Edward Island National Park. More information panels are found bracketing the km 219 marker.

The trail re-enters a forested area for another 1 km (0.6 mi), where there is another panel placed at a clay-surfaced road crossing. Still another panel is found 300 m/yd after that, near a sheltered picnic table. By this point, the trail is quite close to St. Peters Bay, and it remains in sight of the water for the remainder of the route, excepting a few occasions when thick trees obstruct the view.

At 19 km (11.8 mi), the trail crosses Dingwell Road, after which neatly cultivated fields swathe the low hills to the right. It is a pleasant ride with St. Peters Bay on the left and pastures and meadows on the right for the next 1.6 km (1 mi).

20.6 km (12.8 mi) The trail reaches the Marie River, which is crossed on another fairly large bridge. The ubiquitous PEI information panels are positioned just before and after this structure. The trail curves left along the shoreline and climbs ever so slightly. A barrier of trees blocks the view of the ocean, though there are frequent gaps; as they are mostly hardwoods, they are no obstacle in the autumn. When the trail reaches Cemetery Road 1.3 km (0.8 mi) from the bridge, there are views both into St. Peters Bay and to the fields inland.

The next picnic shelter, supplemented by two more interpretive panels, sits 800 m/yd further along in a small copse. Alongside it can be found a special bronze plaque commemorating Adam Mermuys, a dedicated local trail volunteer, who is now deceased.

23.2 km (14.4 mi) The third major bridge of this section crosses the Midgell River and is quite close to Highway 2. It features only one interpretive panel, and its best views are over the water. For the remaining 3.3 km (2.1 mi), the trail runs very close to the water's edge. Broad views are available of St. Peters Bay and the farms decorating the hills opposite. The large St. Peters Bay Roman Catholic Church, gleaming whitely in the sunshine on the hillside above the community, acts as a beacon and measure of progress. Just before reaching the community, there is a fairly large campground alongside the trail, and camp users – including children – frequently pop onto the path without warning, so be cautious.

For the final 850 m/yd, as it enters the community, the trail is squeezed between Highway 2 and the ocean. The road is higher, and there is a wall separating the parallel tracks. The area is wide open without trees, and high winds are common at the bay's end.

Where the trail reaches Highway 2, there is a T junction road intersection just to the right. This can be tricky since there is no crosswalk, and the vehicles making a left turn are behind your right shoulder. This is the most dangerous road crossing of this route.

26.5 km (16.5 mi) Once across Highway 2, the trail reaches the attractive Visitor Information Centre, which has bike racks and washrooms. A boardwalk and bridge lead from there to the stores and services in the community of St. Peters Bay, including the local favourite Rick's Fish & Chips. Either snack at a picnic table or visit one of the local eateries, then retrace the route to Mount Stewart.

Further Information:
Confederation Trail: www.tourismpei.com/pei-confederation-trail
Island Trails: http://islandtrails.ca
Tourism PEI: www.tourismpei.com

Ring-necked Pheasant

Native to Asia, ring-necked pheasants were introduced in North America in the 1800s and have long been one of the continent's most-sought-after game birds, renowned for their succulent meat. The male is particularly colourful and is one of the most distinctive bird species. It is often seen running alongside the road or flying away in a low-altitude near-glide.

A ground dweller, pheasants prefer agricultural landscapes where waste grains from crop fields provide a substantial percentage of their diet. Ring-necks require a nesting cover of grasses and stubble high enough to conceal nests but allow for easy ground travel.

8. Fundy National Park

Eastern Hemlock

The eastern hemlock prefers shady cool and humid climates with rainfall exceeding 750 mm (30 in) a year. In these convivial conditions, the long-lived hemlock can reach heights exceeding 50 m/yd in the Appalachians, although 30 m/yd is more common in Canada.

Hemlocks can live up to six hundred years and during that time create a pure stand that crowds out other species. In an old stand, often found on the north-facing slope of a steeper hillside with a canopy high overhead, the ground beneath the towering trees supports no other life than mosses and lichens.

8. Fundy National Park

The Great Trail only passes through one National Park in eastern Canada: Fundy. Opened in 1948, Fundy National Park encompasses more than 207 km^2 (128.6 mi^2), including more than 20 km (12.4 mi) of Bay of Fundy coastline. Having the highest tides in the world, commonly varying by 12 m (39 ft) from low to high – the height of a four-storey building! – the Bay of Fundy is a major attraction.

Fortunately, this park maintains some excellent hiking paths, and none is superior to the Coastal Trail that constitutes a significant portion of The Great Trail inside the park. From the end of the Coastal Trail at Point Wolfe River, the Goose River Trail extends the hike and connects to the Fundy Footpath, a 41 km (25.5 mi) coastal wilderness trek from Fundy National Park to the Fundy Trail at Big Salmon River.

This is a strenuous hike over difficult terrain. However, it can also be broken down into as many as three separate day trips for those with the time: Dickson Brook to Herring Cove 6.5 km (4 mi) return, Herring Cove to Pointe Wolfe River 12.8 km (8 mi) return, and Pointe Wolfe River to Goose River 17.8 km (11.1 mi). Personally, I recommend hiking from Dickson Brook to Goose River, camping overnight, and returning the following day.

Cycling was once permitted on the Goose River Trail. However, severe erosion has made some sections impassable, so the path is now walking only. Over the next several years, the Goose River Trail will be moved away from the former road and onto a newly constructed footpath. It is possible to cross-country ski on the Goose River Trail; it probably is not possible on the Coastal Trail.

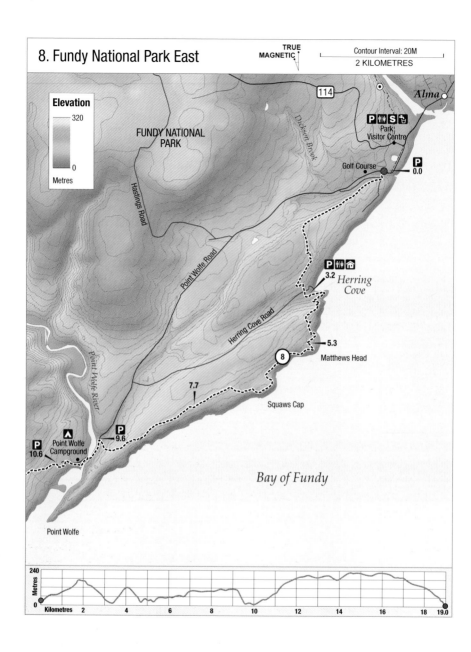

8. Fundy National Park East

TRUE
MAGNETIC

Contour Interval: 20M
2 KILOMETRES

Elevation
320

0
Metres

FUNDY NATIONAL
PARK

Dickson Brook

114

Alma

P ŵ S ⚑
Park
Visitor Centre

Golf Course

P
0.0

Hastings Road

Point Wolfe Road

P ŵ ⌂
3.2 *Herring Cove*

Herring Cove Road

5.3
Matthews Head

8

7.7

Squaws Cap

Point Wolfe River

P
9.6

⛺
Point Wolfe
Campground

P
10.6

Bay of Fundy

Point Wolfe

240
Metres

0
Kilometres   2   4   6   8   10   12   14   16   18   19.0

8. Fundy National Park

Distance: 18.9 km (11.7 mi) – one way
Ascent: 769 m (2,523 ft)
Descent: 797 m (2,615 ft)

Trail conditions: asphalt, crushed stone, natural surface
Cellphone coverage: partial
Hazards: road crossings, wildlife

Permitted Uses							
Walking	Biking	Horseback Riding	Inline Skating	ATV	Snowshoeing	Cross-country Skiing	Snowmobiling
✔	—	—	—	—	✔	✔*	—

Finding the trailhead: The Coastal Trail begins beside a parking area on the Point Wolfe Road next to Dickson Brook. Head back in the direction of Alma, then turn right and cross the bridge over Dickson Brook. The trailhead gateway with map and trail sign affixed is on the far side to the right.

Trailhead: 45°35'29.3" N, 64°57'17.9" W (Start — Dickson Brook)
45°31'35.6" N, 65°05'39.8" W (Finish — Goose River)

Observations: I hiked this section over two days in late October. As often occurs next to the ocean, the weather changed frequently, sometimes sunny and warm, other times cool and cloudy. With its many steep hills, I found the first half of the route, to Point Wolfe River, quite physically demanding. Nevertheless, I enjoyed the ocean views from the hilltops, no matter how much effort was required. From there to Goose River was relatively easy, if less scenic, because the route kept inland. Goose River was an excellent campsite, and it was tempting to continue from there onto the Fundy Footpath. Be aware there are cellphone dead zones on the Coastal Trail on the Bay of Fundy shore, and there is only occasional coverage on the Goose River Trail.

Route description: The Coastal Trail is a naturally surfaced footpath that climbs straightaway after passing beneath the trailhead gateway. Thick vegetation soon enfolds you, particularly spruce, which limits visibility. For the first 1.9 km (1.2 mi), the hike follows near the top of a ridge, named Devils Hill, although on the inland side of the crest. Occasionally, the road or even the golf course can be sighted in gaps among the trees. There is one place, about 1.6 km (1 mi) from the start, where the path is wedged between rocky outcroppings on the left and an almost sheer slope on the right.

At 2 km (1.2 mi), just after the footpath crosses over the crest, the Bay of Fundy is sighted. The hill is thickly wooded with quite tall spruce and hemlock, and the drop on the left is very steep. About 350 m/yd later, there is almost a look-off through a wider opening in the vegetation on a cliff more than 150 m/yd above water level.

After another 300 m/yd of fairly level walking, the trail descends rapidly to reach the junction with the Tippen Lot Trail at 2.9 km (1.8 mi). There is clear signage, a map, and even a TCT marker — one of many along this route. Head left towards Herring Cove.

In the remaining 200 m/yd, you pass through small meadows that are a sea of ferns in summer and emerge at a large clearing where there is another gateway with a map beside it. Should you wish to stop and rest, there are shelters at Herring Cove — at least one with a woodstove — along with washrooms, picnic tables, and a beach.

3.2 km (2 mi) To continue, cross the large field to the trailhead gateway on the far side. The information panel accompanying the map beside the gateway is quite explicit about the challenges of the next 6 km (3.8 mi) or more: "Difficult, steep uphill to the top of a ridge followed by a steep descent." This is perhaps not encouraging but useful information.

The first few hundred metres/yards are quite easy, however, as the trail crosses a tiny brook and works around a headland. There are good views of Herring Cove Beach and the coastline back towards the community of Alma, and several side paths allow access to the water and to the very tip of this small point. You can probably also notice some foundation ruins in the adjacent woods.

After 400 m/yd, the route turns right more than 180°, and about 50 m/yd further, look to the left, where there is a look-off and two Parks Canada Red Chairs, part of the Red Chair Program. Enjoy the view because the steep climb begins immediately afterwards, although only for about 400 m/yd before the slope eases.

At 4.4 km (2.7 mi), a descent that is much steeper than the climb begins with multiple switchbacks. It is also quite rough with exposed tree roots and loose, slippery soil. The hardwoods at the top of the ridge have given way to thick white spruce.

At the bottom of the hill, 600 m/yd later, the path emerges at a look-off near water level next to a small cove. Two more of the Red Chairs sit facing a wooden fence that is posted with warnings of slippery rocks and high waves. The trail makes another sharp turn, veering away from the water.

5.3 km (3.3 mi) You reach the first junction with the Matthews Head Trail, which features a map and directional signs. Turn left where the path returns to the coastline at Matthews Head, 150 m/yd later.

The next stretch of trail is quite scenic as it mostly remains close to the water

and provides frequent views of both the Bay of Fundy and the rugged shoreline. As the edge is often cliff, there are usually fences on the ocean side whenever the path comes close. The ground is quite uneven, and there are frequent wet areas as well, but as the trail contours along the ridge, it is quite enjoyable.

At 6.9 km (4.3 mi), there is a look-off quite high up the slope with a bench — and two more Red Chairs located where it would have been a major challenge to pack them in. About 100 m/yd further is the Squaws Cap Look-off with another bench.

Not long afterwards, the trail moves slightly away from the water and enters a gorgeous area where there is a high overhead canopy of mature spruce and a dense secondary covering of younger trees. These are so thick that it feels as if you are traversing a hedge maze. This interesting section is very short, however, and very soon the claustrophobic is able to relax.

7.7 km (4.8 mi) You reach the second junction with the Matthews Head Trail, where there is another map. It heads right, but your route continues straight. The path is quite high again at about 100 m/yd above the water. However, the hillside is not as steep, and the trail is further back from the coastline. The Bay of Fundy is still often visible, but the views are less striking.

For about the next 1.3 km (0.8 mi), the trail is a pleasant meander through the forest, undulating and curving slightly but not requiring great effort. At 9 km (5.6 mi), this changes when the route makes a sharp turn right and begins to descend.

For the next 600 m/yd, the trail drops down the hillside with the sheer slope requiring numerous switchbacks. Fortunately, the treadway is in good condition

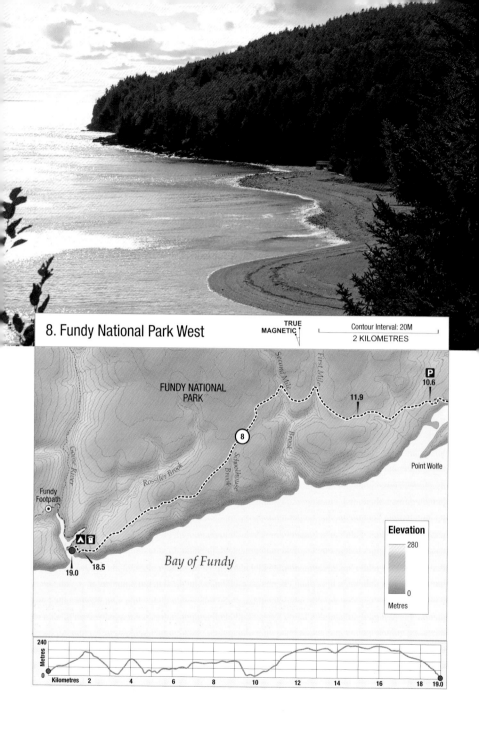

8. Fundy National Park West

TRUE
MAGNETIC

Contour Interval: 20M
2 KILOMETRES

FUNDY NATIONAL
PARK

Grouse River

Rossiter Brook

Schoolhouse Brook

Second Mile

First Mile

Brook

P
10.6

11.9

8

Point Wolfe

Fundy
Footpath

19.0 18.5

Bay of Fundy

Elevation

280

0

Metres

240
Metres
0
Kilometres 2   4   6   8   10   12   14   16   18 19.0

although often deeply etched into the ground; otherwise the sharp grade would be even more challenging.

9.6 km (6 mi) The footpath ends at the side of the Point Wolfe Road, directly across from a parking area with a large interpretive display. The Point Wolfe River can be reached easily from the parking area.

From the end of the Coastal Trail, turn left and walk along the road. Be cautious as the Point Wolfe campground is on the other side of the river, and this road can be quite busy in the summer. Fortunately, it is only 350 m/yd to the covered bridge spanning Point Wolfe River, and as soon as you have crossed, there is a footpath on the left called the Shiphaven Trail.

This is quite an elaborately developed footpath. There are numerous interpretive panels, look-offs, and observation decks. Long boardwalks and stairs keep the walking easy, and where there is no boardwalk, the path is wide and surfaced in crushed stone. There are several excellent views of the mouth of the Point Wolfe River. You might also notice the road from time to time to the right.

At 900 m/yd there is a major, well-signed junction. If you wish a short diversion, walk the 400 m/yd to Point Wolfe Beach. For Goose River, continue straight for 1 km (0.6 mi) towards the Point Wolfe Parking Lot.

10.6 km (6.6 mi) Cut diagonally across the parking lot to reach the trailhead. There is a TCT sign and maps. To the left is the route to the Coppermine Trail; to the right, the list of trails above the gateway mentions Foster Brook, Marven Lake, Bennett Lake, and Goose River, the path that you take.

As soon as you start up the path, there is a sign that states that it is 7.9 km (4.9 mi) to Goose River. Within 100 m/yd, the footpath connects with the former road, which is wide and surprisingly rocky. The area is thickly forested, and this route is far from the ocean, so there are no views through this section.

The trail climbs steadily; the first feature of note, other than some interpretive panels, is Hastie Brook at 11.3 km (7 mi). By 11.6 km (7.2 mi), the erosion of the roadbed is quite severe and care must be taken to avoid the deeper ruts.

📍**11.9 km (7.4 mi)** You reach the junction with the Marven Lake Trail, which veers to the right and continues uphill. There is a map, but the large TCT sign on the path should guide you correctly. Most of the thick forest around you is softwood, though some hardwoods are sprinkled among them. There is no view at all now, except what is directly ahead.

When the trail begins to descend, that is your warning that you are approaching the sturdy bridge crossing First Mile Brook, which you reach at 13.2 km (8.2 mi). Once across, the climb resumes with another deeper drop to the bridge crossing Second Mile Brook at 14 km (8.7 mi). The climb on the far side is much steeper, and the next 400 m/yd is severely eroded with more than half the width of the pathway scoured out, sometimes as deep as one metre/yard.

Once the trail levels, the erosion runnels disappear, and the next section is uneventful, except for occasional undulations. Generally, the ground to the right is higher, and it falls off on the left. At 16.7 km (10.4 mi), the trail crosses tiny Schoolhouse Brook, which is in a culvert. The next 2 km (1.2 mi) is rather pleasant but unexciting. Occasional glimpses of the ocean can be had, and where the vegetation is thinner, you might even regain cell coverage.

📍**18.5 km (11.5 mi)** You arrive at the Goose River campsites with outhouses, firewood, and tables. The trail continues and after 100 m/yd reaches a junction. To the right, it is 2.1 km (1.3 mi) to the start of the Fundy Footpath; directly ahead, it is 400 m/yd to Goose River Beach.

Continue straight. The road ends, changing into a narrow footpath. As it descends the hillside to the beach, it actually becomes one of the most challenging portions of the walk – steep and narrow with difficult footing and switchbacks. Fortunately, this difficult fragment is short.

📍**19 km (11.8 mi)** The trail ends at Goose River Beach, an attractive sand-and-gravel bar, sheltered by low rocky headlands. At least two of the campsites are located there – above high water, naturally. This is a wonderful place to rest, have a meal, and maybe take a swim. If you are not camping and are ready to return, retrace your route back to the Dickson Brook trailhead.

Further Information:
Fundy National Park: http://www.pc.gc.ca/en/pn-np/nb/fundy
Bay of Fundy Tourism: http://bayoffundytourism.com
Village of Alma: http://www.villageofalma.ca

Boreal Chickadee

The least common of the two species of chickadee living in eastern Canada, the boreal chickadee is one of the few species to be found in the deep woods throughout the year. In winter, it often travels in company with golden-crowned kinglets and red-breasted nuthatches, the small grey-brown birds flitting among the spruce and fir.

Curious and very comfortable around people, chickadees are hikers' frequent companions. In the more northerly softwood forests, particularly at higher altitudes, the boreal chickadee is often found. It can be distinguished from its black-capped cousin by its brownish-grey head and slower, wheezier *chick-a-dee-dee* call.

9. Fundy Trail

Since it first opened in 1999, the Fundy Trail has been an attraction for visitors to the province. With the creation of a planned coastal access network on an undeveloped stretch of the Bay of Fundy shoreline, New Brunswick hoped to create a tourism destination, including a low-speed auto parkway with scenic lookouts – all wheelchair accessible – a pedestrian/bicycle trail, footpaths to beaches and river estuaries, and an Interpretive Centre.

This trail is definitely worthwhile, encompassing scenic views from headlands and winding descents – and climbs – into deep, lushly forested ravines and side paths with access to wonderful beaches. It is also surprisingly difficult. Much of the Bay of Fundy coastline is cliff, often 150-250 m (492-820 ft) high. Every stream and creek that enters the Bay of Fundy has gouged a deep, steep-sided gorge that requires considerable effort to traverse, and while the road often remains on the crest, the trail explores every ravine. You get good exercise completing this trail.

Families and novice hikers/bikers should approach this trail with caution and not expect to be able to complete the entire trail and return in one day. The Fundy Trail Parkway is operated by a non-profit organization and charges fees per person for entry, varying with age. In addition, it is only officially open between mid-May and mid-October and for certain hours, 8:00 a.m. to 8:00 p.m. during the height of summer. Consult the trail website for up-to-date details.

9. Fundy Trail

TRUE
MAGNETIC

Contour Interval: 10M

1 KILOMETRE

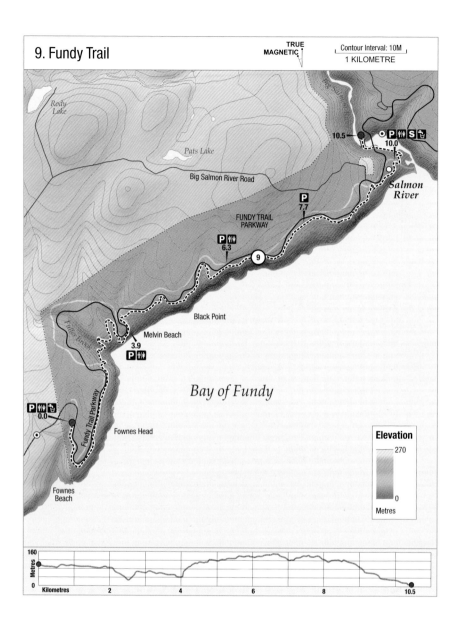

Rody Lake

Pats Lake

Big Salmon River Road

FUNDY TRAIL PARKWAY

10.5

P ｉ S ♻
10.0

Salmon River

P
7.7

P ｉ
6.3

9

Black Point

Fuller Brook

Melvin Beach

3.9
P ｉ

Bay of Fundy

P ｉ ♻
0.0

Fundy Trail Parkway

Fownes Head

Fownes Beach

Elevation

270

0

Metres

9. Fundy Trail

Distance: 10.5 km (6.5 mi) – one way
Ascent: 308 m (1,010 ft)
Descent: 358 m (1,175 ft)

Trail conditions: crushed stone, asphalt, natural surface
Cellphone coverage: partial
Hazards: wildlife

Permitted Uses							
Walking	Biking	Horseback Riding	Inline Skating	ATV	Snowshoeing	Cross-country Skiing	Snowmobiling
✔	✔	—	—	—	✔	✔	—

Finding the trailhead: Start at the parking lot just past the entrance kiosk, where there are washrooms, garbage cans, a pay phone (!), and interpretive panels. A paper map of the trail is available at the kiosk on request.

Trailhead: 45°23'17"N, 65°27'35.2"W (Start — Fundy Trail Parkway Entrance)
45°25'23.1"N, 65°24'38"W (Finish — Big Salmon River)

Observations: This was the first section of The Great Trail that I hiked/biked for this book. I say "hiked/biked" because, although I tried to bicycle the Fundy Trail, I found several of the hills too steep to cycle up and, with the humidity and moss, too slippery to ride down. As well, cellphone reception was uncertain at the bottom of some ravines. As a result, I walked a significant percentage of the total distance. And "hike/bike" might be the best way to travel this trail because it would require a long day to walk it without the bicycle to assist on the more level sections. Other than the practical challenges, it was very scenic, and some of the side paths should be explored, certainly to the waterfall and one or two of the beaches.

Route description: Although surfaced in crushed stone, grass has grown in to cover much of the pathway, which is wide like a rail trail but undulating. Within 500 m/yd, the trail reaches the first observation deck at Fox Rock with views from high above the water. Less than 200 m/yd later, there is a shelter, a map, more interpretive panels, and washrooms. You can also see a km 1 marker; the trail actually starts a short distance outside the parkway and perhaps it is measured from there.

The road continues to be close on the left as you pass or stop at: the Fownes Head Lookout at 1.1 km (0.7 mi), the side trail to the Sea Captains' Burial Ground

Big Salmon River

Although abandoned today, the rugged Bay of Fundy coastline was a hub of industry in the late 1800s. Big Salmon River, where the Interpretive Centre is located, was a flourishing logging, fishing, and shipbuilding community well into the mid-1950s. Today, the forest has reclaimed the once-cleared slopes, and there are few signs that people once lived and worked here. From the suspension bridge, you can see crib work of the old wharves where the sawmill used to be and the remains of the sluice down which logs were sent to the mill; near the Interpretive Centre is the foundation of the one-room schoolhouse.

at 1. 5 km (0.9 mi), the Melvin Beach Lookout at 1.9 km (1.2 mi), and the multiple observation decks for Flower Pot Rock. This short section is packed with tables, benches, interpretive panels, and other facilities.

At 2.1 km (1.3 mi), road and pathway diverge as the trail begins a steep descent. The grade is so severe that the surface has been asphalted to reduce erosion. About 200 m/yd later, there is a junction with the Flower Pot Rock Footpath. As the trail descends into the ravine, the grade steepens, the vegetation gets thicker, and spots of moss grow on the asphalt – making quick bicycle stops more hazardous. The increase in humidity is noticeable as you navigate the curving, steep pathway.

The bridge at the bottom of the hill, crossing the west branch of Fuller Brook, is reached at 2.7 km (1.7 mi). Just before it is a junction with the Bradshaw Scenic Footpath. The s-shaped bridge is fairly long and built massive and strong, testimony to the power of the spring runoff, but difficult to imagine looking at the modest trickle in the brook in July.

Once across, there is an outhouse and a short side trail to Melvin Beach that is worth reconnoitring. You might enjoy a short breather on the beach because, after that, the trail climbs about 200 m/yd back out of the ravine and on a grade so steep that I could not cycle it. At the top of the hill, there is an intersection with a side trail to parking area P3 – a good opportunity to abandon the trail, if necessary.

The pathway turns right and becomes nearly level again, regaining its crushed-stone surface. At 3.4 km (2.1 mi), another sturdy bridge is crossed, this time over the east branch of Fuller Brook. Another 250 m/yd after that, there is an intersection with a side trail to Fuller Falls. This is an interesting short detour, but only undertake it if you are prepared for a steep descent on a cable ladder.

3.9 km (2.4 mi) When you see the km 4 marker, you have reached the Pangburn Beach Lookout. The road and pathway reconnect here, and there are a variety of facilities, including a washroom, benches, and covered tables. Parking lot P4 is the access point for motorists to reach Fuller Falls, so cyclists should use extra caution in this area.

Once past this lookout, the trail resumes its climb, with asphalt covering the steepest sections. Thick forest limits your view of the ocean as the trail ascends more than 75 m (246 ft) to the Black Point Lookout at 5.3 km (3.3 mi). There is another stop for cars here and the usual observation deck, picnic tables, garbage cans, and interpretive panels. More wooded pathway follows, hidden from view of the road and more level now with two short bridges providing some variation. However, views of the ocean remain restricted.

6.3 km (3.9 mi) Trail and road reconnect at parking area P5 where, in addition to other amenities, there is a washroom. The trail returns to the thickly wooded hillside and begins one of the sections I most enjoyed with a gently rolling, sinuously winding route. Hearst Lookout, about 250 m/yd from P5, did not have a particularly great view.

The trail through here is relatively easy riding, although at 7 km (4.3 mi) a sign warns – fittingly – of a steep downhill. The Pejepscot Lookout at 7.1 km (4.4 mi) is another with a restricted vista. About 250 m/yd later, after crossing a small bridge, the least pleasant section of the trail begins. Instead of crushed stone, a layer of deep unpacked sandy aggregate covers the pathway. My bicycle tires sank into it. Like turning the resistance high on a stationary bike, the effort required to continue is much greater.

7.7 km (4.8 mi) Pathway and road reunite at the Davidson Lookout, where there are the usual shelters, garbage cans, interpretive panels, and benches. For the best view, climb to road level. The challenging trail surface persists over the undulating terrain, and two small lookouts, accessed only from the trail, are reached in the following 1 km (0.6 mi).

At 8.9 km (5.5 mi), where there is a gate for service vehicle access, the pathway begins a winding descent. Caution is strongly advised because the slope is quite steep with fences bordering both sides of the trail. At 9.3 km (5.8 mi), there is a 180°-hairpin turn, leading almost immediately to a bridge. Less than 200 m/yd further, the trail reaches parking area P6 and the site of the Cookhouse, the Heritage Sawmill Display and School Foundation, and the Green Picnic Area. Still descending, but much more gradually, the trail reaches P7 and intersects the road.

♀ **10 km (6.2 mi)** Turn left and follow the trail with the wooden-rail fence on the right for another 150 m/yd to the Interpretive Centre, where there is a snack bar along with all the other amenities. It also has displays of original artifacts and photographs from when the area was settled, including a video outlining some of the community and province's historical background. At that time, the Pejepscot Paper Company provided housing, a schoolhouse, a community centre, and even electricity for the settlement at Big Salmon River. Regular presentations by staff provide additional detail about the exhibits of photos and memorabilia. And should you so desire, you can purchase Fundy Trail T-shirts, bush hats, caps, sweatshirts, and tote bags, as well as the Fundy Trail postcards at the Interpretive Centre.

The pathway ends at the Interpretive Centre, so follow the road as it continues downhill to parking lot P8 on the bank of the Big Salmon River. Follow it upstream and underneath the road bridge. Just beyond, you sight a magnificent suspended bridge. It is placed where the original covered bridge crossing the river once was located. Continue to it where you see a sign for the Fundy Footpath, a challenging 41 km (25.5 mi) hiking trail along the Bay of Fundy shoreline to Goose River at Fundy National Park.

♀ **10.5 km (6.5 mi)** Cross the bridge, which is very enjoyable. It can only be walked, so if you cycled the Fundy Trail you must leave your bike behind. Once across, I recommend you go no further. The Fundy Footpath is a far more rugged proposition that the Fundy Trail; it is entirely without services and requires at least three days to complete. It should only be attempted after careful preparation. Instead, enjoy the bridge and the scenery, and retrace your route back to the starting trailhead.

Further Information:
Fundy Trail: http://fundytrailparkway.com
Tourism Saint John: http://www.discoversaintjohn.com
Bay of Fundy Tourism: http://bayoffundytourism.com

Blue Jay

One of the most colourful – and noisy – birds in the forest is the blue jay, which is slightly larger than a robin and is also one of the relatively few species that does not migrate. There are few contrasts greater than the jay's startlingly brilliant cobalt feathers among the greys and browns of a winter forest. In fact, the blue jay's feathers are not actually blue, but only appear so because of a peculiar distortion of sunlight by their feathers.

10. Grand Falls to Florenceville

New Brunswick has several iconic topographical features, such as the Bay of Fundy and the Acadian Peninsula, but none is more central to the province's identity than the Saint John River. Although its headwaters are in Maine and Quebec, nearly its entire 673 km (418 mi) length lies in New Brunswick. On a map, it appears like a spine alongside the United States border, supporting the province. It has been popularly christened rather grandly as the Rhine of North America for its scenery.

The rail line that operated alongside the Saint John River was an amalgamation of small independent railroads that were acquired and operated by CP Rail. But after the bridges spanning the river in Woodstock and Perth-Andover were washed away in the spring of 1987, the line was soon abandoned. With the formation of the New Brunswick Trails Council in 1994, this corridor became a critical element of its objective of developing the Trans Canada Trail and the new Sentier NB Trail (SNBT). In 1996-1997, most of this section was officially opened for recreational use.

Almost all of this route is restricted to snowmobile use in winter, but within larger communities such as Grand Falls, Perth-Andover, and Florenceville-Bristol, snowshoeing and cross-country skiing are permitted. Similarly, dogs are permitted off-leash on most of the trail but are expected to be on a lead within urban areas.

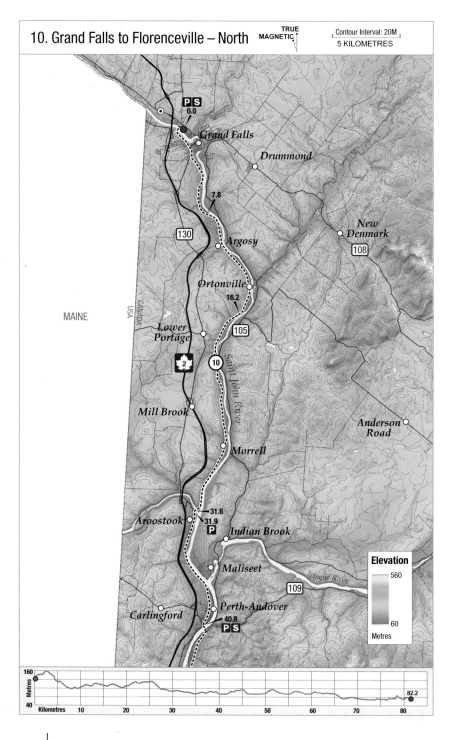

10. Grand Falls to Florenceville – North

TRUE
MAGNETIC

Contour Interval: 20M
5 KILOMETRES

P S 0.0

Grand Falls

Drummond

7.8

130

Argosy

New Denmark

108

Ortonville

16.2

105

Lower Portage

MAINE

CANADA

USA

2

10

Saint John River

Mill Brook

Anderson Road

Morrell

31.6
31.9
P

Aroostook

Indian Brook

Maliseet

Tobique River

109

Carlingford

Perth-Andover

40.8
P S

Elevation

560

60

Metres

160
Metres
40

Kilometres   10   20   30   40   50   60   70   80

82.2

10. Grand Falls to Florenceville

Distance: 82.2 km (51.1 mi) — one way
Ascent: 426 m (1,406 ft)
Descent: 497 m (1,640 ft)

Trail conditions: asphalt, compacted earth, crushed stone
Cellphone coverage: yes
Hazards: road crossings, wildlife

Permitted Uses								
Walking	Biking	Horseback Riding	Inline Skating	ATV	Snowshoeing	Cross-country Skiing	Snowmobiling	
✔	✔	✔	—	—	✔*	✔*	✔	

Finding the trailhead: This route starts at the Grand Falls Marina, where there is a parking area, restaurant, and picnic tables at river level.

Trailhead: 47°03'25.5" N, 67°45'23.3" W (Start — Grand Falls)
46°26'23.8" N, 67°36'54.3" W (Finish — Florenceville)

Observations: There are many scenic stretches, particularly where the trail follows the shore of the Saint John River, bounded on either side by vividly green, tree-covered hills. I found it tranquil and delightful, and while I might not compare it to the Rhine, the Saint John River is broad, and its adjacent communities and farms are charming. Generally, I found this relaxing and an easy ride.

Unfortunately, this was the only section of The Great Trail where I really encountered problem ATVs. Although not permitted on this trail, they were active in numerous places, and several times, I had to scramble out of the path of vehicles moving at high speed. I also managed to crash when I encountered an unexpectedly deep rut that these vehicles had scoured into the treadway where they turned off the trail and onto a highway.

The signs on the trail are a mix. Most have been put up by the New Brunswick Federation of Snowmobile Clubs, but the brown ones are by the NB Trails Council, which manages the SNBT.

Route description: The bridge crossing the Saint John River is almost 400 m/yd long and provides one of the most dramatic vistas on this entire trail. The structure is itself impressive, steel spans connecting to massive concrete pillars with one Subdivided Warren Truss bridging the widest passage.

Across the bridge, the trail passes underneath Main Street, curves left, and heads into a residential area. It crosses a few streets and passes several picnic tables and an interpretive panel before it crosses Highway 130, also Portage Street, at 2.5 km (1.6 mi). Take advantage of the nearby convenience stores as the next are at Perth-Andover, nearly 40 km (24.9 mi) away.

The asphalt surface is replaced by crushed stone as the trail parallels the road for 400 m/yd until crossing busy River Road. Then it curves left into the first wooded section of the route, passing beneath a powerline 300 m/yd later. At the next (gravel) road, a brown sign indicates Aroostook (Maine, USA) in 35 km (21.7 mi) and Perth-Andover in 40 km (24.9 mi).

The trail soon moves back alongside West River Road. At 3.8 km (2.4 mi), it crosses the entrance road to a construction company, and 350 m/yd later reaches the first entrance to Northern Construction Inc. For the next 2 km (1.2 mi), the path passes alongside this massive quarrying operation where several roads cross the trail. There are deep excavations on both sides of the path, sometimes with fencing, but truck traffic appears to pass quite freely over the trail. At 6.3 km (3.9 mi), there is a particularly chewed-up spot where I had to walk my bicycle over a wet area.

About 100 m/yd later, the trail moves onto an excellent, crushed-stone surface. Houses soon appear, including one where a homeowner has lawn on both sides of the trail, reducing the path to a barely distinct track. Another quarry is on the right at 7.3 km (4.5 mi), and at the entrance, the path turns left and crosses West River Road.

7.8 km (4.8 mi) There is no trailhead here, but a gate restricts vehicle access, and there are SNBT, TCT, and Provincial Park signs identifying the pathway. Once across the road, it is back into a thickly forested area, where the trail soon runs alongside the river, perhaps 10 m (32.8 ft) above water level. No longer crushed stone, the treadway is a bit rougher biking but has few potholes.

At 8.8 km (5.5 mi), there is a viewing place; a fence protects riders from the steep river embankment. About 200 m/yd later, the trail moves away from the riverbank with a large field between trail and water. After another short stretch of thick forest, the trail crosses the West River Road once more and passes some now-unused train sheds. Argosy Road, which it crosses 300 m/yd later, connects to the Trans-Canada Highway.

At 10.5 km (6.5 mi), there is a fenced, rebuilt section of the trail, which makes a sudden curving drop. The trail then settles into a pleasant ride through a sparsely populated countryside. Sometimes it is close to both road and river; sometimes the water is out of sight.

One of the roughest places on this route is found at 12.3 km (7.6 mi). There is another quarry and a 50 m/yd section of trail full of deep ruts and large gravel. Bicycles must be carried across, and the footing is like a boulder field. The next cluster of houses at Ortonville is passed at 13.3 km (8.3 mi), where farm machinery clearly shares the trail with recreational users. From there, it runs through a mixture of forest and fields until Streets Brook.

16.2 km (10.1 mi) You may reach a "trail closed" sign. The former bridge and much of the soil on either bank has washed away, leaving a wide rocky gully. When I was there in 2015, even the road bridge was a temporary structure. I picked up my bicycle and crossed without getting my feet wet; if not possible, you might need to cross at the highway.

The trail remains wooded for only a few hundred metres/yards before reaching the collection of farms and homes that constitute the community of Limestone. This is quite a pretty section, although heavily used by ATVs. At 18 km (11.2 mi), an informal track branches from the trail towards the Brooks Bridge Road, which crosses the Saint John River. I crashed here after hitting an unexpectedly deep ATV rut.

About 250 m/yd later, you cross Limestone Siding Road. The trail continues to run parallel to and above the West River Road, which is higher than the river. This continues until 19.9 km (12.4 mi), where the highway makes a sharp 90° right turn, and the trail crosses it.

A combination of thick forest and high ground hide the road for the next 3 km (1.9 mi). More farms, fields, forests – and another gravel pit – are passed. It is quite pastoral and pleasant. At about 23 km (14.3 mi), road and trail converge again, but the road is on the right now. There are no benches or other facilities anywhere along the path, but at 24.6 km (15.3 mi), a lone interpretive panel may be found.

At 27.2 km (17 mi), the trail crosses the West River Road again, then a final time at 28.6 km (17.8 mi). The companion highway since Grand Falls heads inland here while the trail edges closer to the river. This is the most scenic area thus far with no houses visible on either bank for nearly 3 km (1.9 mi). Enjoy this undisturbed space until 31.3 km (19.4 mi), where the trail curves right and passes through the first rail cut with higher land on both sides.

31.6 km (19.6 mi) The trail emerges from the forest onto a massive structure: the Aroostook River Bridge. It is 200 m/yd long, with impressive views of the Saint John River and the United States border upstream, barely 5 km (3.1 mi) away.

Once across the bridge, another 300 m/yd brings you to a parking area and a dirt road – Jewett Drive – that leads uphill to Highway 130 and the small community of Aroostook, where nothing but lawns and gardens abut the treadway. The remains of the former train station, collapsed and overgrown with vegetation, sit at 32.4 km (20 mi). Except for the church steeple, peeking above the lush hardwoods, it is difficult to even tell that you are passing through a community, although the road is actually quite close.

Despite the many cultivated fields and frequent ATV and farm equipment crossings, the next section feels relatively isolated. Vegetation is thick, and few signs of human habitation are visible alongside the Saint John River. The tread-way is quite good though prone to being muddy after a rainfall.

The highway is close enough above and to the right that you often hear cars but don't see them. At 37.6 km (23.4 mi), the trail crosses the highway at a diagonal; be wary of fast-moving traffic. A sign on the far side announces that you have arrived in Perth-Andover.

Several driveways and small streets are crossed and a major intersection where there are trail gates at Fort Road, 39.4 km (24.5 mi). The Trans-Canada Highway is 1 km (0.6 mi) uphill with restaurants and grocery stores. Once across Fort Road, the treadway is asphalt, making deliciously smooth riding through this pleasant community for the next 1.4 km (0.9 mi).

📍 **40.8 km (25.3 mi)** The trail arrives at West Riverside Drive beside the Town Hall and a large trailhead kiosk—and ends. The rail bridge that crossed the Saint John River here was washed away in the 1980s; however, a map at the kiosk reveals that the pathway resumes on the opposite side of the river.

Your route across the road bridge is quite narrow and several hundred metres/yards long, so you might wish to cross on the sidewalk, especially if traffic is heavy. On the east bank, turn right—not surprisingly—on East Riverside Drive. (The Railcar Brewing Company is directly ahead should you require "refreshment"!) The businesses along East Riverside Drive are the only stores until Florenceville-Bristol, so stock up on water and food.

Continue for 200 m/yd to Station Road and turn left. Another 150 m/yd delivers you back to the SNBT, where you turn right. Shortly after, a snowmobile sign states that Florenceville is 35 km (21.8 mi) distant. This is a lovely paved section and is smooth riding past many residences and the local hospital for the next 2.1 km (1.3 mi). There are a few road crossings, all gated and with stop signs on the trail, as well as SNBT and TCT emblems.

At Beech Glen Road, 43.5 km (27 mi), the asphalt ends. The path moves into thick forest, crossed by driveways occasionally and ATV tracks. The ground on the right is lower, but trees mostly block any view of the river. It is not for another 2.3 km (1.4 mi) that a clear sight of the water appears. Then 300 m/yd later at 46.1 km (28.7 mi), the trail crosses Highway 105—at a very dangerous angle in an 80 kph (50 mph) zone.

A sign indicates that Muniac is 10 km (6.2 mi) away and Upper Kent is 16 km (10 mi). The trail now tracks along the river's edge, and for the first time, the water can be easily accessed from the pathway. Oddly, the treadway is in poor condition, bumpy and almost completely grass covered. This is also a fairly isolated section as the trail becomes a causeway with a small pond on the left that separates it from road and houses. More than once, I needed to stop and wait for gaggles of geese, the young not yet able to fly, waddling away down the trail ahead of me until they decided to take to the water to escape.

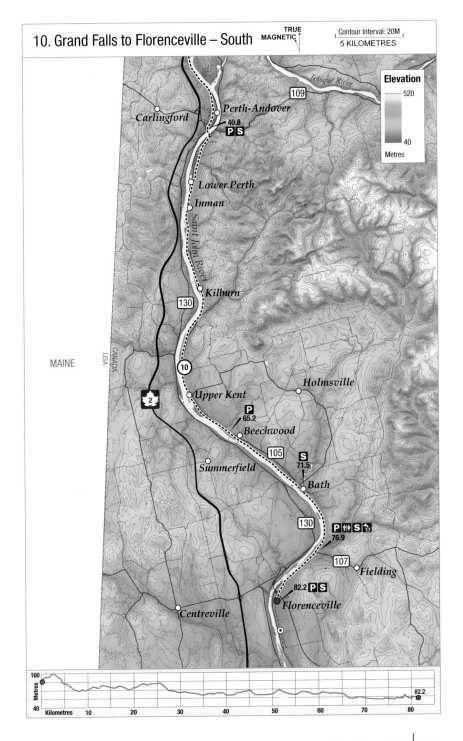

At 48.2 km (30 mi), the path crosses a small bridge at Bishop Brook, after which the road and trail converge again. About 200 m/yd later, there is an old cemetery on the right, and for most of the next kilometre, the river is obscured by thick vegetation. Then the trail is riverside again although it climbs somewhat above water level.

The path works away from the river and into a forested area. There are occasional driveways and a few houses, but it is mostly thick hardwood. The river is usually visible through the leaves. At 50.3 km (31.3 mi), snowmobile Route 124 branches to the left, and 700 m/yd later, the trees give way to fields and houses, and the trail reaches the end of the Kilburn Road.

Houses and fields are much more common as the trail moves into the hamlet of Kilburn. The ground on both sides of the trail is cleared, and for the next 1.5 km (0.9 mi), the route is out in the open. Although Kilburn has no store, there is an elaborate playground – in case you want to stretch.

As the trail leaves Kilburn, it squeezes between river and road with excellent views of the opposite bank until reaching the junction with the Muniac Road at 54.8 km (34 mi). At this junction, there is no formal trailhead, but an informal track connects the 5 m/yd between road and pathway.

The treadway is in excellent condition through here. At 56 km (34.8 mi), there is an interesting area where the ground is quite sandy, and a talus slope on the left has a few scraggly white birches. Shortly after, a set of gates is followed by one of the largest cultivated fields yet encountered. For more than 2 km (1.2 mi), no trees border the path as it crosses this open area.

At a dirt road crossing at 58.4 km (36.3 mi), Snowmobile Trail #44 turns off to the left. Highway 105 is again quite close, and on the opposite bank of the river, cliffs are noticeable. About 900 m/yd later, trail and river converge at a small marshy area. At 60.6 km (37.7 mi), the trail reaches the far end of the Upper Kent Road and the first houses of the tiny rural community.

Most of the houses are to the right, and the river is once again concealed. About 700 m/yd later, the trail crosses paved Upper Kent Crossing Road. There are more houses now, some with their lawns – and buildings – spreading over both sides of the track. However, the trail quickly returns to thick forest with higher ground on the left and crosses Upper Kent Road at 63.2 km (39.3 mi).

Shortly after this, the river comes into view again along with a couple of new, quite elaborate cottages – or homes. After the second of these, the Hillman Road nearly touches the right side of the trail, crossing it and the entrance to the Beechwood Generating Station at 64.1 km (39.8 mi). A variety of snowmobile information signs decorate this junction.

The next bit of treadway is excellent as it runs alongside the grounds of the Beechwood Dam. The is one of three hydroelectric generating facilities impounding the Saint John River and first opened in 1957, raising water levels for 18 km

(11.2 mi) upstream. On the right of the trail are open grounds with extensive lawns.

65.2 km (40.5 mi) A metal staircase comes down to the trail from a parking area on Highway 105, and there is a foot entrance to the Dam grounds. I did not see any tables or benches, but there is a lovely lawn and garden area if you wish to rest or snack, as well as a good view of the dam and the many powerlines and power transmission facilities.

Once through another set of gates and past the dam, the trail enters one of the most remote sections of this route. It runs alongside and well above the river on a fairly steep hillside. To the left, the ground is higher and thickly forested, concealing the highway and any houses. Across the river, very few buildings can be seen, although there is considerable farmland.

Tall hardwoods shade the trail, and the treadway is in excellent condition except for a few rebuilt embankments. It is a pleasant ride with very little sign of human activity for several kilometres – although there is a cemetery at 70.1 km (43.6 mi) that uses the preceding 250 m/yd of the trail as its access road. About 400 m/yd later, there is a large trucking business on the left, and the pathway intersects Hallett Road. After a straight ride for another 950 m/yd, the trail crosses Monquart Stream over a steel truss bridge.

71.5 km (44.4 mi) Just 50 m/yd beyond the bridge, the trail reaches a set of gates and Highway 105 at the community of Bath. To the right is a river look-off with a Trail interpretive panel and benches. Across the road to the left is a grocery store.

The trail crosses the highway, and for the next 1.5 km (0.9 mi) runs through the middle of the village, crossing several streets and passing by the former train station, at least one restaurant, and the large Bath Middle School. As it leaves the community, the trail is in open grassland and very close to the highway, which is now between the pathway and the river.

At 73.5 km (45.7 mi), there is another interpretive panel at the entrance to a group of ballfields. Just 200 m/yd later is a very dangerous spot, where several automotive businesses have driveways and parking areas across the trail.

The path passes by a wastewater treatment facility and over a few more driveways, then at 74.5 km (46.3 mi) crosses Highway 105 once again. This is another dangerous road junction at an odd angle where the road curves, and the speed limit is 80 kph (50 mph). Use extreme caution.

An excellent, crushed-stone treadway awaits on the far side, and the trail re-enters a forested area. No houses are visible for some time, but at 76.3 km (47.4 mi), the trail comes back to the road and crosses the Shikatehawk Stream. Signs on both the road and the trail welcome you to Florenceville-Bristol, the "French Fry Capital of the World"!

The road boasts a sidewalk now, and there are many homes and businesses.

About 600 m/yd from the bridge, the trail reaches the Visitor Information Centre and the Shogomoc Railway Site. The former has water, washrooms, picnic tables, a playground, and a large parking area. The latter features a restored 1914 Canadian Pacific Railway station and three rail cars – one of which is a restaurant. There is even a short stretch of asphalt treadway, and Riverside Park offers more benches with good views of the Saint John River.

The trail crosses Highway 105 for the final time at 77.3 km (48 mi), just after the park and another short bridge. The SNBT then runs behind and above many houses for almost a kilometre. As it emerges from this built-up area, it actually has to climb a small hill – quite unusual given the originally level railbed.

The trail runs alongside the road, separated only by a shallow ditch, and at 79.2 km (49.2 mi) enters Florenceville. Driveways are frequent, and a number of business entrances cross the trail, including a large mall with a Co-op, Subway, Liquor Store, and Tim Hortons. Motorists are not watching for cyclists, so this might actually be the most hazardous section of this entire route.

At 80.2 km (49.8 mi), the trail curves left away from Highway 105 and behind the massive McCain Foods processing plant. It skirts the Florenceville Middle School athletic track and passes underneath Highway 2 at 81.3 km (50.5 mi).

You remain on the SNBT for another 400 m/yd until McCain Street then turns right. Continue on this road past the Northern Carleton Civic Centre for 350 m/yd to reach Highway 105, which runs alongside the river. Use the crosswalk and then turn right and follow the sidewalk through the town centre.

82.2 km (51 mi) You arrive at the junction of Highway 105 and Old Florenceville Bridge Road. There are many restaurants and convenience stores nearby. A look-off with benches and interpretive panels faces the (partially) covered bridge spanning the Saint John River. This is a lovely location in an attractive community to finish this route.

Further Information:
Sentier NB Trail: www.sentiernbtrail.com
Tourism New Brunswick: www.tourismnewbrunswick.ca

Sentier NB Trail

Although the New Brunswick Trail Council originally formed to complete their portion of the Trans Canada Trail, they quickly developed a more ambitious agenda, the Sentier NB Trail (SNBT). The SNBT was conceived as a system of non-motorized, off-road pathways that would connect each region and every major community in the province.

As with every trail project across Canada, the fortunes of the SNBT have waxed and waned depending upon the provincial and national governments of the day and their commitment to the trail development. Despite often wildly fluctuating fortunes, the volunteers of the NB Trail Council and their community partners have created a network exceeding 1,300 km (808 mi) of completed trail with more under development. As of 2017, the SNBT is well supported, and new sections such as the Bathurst to Mount Carleton trail are nearing completion.

above: Lower Shogomoc footbridge; inset: Grand Falls (courtesy Tourism NB)

15. Parcours des Anses

QUEBEC

11. Petit Témis

Since its opening, Petit Témis has been recognized as one of the best rail-to-trail conversions in Atlantic Canada and eastern Quebec. Winding through the hilly and picturesque base of the Gaspé Peninsula, the trail provides a combination of near-wilderness conditions interspersed with charming villages, all on a well-developed and well-maintained pathway.

The full length of Petit Témis is 134 km (83.3 mi), extending from Edmundston, New Brunswick, to Rivière-du-Loup, Quebec. However, for me, its most scenic portion is found where it follows the shoreline of Lac-Témiscouata between the communities of Dégelis and Cabano, which amalgamated with Notre-Dame-du-Lac in 2010 to create the town of Témiscouata-sur-le-Lac.

The Témiscouata area is sparsely populated and more than eighty-five percent covered by forest. The lake is more than 42 km (26 mi) long and is Quebec's second largest lake south of the St. Lawrence River. The trail is well serviced with numerous picnic shelters and rest stops, and there are restaurants, grocery stores, accommodations, and other services available in Dégelis, Cabano, and Notre-Dame-du-Lac. There are even several beaches easily accessed from the pathway. This should be an easy and pleasant bike ride for anyone, especially for a family, and with the abundant scenery, a good hike even though it's on a rail trail.

11. Petit Témis

TRUE
MAGNETIC

Contour Interval: 30M
5 KILOMETRES

PARC NATIONAL
DU LAC-TÉMISCOUATA

P ⛺ S
28.2

Cabano
26.9

Pointe
à Midas

Lac-Témiscouata

Pointe aux
Trembles

Pointe
à Dick

Saint-Juste-
du-Lac

Pointe
à Hayes

16

11

Notre-Dame-
du-Lac
P ⛺ S

11.7

Île Notre-Dame

Cours D' Eau Berube

Ivry

3.6

2.5

1.6

Elevation

380

140

Metres

Dégelis

0.0
P ⛺ S

180
Metres
165

Kilometres   4   8   12   16   20   24   28.2

11. Petit Témis

Distance: 28.2 km (17.5 mi) – one way
Ascent: 142 m (466 ft)
Descent: 120 m (394 ft)

Trail conditions: asphalt, crushed stone
Cellphone coverage: yes
Hazards: road crossings, wildlife

Permitted Uses							
Walking	Biking	Horseback Riding	Inline Skating	ATV	Snowshoeing	Cross-country Skiing	Snowmobiling
✔	✔	—	✔*	—	—	—	✔

Finding the trailhead: This route begins at the former Dégelis train station, which has been converted into an art gallery and during the summer features open washrooms and a pop machine outside facing the trail. There is also a small but attractive park that has a water fountain, benches, picnic tables, garbage cans, interpretive panels, and a map of the entire trail.

Trailhead: 47°32'59.7" N, 68°38'29.3" W (Start — Dégelis)
47°41'06" N, 68°53'18.1" W (Finish — Cabano)

Observations: The treadway was in superb condition, and it was never far between well-maintained picnic tables and benches – which often featured a view – available whenever I wanted to stop. Frequent and clear signage provided information both on current location and distance to the next services or communities. There were large numbers of both cyclists and walkers all along the route, particularly near the communities. I rode effortlessly, relaxing and enjoying the splendid scenery until I finished my ride. Better still, I even obtained an excellent fresh baguette and croissants for lunch at a boulangerie in Cabano.

Route description: At first, the trail surface is asphalt and runs through the small community of Dégelis, passing houses and a few businesses. Several side trails permit local access, and a road parallels closely to the left.

1.6 km (1 mi) The trail leaves Dégelis and moves into a wooded area with the Madawaska River visible to the right. At the first rest area, there is a covered picnic table, garbage can, and an outhouse.

2.5 km (1.6 mi) Where the trail crosses Chemin du Barrage, there are a bench and numerous signs pointing towards community attractions. There are also quite a few houses nearby. Less than 300 m/yd later, Lac-Témiscouata comes into view, and 500 m/yd beyond that, the path reaches the Dégelis Marina, where there are all manner of facilities available – even shuffleboard. Since the trail passes between the buildings and the water, everything is easily accessed.

3.6 km (2.2 mi) Almost immediately after leaving the marina, the asphalt surface ends, replaced by crushed stone. It is mostly thickly forested after the marina and quite hilly, though one or two cottages can still be seen near the lakeshore. The terrain becomes much more rugged, and the trail is a deep railway cut with cedars perched along its edges. Moss-covered boulders line the pathway, while the lake is visible through the vegetation to the right.

The next rest area, with picnic tables and an outhouse, is found at 4.3 km (2.7 mi) in an area of thick forest with high, steep rock walls to the left and the lake maybe 25 m (82 ft) below. The trail reaches a high trestle bridge about 1,000 m/

yd later, which crosses a small brook and is open on the water side. Immediately before the bridge to the left is a spring and on the far side is another picnic area. Just after that, the trail enters a deep cut with steep rock walls on both sides.

A second trestle bridge is crossed 400 m/yd further on, and this provides superb views across the lake to the wooded hills of Parc national du Lac-Témiscouata, where the Sentier national au Québec, Quebec's provincial hiking path, may be found. Yet another rest area, this one with a covered picnic table, is situated just before the trestle. (There are so many rest areas that from now on I am only going to mention the most important.)

A third long trestle bridge is reached at 6.8 km (4.2 mi), and a rest stop immediately afterwards with two covered tables is named Le Trestle. It features lake access and an unsupervised swimming site. The deepest rock cut on the trail begins past this rest area.

At 7.7 km (4.8 mi), the hills recede, and soon after, residences proliferate on both sides of the trail. Most are quite modest rustic cottages with a small dock for a canoe or motorboat, but the further along you travel, the larger and even palatial some are. There are good views of the lake because much of the vegetation on the water side has been cleared.

11.7 km (7.3 mi) The trail nearly intersects Highway 85. Massive road reconstruction has almost crowded the trail into the lake, but it also provided a new bridge crossing the Rivière Creuse and a rebuilt rest stop, overlooking the water. From here, hillier terrain once again squeezes the trail, and there are still many houses adjacent. Within a few hundred metres/yards after crossing Rivière Creuse, the road construction is left behind, and a pleasant overhead canopy of tree branches resumes.

There are several benches and rest stops in the next 2 km (1.2 mi) – and many driveways to cross – but when you reach the rest stop with the sign l'Ancienne Gare de Notre-Dame-du-Lac, the location of the former train station at 14.1 km (8.8 mi), you are inside the town limits. About 250 m/yd later, the trail passes the Auberge Marie Blanche, an inn and café.

Several street crossings follow, and the trail is actually somewhat higher than lake level. At 15.3 km (9.5 mi), there is a large campground on both sides of the trail where the treadway switches from crushed stone to asphalt. There are a shelter, picnic tables, and a canteen.

16 km (10 mi) You reach a major rest area with another marina on the right where the ferry from Notre-Dame-du-Lac crosses Lac-Témiscouata to Saint-Juste-du-Lac. Tables, shelter, interpretive panels, a trail map, washrooms, and water are all available. At the street crossing just before the rest area, signs advertise local businesses, which are to the left in the town centre and less than 100 m/yd away.

The asphalt continues another 450 m/yd, returning to crushed stone as the trail leaves the community.

For the next 6.2 km (3.9 mi), the trail returns to being mostly forested. There are occasional cottages and even one small cluster of houses, but generally it feels rather isolated. There are frequent rest areas, of course, and shelters with outhouses at 20.2 km (12.6 mi), as well as at Le Rocher, 21.5 km (13.4 mi), and La Pointe aux Trembles, 22.9 km (14.2 mi).

Although there is a sign marking the Cabano boundary at 22.5 km (14 mi), the first buildings are not reached for another few hundred metres/yards and they are widespread only after 23.7 km (14.7 mi). By this point, the trail has moved away from the lake, and cultivated fields are visible to the left. Road crossings are also more frequent.

The trail is within the town limits now and passes through an industrial area. Several streets are busy with truck traffic and feature stop signs on the pathway. At 25.2 km (15.7 mi), a side trail branches towards l'Auberge Sur-le-Lac-Témiscouata and at 26.6 km (16.5 mi), the trail crosses the Rivière Cabano.

26.9 km (16.7 mi) In downtown Cabano, the asphalt treadway resumes, and the trail enters a large park area adjacent to the business area. Restaurants, bars, boulangeries (bakeries), and many other businesses line the park to the left. The trail passes several small ponds, sculptures, and painted murals, and there are quite a few benches and picnic tables. This is an excellent place to stop and have a meal, even though the trail continues through the park and crosses several other streets before reaching Cabano's formal trailhead.

28.2 km (17.5 mi) Immediately after crossing Rue Caldwell, the trail reaches the former train station for Cabano, which is now l'Auberge de la Gare. As in Dégelis and Notre-Dame-du-Lac, there are a map and interpretive panels, as well as a shelter, picnic tables, bike racks, and even a few lawn chairs. Best of all, l'Auberge de la Gare operates a small café, serving outdoors in good weather. Retrace your route back to Dégelis or, if you are in no rush, stay overnight in the Auberge and enjoy a leisurely return the following day.

Further Information:
Petit Témis Website: http://petit-temis.ca
Tourism Bas-Saint-Laurent: http://www.bassaintlaurent.ca
Tourism Témiscouata: https://www.tourismetemiscouata.qc.ca

Black Bear

Nearly everyone's greatest fear while hiking is the black bear, an impressively large and dangerous animal. Growing to 215 kg (474 lb), it is capable of bursts of speed up to 30 kph (19 mph) and of climbing trees. It is primarily nocturnal and usually solitary, except for a brief time during mating season and when a mother is caring for cubs.

However, the black bear is itself usually frightened of encountering people. From the beginning of settlement in North America, bears have been hunted and driven from foraging near human habitations. Making noises while you are walking announces to a bear that you are nearby, and it almost certainly withdraws before you see it. However, opinions differ on the best course of action to take should you actually come face to face with a bear. Always remember that they are wild and unpredictable animals that are capable of causing you serious injury or even death.

12. Traversée de Charlevoix

To fully appreciate that The Great Trail is not a uniform entity but an amalgam of hundreds of individual community trails and experiences, you need simply to consider the Traversée de Charlevoix. Unlike any other section of the entire Great Trail system, the Traversée de Charlevoix may only be walked from west to east. Further, it is a closed route; you must register to use it, pay a fee, and stay overnight at prescribed locations and accommodations. Daily use is restricted by the space available in the shelters.

The Traversée de Charlevoix is intended to be a multi-day back-packing experience. Seven days of trekking with six nights of camping are recommended, although it may be done in less time if desired. Its start is nowhere near its finish, and it ends at nowhere at all, so arranging for the transfer of your car is strongly recommended. You may do the experience however you wish, for a fee. Should you wish the organizers to transfer your bags from one shelter to the next, there is a fee for that; should you wish the organizers to bring in your meals, there is a fee for that; and should you decide that you wish to drop out – well, there is a fee for that as well.

The previous paragraph might sound disapproving. In fact, I was highly impressed with the Traversée de Charlevoix and its business model. It is an excellent example of a modestly sustainable hiking tourism resource. It has functioned for longer than almost any other trail of its type in Canada and is prepared for every contingency. The chalets contain cooking utensils, plates, pots, and also have propane stoves, so you do not need to carry kitchen supplies in your backpack. There is abundant firewood for the wood stove. Mattresses are provided, but you still need to carry your own sleeping bag. All the chalets are located near a water source. I did, however, find the maps that they provide hikers were out of date, which caused some minor problems at times.

Hiking is offered from the end of May to the end of October. During hunting season, an orange bib is provided. For mountain biking, the route is often different than for walkers. The cross-country ski route operates from the end of December to the end of March.

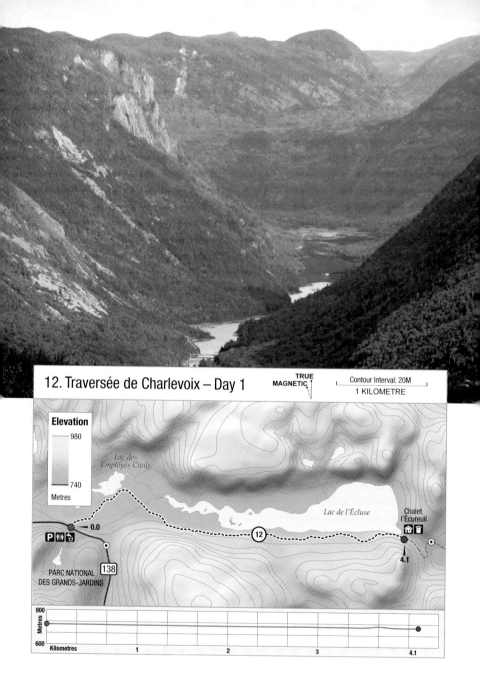

12. Traversée de Charlevoix – Day 1

TRUE
MAGNETIC

Contour Interval: 20M
1 KILOMETRE

Elevation

980

740

Metres

Lac des
Employés Civils

Lac de l'Écluse

Chalet
l'Écureuil

0.0

12

4.1

138

PARC NATIONAL
DES GRANDS-JARDINS

900
Metres
600

Kilometres   1   2   3   4.1

12. Traversée de Charlevoix

Distance: 92.3 km (57.4 mi) – one way
Ascent: 864 m (2,835 ft)
Descent: 3,319 m (10,889 ft)

Trail conditions: compacted earth, natural surface
Cellphone coverage: Partial (numbered cell signal locations on the trail)
Hazards: hunting, rugged terrain, wildlife

					Permitted Uses			
Walking	Biking	Horseback Riding	Inline Skating	ATV	Snowshoeing	Cross-country Skiing	Snowmobiling
✔	✔*	—	—	—	—	✔	—

Finding the trailhead: Begin at the Zec Des Martres, reporting to the Welcome Centre (Accueil Saint-Urbain) beside Highway 381 to confirm registration on the Traversée. From there, follow the wide dirt road behind the Accueil to its end at the dam impounding Lac à l'Écluse, about 4 km (2.5 mi) away.

Trailhead: 47°42'29.1" N, 70°39'31.1" W (Start — Zec Des Martres)
47°46'19.2" N, 70°06'23.7" W (Finish — Mont Grand-Fonds)

Observations: This was tough. The terrain is quite hilly, with plenty of rock to punish your feet. And the extra weight required when backpacking makes all those never-ending hills much more cumulatively challenging than on a day hike. But this was exhilarating to complete, with each day bringing greater peace and contentment. This was also the first time that I had backpacked for such a long time, so I was a little apprehensive about how I would do.

As is my habit, I trekked alone, only meeting my fellow section hikers at the hut at the end of the day. Usually that meant that I saw no other person from dawn to dusk. This was quite agreeable, and I found the return to society at the end of the trip momentarily disorienting and even a little disappointing.

My shelter companions were Quebecers, all quite different people from each other, who probably would never have met or talked under other circumstances. Yet each evening around the wood stove, we chatted and joked long into the night. It was sociable; it was congenial; it was satisfying. In a number of ways, the Traversée was my most enjoyable personal experience of the entire exploration of The Great Trail.

Route description
Day 1: Zec des Martres to Chalet l'Écureuil
Distance: 4.1 km (2.5 mi) – one way
Ascent: 33 m (108 ft)
Descent: 105 m (344 ft)

This first walk is short and easy, ideal for someone travelling from Montréal or arriving after work from Québec City. Along the way, you are introduced to the distinctive red-and-white directional signs of the Traversée. A few indicate distances, but most are directional arrows or indicate the distance travelled from the day's start. There are even occasional TCT – or Great Trail – markers.

You also have the opportunity to observe the rugged terrain of the region. Low hills, apparently composed of unbroken rock, bulge everywhere. Some are entirely tree covered, sprinkled all over with softwoods and appearing deceptively gentle. Others reveal imposing grey cliffs, etched by deep, violent fissures, the trees appearing like survivors clinging to the edges.

For most of the final 2 km (1.2 mi), the trail runs close to the edge of Lac de l'Écluse, providing impressive views of the crags on the opposite shore. Cottages are common, their driveways branching off towards the water, so this area does not feel terribly remote.

At 4 km (2.5 mi), the road ends in a large cleared area. A small dam blocks this end of Lac de l'Écluse, providing something to scamper over if you wish to explore. Directly ahead is a trailhead kiosk for the Traversée and a number of side trails, which are marked by yellow-and-green signs.

The trail continues straight, parallel to the outflow from the lake. However, other signs direct hikers onto a footpath behind the kiosk. Either route delivers you in 100 m/yd to your destination, the chalet.

4.1 km (2.5 mi) You arrive at the Chalet l'Ecureuil, a large cabin which fronts on the footpath and has a porch with two outdoor picnic tables. Sleeping mats are upstairs; at ground level are the kitchen area, wood stove, and tables. Privies are out back. One interesting feature is the sign above the door. It provides the chalet name and also the altitude 750 m (2,460 ft) and the latitude and longitude 47°42'34" N, 70°36'28" W.

Day 2: Chalet l'Écureuil to Chalet de la Marmotte
Distance: 14.7 km (9.1 mi) – one way
Ascent: 346 m (1,135 ft)
Descent: 752 m (2,467 ft)

From the chalet, turn right and follow the wide path. The first of many junctions arrives in only 250 m/yd, where a fiesta of signs decorates the trees. All the side trails are signed in yellow and green; look for the main red-and-white ones. In this case, turn left where the sign indicates that the Chalet de la Marmotte is 14.9 km (9.3 distant). In the first 600 m/yd there are several such junctions – follow the red route only.

At 475 m/yd, the trail crosses a small bridge over the Ruisseau aux Mouches, the outflow from Lac de l'Écluse, and another side track branches off about 100 m/yd later. The area is thickly wooded, but the track is wide, as if occasionally used by ATVs. A solitary interpretive panel sits in a slightly cleared area about 300 m/yd from the bridge.

The vegetation is thick and packed tightly near the trail, so there are few views – except when you reach a junction with a side trail to Mont Eudore-Fortin with its imposing bulk dominating the skyline to the right. The path works along the hillside above the creek, narrowing to a footpath, until 2.4 km (1.5 mi) where it curves left and downhill to another junction 250 m/yd later. Here it makes a sharp turn right and drops downhill.

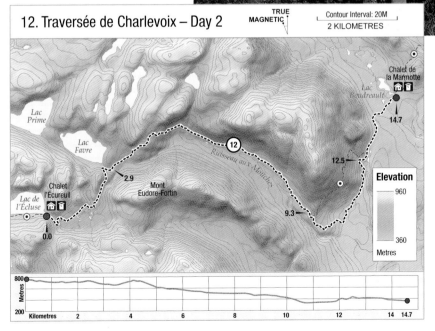

12. Traversée de Charlevoix – Day 2

TRUE MAGNETIC

Contour Interval: 20M
2 KILOMETRES

Chalet de la Marmotte

Lac Boudreault

Lac Prime

Lac Favre

12

Ruisseau aux Mouches

14.7

12.5

2.9

Chalet l'Écureuil

Mont Eudore-Fortin

9.3

Lac de l'Écluse

0.0

Elevation
960
360
Metres

800
Metres
200
Kilometres   2   4   6   8   10   12   14   14.7

2.9 km (1.8 mi) The trail reaches an elaborate bridge over the outflow from Lac Favre. An interpretive panel – ominously, about the blackfly – sits beside the near end. In the opening created by the stream, the nearby towering hills are visible. The path quickly re-enters the thick brush on the opposite bank, and for most of this next section, there are few views. About 350 m/yd later there is a smaller bridge, followed by tiny rivulets with nothing constructed over them.

From the very beginning, there have been kilometre markers, starting with 14 km and counting down the distance to the next refuge, but many are bear-chewed or otherwise mangled. Although mostly downhill, between 3.5 km (2.2 mi) and 4.2 km (2.6 mi), there is a sharp climb of 80 m (262 ft). But after that, the track descends almost nonstop for the next 6.5 km (4 mi).

The footing is quite rugged, with many rocks making it tricky. To the left, the hill slopes steeply with rock faces sometimes being revealed in gaps in the vegetation. Occasionally, boulders that have calved off those cliffs sit next to the trail. To the right, the Ruisseau aux Mouches can always be heard, if rarely observed.

9.3 km (5.8 mi) Reach cellphone coverage site #4. For most of this trek there is no signal available, so phones should be turned off to save the battery. Where coverage is possible, the site is marked with a special sign.

About 100 m/yd after this, there is a junction where a ski-only trail branches left, and the km 5 marker is 400 m/yd after that. At 10.1 km (6.3 mi), there is a sharp 90° turn left, and the descent becomes even steeper. For another 600 m/yd it drops, the footpath becoming a wide former woods road. But with another left turn at 10.7 km (6.6 mi), the route levels out and returns to a slender track.

For the next kilometre, the trail climbs quite gently with quite a bit of swampy ground, surrounded by thick young softwoods. A small brook can be heard on the right. Suddenly the climb becomes much steeper: 80 m (262 ft) in the next 800 m/yd. To the left is a vertical rock face, and the path is littered in large stones.

📍**12.5 km (7.8 mi)** The path crosses the stream on a bridge at the highest point, where there is another cell coverage sign. As soon as it crosses, the trail turns sharply right and makes a quick drop of 20 m (65.6 ft). About 600 m/yd later, there is a trail branching left to Mont des Morios.

From here, the walking becomes much easier. The path becomes a wider woods road, and many hardwoods grow among the adjacent trees. The track continues unimpeded, emerging from the forest into a large clearing beneath a powerline. (There might be an assembly of trailers clustered about for hunters.) A sign directs you to the right with the indication that only 150 m/yd remain.

📍**14.7 km (9.1 mi)** Arrive at the Chalet de la Marmotte, nestled among the trees almost on the shore of Lac Boudreault.

Day 3: Chalet de la Marmotte to Chalet de la Chouette
Distance:10 km (6.2 mi) – one way
Ascent: 490 m (1,607 ft)
Descent: 267 m (876 ft)

As you leave Chalet de la Marmotte, you see a sign indicating that it is 10.3 km (6.4 mi) to your destination, the Chalet de la Chouette. The walk begins on a wide gravel road that crosses the outflow of Lac Boudreault and provides superb views of the surrounding mountains. But just 500 m/yd from the start, the bike route and hike/ski track separate with walkers turning left onto a footpath.

This path climbs through an attractive mixed pine and hardwood forest to a signed lookout at 1.2 km (0.7 mi), which is comically completely overgrown. Immediately after, the path descends, reconnecting with the wide gravel road in another 600 m/yd.

An arrow directs you left. Be cautious as this road is used by logging vehicles, and walkers are probably not expected. At 2.4 km (1.5 mi), the road crosses the Rivière du Gouffre, which is a quite modest flow at this point. The km 8 marker is about 100 m/yd further along, and just after that, there is a "T" junction; turn left. There are few trail markers along the road but continue along this route for about 1 km (0.6 mi).

📍**3.5 km (2.2 mi)** You arrive at the km 7 marker, where the hike/ski route leaves the road and resumes on a narrow footpath. As soon as you leave the road, you begin

12. Traversée de Charlevoix – Day 3

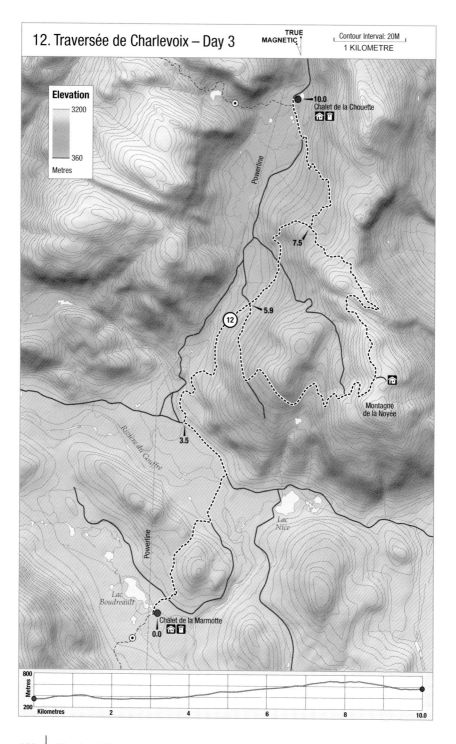

TRUE / MAGNETIC

Contour Interval: 20M
1 KILOMETRE

Elevation

3200

360

Metres

10.0
Chalet de la Chouette

7.5

⑫

5.9

Powerline

Montagne
de la Noyée

3.5

Rivière du Gouffre

Lac
Nice

Powerline

Lac
Boudreault

Chalet de la Marmotte
0.0

to climb. There are numerous unsigned side trails; continue left. The trail makes a brief dip, and there is an interpretive panel for trembling aspen.

The narrow footpath soon resumes its climb over some flat rocks but also through a lovely section of densely packed trees with the path a thin ribbon of green between them. The ascent is steep at times, and at 4.3 km (2.7 mi), there is a flat spot where you have views of the hills around and ahead.

The trail is rough at times, but not excessively challenging. Much higher ground is to the right, and a steep down slope on the left. At the km 5 marker is a semi-open area of rock and spruce with something of a view; there is also a cell coverage sign at 5.4 km (3.4 mi), so this makes a good place for a break.

5.9 km (3.7 mi) You arrive at the junction with the side trail (loop) to Montagne de la Noyée, which is a gravel road. The sign indicates that the main path is directly ahead and that it is 4.2 km (2.6 mi) to the Chalet de la Chouette. There is also an excellent view of the rocky hill to the left.

From the main trail's nearly overgrown state, it is clear that most people follow the Montagne de la Noyée loop. Vegetation grows almost to the centre of the path, and there are few signs. In this dense brush there are no views, and the climb continues. The most difficult walking of this day's route is through here.

I hiked both the main trail and the loop, and I strongly recommend the latter. True, it adds more than 9 km (5.6 mi) to the day's trip, but the views at the cabin on the summit of the mountain, including looking over the St. Lawrence River, are the most dramatic of the entire Traversée.

7.5 km (4.7 mi) You arrive at the second junction with the Montagne de la Noyée loop, although you might not notice as it is not signed from this direction, except with a directional arrow that points left. As the Traversée is always walked west to east, this junction permits hikers on the loop to rejoin the main trail.

The worst of the climb ends here, even though after the first short descent, there follows an equally short climb. However, by 8.2 km (5.1 mi), the final descent begins, which at times crosses loose rocks and leads through wet areas. As you lose altitude, the vegetation switches from primarily conifers to thick groves of young hardwoods.

At 9.3 km (5.8 mi), the descent ends where the footpath intersects a gravel road, and an arrow directs you to the right. Though essentially level, even the minor undulations of this road may be demanding. Along the way, there are a few junctions, but there are frequent arrows and signs to keep you on the correct track.

10 km (6.2 mi) Arrive at the Chalet de la Chouette, which is located slightly off the gravel road and just above a small lake with excellent views of the mountain on the far side of the water.

Day 4: Chalet de la Chouette to Chalet du Geai-Blue

Distance: 18.8 km (11.7 mi) – one way
Ascent: 587 m (1,926 ft)
Descent: 943 m (3,094 ft)

From the chalet, return to the gravel road. The bike route heads right while hikers/skiers turn left. After 100 m/yd back the way you hiked in, a sign directs you to the right. Ahead is an intimidating wall of rock, but the path is a former woods road that crosses a small bridge and runs beneath an also intimidating electrical powerline.

About 350 m/yd further, the trail returns to forest and begins to climb. Among the trees, massive boulders, split from the adjacent cliffs, loom menacingly amid the early morning shadows. The trail climbs into a narrow ravine bisected by a small creek and at 1.2 km (0.7 mi) reaches the decidedly rustic Refuge du Bihoreau. The road ends here with the trail narrowing to a rough footpath.

For the next 400 m/yd, the route works around a small pond with towering hills enfolding it. Although still climbing, the grade is slight. However, the trail is quite rough and winds its way over moss-covered rocks, deadfalls, and rotting stumps.

As the trail turns away from the pond, it once again climbs steeply. For the next kilometre, you ascend, working into the narrow pass between two crests. When the trail next levels, you have climbed more than 300 m (984 ft) in the first 2.6 km (1.6 mi). Not surprisingly, there is cell coverage in this area.

The route cuts between the hills and enters into a shallow remote valley, dropping 60 m (197 ft) before making a sharp right turn at 3.8 km (2.4 mi). The path is often indistinct and is difficult to follow at times in the thick undergrowth, and several re-routings were required to avoid beaver activity. The trail follows the ravine near its base for another 1.4 km (0.9 mi) before reaching an old woods road, where it makes another 90° right turn and climbs back out.

6 km (3.7 mi) The trail reaches its high point of the entire trek – unless you included the Montagne de la Noyée loop – 857 m (2,812 ft) above sea level. There are no great views at this point, unfortunately, although tantalizing glimpses of deep ravines to the left are possible through the vegetation. It is only 600 m/yd

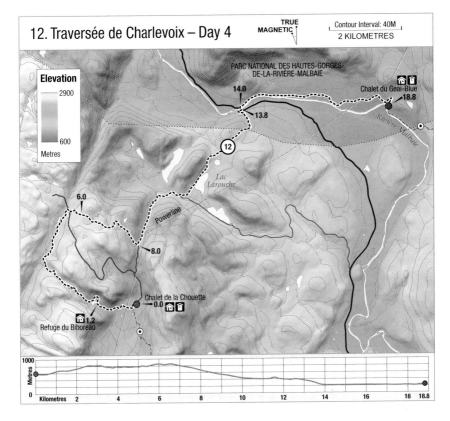

12. Traversée de Charlevoix – Day 4

TRUE
MAGNETIC

Contour Interval: 40M
2 KILOMETRES

PARC NATIONAL DES HAUTES-GORGES-DE-LA-RIVIÈRE-MALBAIE

Elevation

2900

600

Metres

14.0

Chalet du Geai-Blue
18.8

13.8

Rivière Malbaie

(12)

Lac
Larouche

6.0

Powerline

8.0

Chalet de la Chouette
0.0

1.2
Refuge du Bihoreau

1000
Metres
0
Kilometres 2   4   6   8   10   12   14   16   18 18.8

later, once into a steep descent, that a gap in the trees permits an unobstructed view of the dramatic Hautes-Gorges-de-la-Rivière-Malbaie.

The trail begins a long descent more than 4 km (2.5 mi) long. As you lose elevation, the trees once again shift from softwoods to hardwoods as the path enters a more protected valley.

8 km (5 mi) Reconnect with the bike route from Chalet de la Chouette, which is well signed, including the cell coverage marker #12. Turn left, continuing to descend on the very rocky, wide track. To the right, tall, high-voltage electrical towers parallel the path, and thick vegetation crowds the edges. A small creek to the left grows wider and more powerful as you drop down the hillside.

At 9.9 km (6.2 mi), you reach a wider road where an arrow directs you right. You follow this for 300 m/yd before turning left onto a footpath – cyclists keep to the road – where there is a TCT interpretive panel (pileated woodpecker). Almost immediately, a small bridge conveys you across a narrow but lively brook, and the route turns right again.

About 500 m/yd from the bridge, the path levels for a few minutes through luscious hardwoods as it runs alongside picturesque Lac Larouche. Once past this lake, there is a short climb – skirting past some impressively large boulders – before the trail begins another long and challenging descent.

The vegetation is thick with many young trees, mostly hardwood. At 12 km (7.5 mi), you cross the tiny Ruisseau Larouche, which is unbridged. After another short uphill, the trail drops down its steepest decline yet through the darkest, densest spruce thicket of the day. The path switchbacks down the slope until it intersects with the wide, crushed-stone Sentier le Riverain at 13.8 km (8.6 mi). You have reached the Rivière Malbaie in the Parc national des Hautes-Gorges-de-la-Rivière-Malbaie.

Turn right and follow the path for about 100 m/yd to the paved road. Turn left and cross the vehicle bridge (no sidewalk) to the opposite bank of the wide river. Take a moment to enjoy the excellent views of the surrounding mountains.

14 km (8.7 mi) Arrive on the north bank of the Rivière Malbaie where there are benches and a covered sitting area at the junction of the paved park road and a gravel road follows the river's north bank. A Traversée sign indicates that the Chalet du Geai-Bleu (Blue Jay) is to the right 5.9 km (3.7 mi) further.

Now comes confession time. Somewhere along the gravel road, the Traversée turns left onto a footpath. This runs through what I was told are the most attractive hardwood forests of the entire day. This footpath reconnects to the gravel road about 200 m/yd from the chalet. I, however, did not find the junction and ended up trekking the gravel road the remaining 4.8 km (3 mi).

Actually, this was my third time lost this day. One of these side trips, someone had "playfully" rotated one of the directional arrows at a junction to point to the wrong route and had added more than 5 km (3.1 mi) to my walk. Somehow, I missed this last junction even though I backtracked to the paved road and even tried some park trails. I finally gave up and trudged the road to the day's finish. For the first 1.5 km (0.9 mi), when alongside the river, it is quite pleasant. A sign indicates that the chalet is 200 m/yd off the gravel road to the right.

18.8 km (11.7 mi) Arrive at the Chalet du Geai-Blue, which is attractively situated on an open hill overlooking a bend in the Rivière Malbaie. A discovery panel, appropriately about the blue jay, is beside it. There is even a rare TCT marker. This

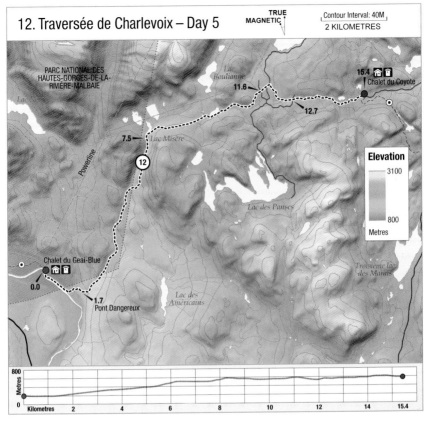

12. Traversée de Charlevoix – Day 5

TRUE
MAGNETIC

Contour Interval: 40M
2 KILOMETRES

PARC NATIONAL DES
HAUTES-GORGES-DE-LA-
RIVIÈRE-MALBAIE

Lac Boulianne

11.6

15.4 🏠🚻
Chalet du Coyote

12.7

7.5 — Lac Misère

12

Elevation
— 3100

800

Metres

Lac des Panses

Chalet du Geai-Blue 🏠🚻

0.0

Troisième lac
des Marais

1.7
Pont Dangereux

Lac des
Américains

Powerline

800
Metres

0

Kilometres   2   4   6   8   10   12   14   15.4

was my favourite overnight site, providing excellent views and the best place to swim on the entire Traversée.

Day 5: Chalet du Geai-Blue to Chalet du Coyote
Distance: 15.4 km (9.6 mi) – one way
Ascent: 621 m (2,037 ft)
Descent: 254 m (833 ft)

From the chalet, the footpath drops down the slope to run alongside the Rivière Malbaie, which is wide, shallow, and lively. About 1 km (0.6 mi) from the start, the trail turns inland and crosses the much smaller Ruisseau du Pont over two sturdy bridges in an area where the spring runoff has scoured the low land.

Once across, the trail begins a snaking meander round some rock faces and begins what is an almost continuous climb throughout the entire day. At 1.7 km (1.1 mi), you cross what is signed as a "pont dangereux" (dangerous bridge) over the tiny Ruisseau Chouinard. After this, the trail turns left and follows the creek upstream.

The ravine is narrow, wedged between towering hills. Although there is a designated lookout shortly after the bridge, views are limited in the thick vegetation. There is a variety of tree species along the route, and at 2.7 km (1.7 mi), an interpretive panel is about the yellow birch.

The climb is challenging at times, particularly as there is considerable deadfall impeding the path. In the humid ravine, most rocks were moss covered and slick, encouraging your feet to slither off in unplanned directions. There is an overhead canopy of leaves for the entire distance alongside the brook.

The creek is a constant companion on the left for a considerable distance, although the path occasionally drifts out of sight of it for a few minutes. There was one fresh beaver dam at 4.1 km (2.5 mi), but I imagine these change from year to year. At 5.6 km (3.5 mi), the trail makes a 180° switchback and ascends more steeply, turning decisively away from the brook.

At 6.3 km (3.9 mi), the climb ends (temporarily) on a viewing area of open rock, and sure enough, there are good views of the neighbouring jagged, tree-covered hills. Signs announce it as cell coverage point #12, although I did not have a good signal.

7.5 km (4.7 mi) Arrive at the mouth of Ruisseau Chouinard, draining from small Lac Misère. The trail turns right, skirting the edge of the lake and providing more views of the rocky hills – the ubiquitous powerline at their base. Another cell coverage sign is located overlooking the water.

At it leaves the lake, the trail resumes climbing steeply, almost 70 m (230 ft) in the next 800 m/yd. However, after that, the walking becomes much easier and even descends slightly. The treadway is gratifyingly clear with few obstructions or even rocks. The surrounding forest has become mostly thick spruce.

A rough bridge crosses a small creek at 9.4 km (5.9 mi), and the km 6 marker is almost in sight of it. Just 400 m/yd beyond that, the trail diverts because of a large beaver pond. Expect that a new path needs to be cut to avoid this growing hazard. After this, the path meanders through the forest, climbing another small knoll and working through several wet messy areas.

11.6 km (7.2 mi) After 500 m/yd of difficult downhill, the trail connects to a wide, gravel logging road. Look carefully on the opposite side; you should see a footpath, but there was no sign or marker until further into the forest. (This looked as if it is a newer road and might not appear on maps.)

There are two more road crossings, one at 11.9 km (7.4 mi) and another at 12.7 km (7.9 mi), but they are better marked. After these, the trail appears to be more like an old woods road, and for the first time this day, the walking and biking routes are the same.

The final few kilometres are easy walking, even though the path climbs for the next 2 km (1.2 mi). This gradual ascent is noticeable only in your quadriceps, however, as the thick forest blocks any views of the surrounding terrain. There are even a couple of nice bridges.

The final 500 m/yd are on a woods road clearly used by vehicles, though not commercially, so the adjacent vegetation is lush. Side tracks are frequent, but the directional markers at each junction are clear.

15.4 km (9.6 mi) You arrive at the night's shelter, the Chalet du Coyote, which is 60 m/yd off the main trail. Though situated next to a small creek, this is the least attractively situated chalet of the Traversée, being hemmed in by forest and with no views whatsoever.

Day 6: Chalet du Coyote to Chalet de l'Épervier
Distance: 19 km (11.8 mi) – one way
Ascent: 499 m (1,637 ft)
Descent: 639 m (2,096 ft)

Departing from the Chalet du Coyote, return the 60 m/yd to the last junction where the directional signs point you onto a wooded footpath. Although the trail guide assures a net descent today, the hike begins with a climb. At 300 m/yd, where there is an interpretive panel, the footpath connects to an old woods road, and turns left.

This old road is clearly no longer used, and vegetation has grown in so much that it appears more like a wide footpath. The walking is easy with only a few tree roots and even fewer rocks to trip on. In the thick mixed forest, there are no views.

At 450 m/yd, the trail turns left again, returning to a footpath and descending. Sentier national au Québec markers (white over red squares) are frequent. At 1 km (0.6 mi), the trail makes another sharp turn, this time to the right, and starts to climb again. Soon there is a small creek alongside on the left and plenty of beaver activity in the marshy ground. In fact, there are several large ponds that they have created that do not appear on your map. The path climbs a little to avoid these gradually expanding water hazards.

At 2.3 km (1.4 mi), the trail reaches a small lake and begins another descent through difficult ground. However, only 200 m/yd later, the footpath connects to a wide woods road, and the walking becomes easier. At the next junction to Lac de l'Hermine, keep straight. (There is an arrow, but it was obscured by vegetation.) The road soon begins a very steep descent, somewhat tricky on the small loose rocks in the treadway.

3.9 km (2.4 mi) The trail leaves the road, continuing on a footpath. This is well signed and includes another interpretive panel on the moose. Just 100 m/yd after you reach the end of this downhill, you cross a small brook on a very rickety

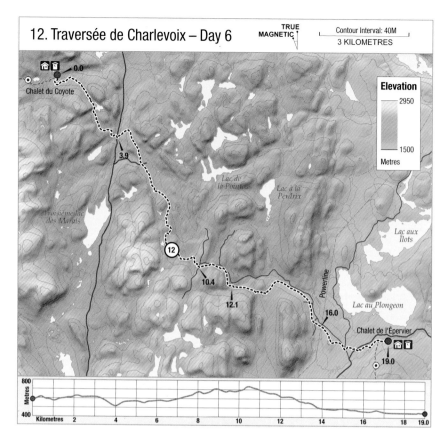

12. Traversée de Charlevoix – Day 6

TRUE
MAGNETIC

Contour Interval: 40M
3 KILOMETRES

Chalet du Coyote — 0.0

3.9

Lac de la Pointe
Lac à la Perdrix
Troisième lac des Marais
Lac aux Îlots

12

10.4
12.1

Powerline

Lac au Plongeon

16.0

Chalet de l'Épervier
19.0

Elevation
2950
1500
Metres

800
Metres
400
Kilometres   2   4   6   8   10   12   14   16   18 19.0

bridge. The next section is quite lovely, especially the first climb up a hill of tall spruce with a forest floor of sphagnum moss.

The footpath connects to another road at 5.3 km (3.3 mi) and turns right to cross a brook – the same brook as before, actually – before returning to a footpath on the opposite bank less than 200 m/yd later. This is almost the only place where the cycling route and walking/skiing route intersect on today's hike.

The trail now follows a pleasant footpath, actually quite close to a gravel road that is often in sight on the right for nearly a kilometre. The route is almost level, as well, with only the minor undulations of the natural landscape. A pale light shines through the thick forest canopy of mostly softwoods.

At 6.6 km (4.1 mi), the trail crosses a tiny brook – a good water source – and begins to move away from the road. It also begins what is a quite challenging climb, the easy treadway gradually replaced by moss-covered rocks. There is a brief break at 8 km (5 mi) when it descends briefly to reach and cross a tiny creek 600 m/yd later. The climb resumes for another 400 m/yd before dropping again to cross a woods road and wet area.

The path appears to cross a succession of low ridges, especially around the km 9 marker, but there is one steep ascent up a hillside completely covered in spruce.

10.4 km (6.5 mi) The trail crosses a very wide new forestry road – one of several which do not appear on the map. The trail immediately re-enters the forest cover, although it allows views from the middle of the road. Shortly afterward, the long descent to the Chalet de l'Épervier begins.

Recent clearcuts are sometimes visible to the right, and by 10.9 km (6.8 mi), a forestry road can be seen to the left and slightly below. In fact, the trail remains quite close to this road, although separated by a buffer of vegetation, for a considerable distance. The trail is quite uneven walking, poorly grubbed into the slope with many rocks in the treadway. There is even a bridged walkway over one very rough spot.

12.1 km (7.5 mi) You arrive at a lovely brook, spanned by a sturdy new bridge. This was my lunch spot, an attractive, shaded glade beside a bubbling brook with a few stools fashioned from cut trees. From here, the path continues its descent except for a minor rise immediately after the creek.

The trail continues to work along a hillside with higher ground on the right. The vegetation is thick, and the footing is often quite rugged. Another nice bridge crosses the next brook at 13.2 km (8.2 mi), where beavers have built a dam beneath it. The path after this point becomes even easier.

Around 13.9 km (8.6 mi), the trail curves sharply right and the rate of descent diminishes. To the left, a creek and marshy area are quite close, so several puncheons (plank boardwalks) are used to cross the wettest spots. The trail crosses a woods road 300 m/yd later, with the gravel forestry road visible to the left.

The trail remains relatively close to the gravel road and crosses side roads at 15.2 km (9.4 mi) and 15.8 km (9.8 mi). This last one is particularly tricky as it does not appear on the map, and the path on the far side was almost completely hidden by vegetation. (Another hiker and I both initially followed the road for a few hundred metres/yards before we decided that was incorrect.)

16 km (10 mi) After an easy 200 m/yd in the forest, the trail reaches a broad clearing beneath several powerlines. A row of high posts tipped with arrows marks the route across the 250 m/yd-wide clearing.

The next kilometre is easy walking, even though there is a short climb. At 17.3 km (10.7 mi), after having been quite close to the road for several hundred metres/yards, the trail crosses a gravel road. Another 100 m/yd later, it crosses another. Fortunately, the signage in this confusing area is excellent.

At 17.8 km (11 mi), there is yet another road crossing, but this is the final one for the day. The trail continues through the forest, and gradually the sounds of the Rivière Noire Sud-Ouest swell into audibility. This winding, weaving section, though not difficult walking, seems interminable after the long day's hike.

Finally, at 18.7 km (11.6 mi), you reach a junction where several signs indicate that the end of the Traversée at Mont Grand-Fonds is to the right. Tonight's chalet, however, is straight ahead. As you continue, you can see the slow-moving river off to the right.

19 km (11.8 mi) You arrive at the Chalet de l'Épervier, the final chalet on this route.

Day 7: Chalet de l'Épervier to Mont Grand-Fonds
Distance: 10.3 km (6.4 mi) – one way
Ascent: 287 m (941 ft)
Descent: 358 m (1,175 ft)

From the Chalet de l'Épervier, return the 300 m/yd to the junction with the main trail. Turn left and cross the long bridge – the longest on the Traversée – across the wide but sluggish Rivière Noire Sud-Ouest.

On the far bank is a junction and a plethora of signage. In addition to the directional signs, showing that the cyclists turn left but the walkers or skiers continue straight, there is an interpretive panel, a TCT marker, and a map of the Sentier de l'Orignac, which shares some of the Traversée route.

Actually, this is the end of The Great Trail on the Traversée de Charlevoix. It now follows the Sentier de l'Orignac for the 33 km (20.5 mi) to its end on the St. Lawrence River at Saint-Siméon with the ferry to Rivière-du-Loup on the opposite bank. However, the trek must finish, and the remaining portion of the Traversée is also the sentier d'accès (access trail) for the Sentier de l'Orignac.

Naturally, our path starts climbing steeply, in fact ascending nearly 200 m/yd in the following 2 km (1.2 mi). Although there are occasional glimpses of the neighbouring hills, this climb is done mostly within a thick enclosing barrier of spruce.

The grade moderates at around 2.4 km (1.5 mi) and shortly afterwards, there is enough of a clearing that you can view the hills to the right. At 2.7 km (1.7 mi), the path crosses a small woods road. For some time, the trail is nearly level and undulating slightly. The ground is higher to the left, but views to the right over a deep ravine are occasionally possible through the vegetation. This is especially true in several stands of white birch that you pass through on the hilltop. The final cell coverage marker, #20, is found at 4 km (2.5 mi).

4.5 km (2.8 mi) The trail begins to descend, gradually at first but with increasing steepness. It soon enters a series of switchbacks over some rougher ground. Quite quickly, we lose almost all the elevation we gained at the start. The trees on this slope are almost all spruce and fir.

At a junction at 6 km (3.7 mi), hikers branch left while skiers head right. Our trail remains in the mixed wood forest but crosses several clearings and narrow

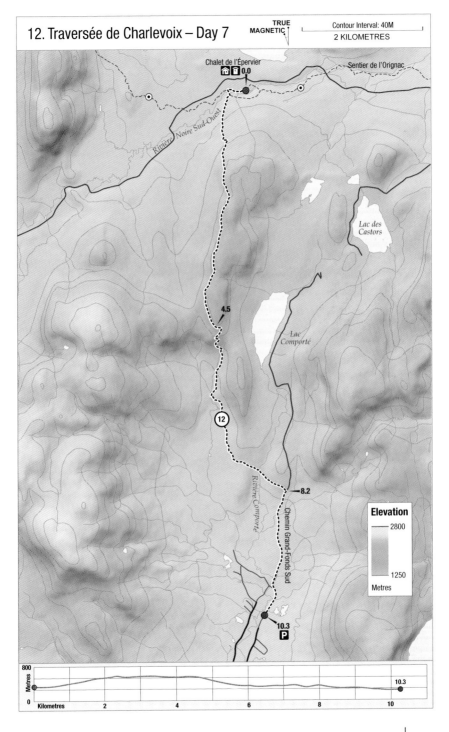

12. Traversée de Charlevoix – Day 7

TRUE
MAGNETIC

Contour Interval: 40M
2 KILOMETRES

Chalet de l'Épervier
0.0

Sentier de l'Orignac

Rivière Noire Sud-Ouest

Lac des Castors

4.5

Lac Comporté

12

Rivière Comporté

8.2

Chemin Grand-Fonds Sud

Elevation
2800
1250
Metres

10.3
P

Metres 800 / 0
Kilometres 2 4 6 8 10

10.3

woods roads. Some are signed as cross-country ski trails; you have reached Mont Grand-Fonds, a small ski resort.

The trail then actually crosses some of its rockiest and most difficult terrain, especially near the bridge crossing the Rivière Comporté at 7.6 km (4.7 mi). The drop into – and climb out of – its narrow ravine are quite ugly. Do not accidently turn onto one of the many ski runs that intersect the path!

8.2 km (5.1 mi) The footpath ends, connecting to the Chemin Grand-Fonds Sud, a wide dirt road. Turn right; this is your route for the remaining portion of the Traversée. Be cautious as this is used by large logging trucks, two of which passed me as I finished my trek. They move at high speed and do not expect walkers.

There are several road junctions and cross-country ski paths that intersect with this road, but your route continues straight. In the last few hundred metres/ yards, there are some houses on the left, as well as a sizable stable and exercise yard for horses. On the hill behind that, you can see the downhill ski runs for Mont Grand-Fonds.

10.3 km (6.4 mi) Arrive at the official end of the Traversée de Charlevoix in a small parking lot, where the paved road begins, just opposite the entrance to Les Chalets de Môh. There is a new trailhead kiosk there, which features a map of The Great Trail route in the Charlevoix region, an interpretive panel, and a map of the Sentier de l'Orignac. However, it would be wise to make arrangements for your vehicle to be transported here from the Zec des Martres as it is still 14.2 km (8.8 mi) from Highway 138 and La Malbaie, the closest community with most services.

Further Information:

Mont Grand-Fonds: www.montgrandfonds.com

Parc national des Hautes-Gorges-de-la-Rivière-Malbaie: www.sepaq.com/ pq/hgo

Traversée de Charlevoix: www.traverseedecharlevoix.qc.ca

Tourism Charlevoix: www.tourisme-charlevoix.com

Zec des Martres: https://zecdesmartres.reseauzec.com

Zec Lac-au-Sable: https://zeclacausable.reseauzec.com

Eudore Fortin's Life-Long Passion

In 1978, Eudore Fortin began his development of a long-distance cross-country ski trail in the Charlevoix region. Born in nearby Saint-Urbain, Eudore was an experienced outdoorsman who had worked in the forest for most of his life. He had built trails before, in what is now Parc national des Grands-Jardins, but never before had a multi-day ski route been created in Quebec. In partnership with the Fédération québécoise  de la montagne, he soon completed a 105 km (65.2 mi) pathway.

In 1991, the Traversée de Charlevoix Inc., a private, not-for-profit organization whose objectives are to contribute to the development, maintenance, and administration of the trail network, formally took control of the Traversée de Charlevoix. Eudore naturally became its President. That was also the year when the six chalets were first built. Since then, the Traversée de Charlevoix has become a component of the Sentier national au Québec (1998), the National Hiking Trail, and The Great Trail. This trail has been repeatedly recognized for its excellence and contribution both to tourism and the outdoors community.

And Eudore? When I went to the office to register in September 2015, the 85-year old was in the yard, splitting wood for the chalets and still the President of the Traversée. He shyly greeted us, thanked us for hiking his trail, and returned to his work.

Pileated Woodpecker

Anyone old enough to remember the Woody Woodpecker cartoons can instantly recognize this red-crested bird as it flits between trees in search of the carpenter ants that are its favourite food. The pileated woodpecker is also distinctive because of its size, about as large as a crow and much larger than any other eastern woodpecker. Since they require larger mature trees for nesting, pileated woodpecker populations declined sharply with the harvesting of old-growth forests. However, as regrowth tree populations have matured, pileated woodpeckers have become more common.

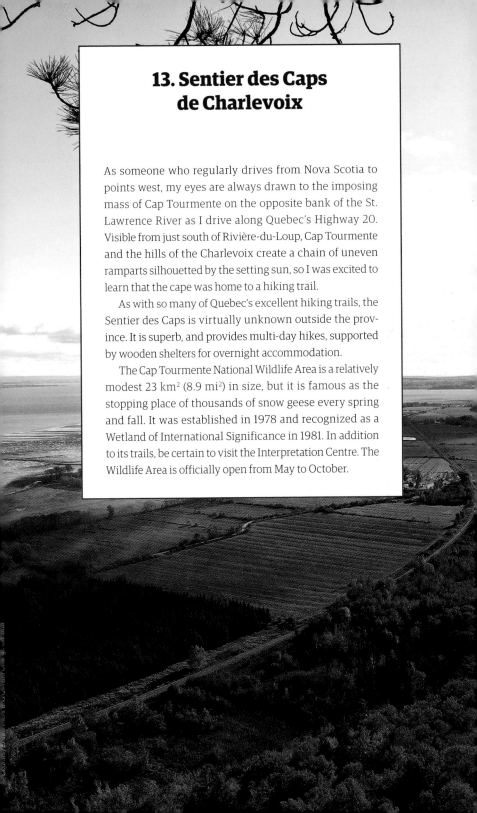

13. Sentier des Caps de Charlevoix

As someone who regularly drives from Nova Scotia to points west, my eyes are always drawn to the imposing mass of Cap Tourmente on the opposite bank of the St. Lawrence River as I drive along Quebec's Highway 20. Visible from just south of Rivière-du-Loup, Cap Tourmente and the hills of the Charlevoix create a chain of uneven ramparts silhouetted by the setting sun, so I was excited to learn that the cape was home to a hiking trail.

As with so many of Quebec's excellent hiking trails, the Sentier des Caps is virtually unknown outside the province. It is superb, and provides multi-day hikes, supported by wooden shelters for overnight accommodation.

The Cap Tourmente National Wildlife Area is a relatively modest 23 km² (8.9 mi²) in size, but it is famous as the stopping place of thousands of snow geese every spring and fall. It was established in 1978 and recognized as a Wetland of International Significance in 1981. In addition to its trails, be certain to visit the Interpretation Centre. The Wildlife Area is officially open from May to October.

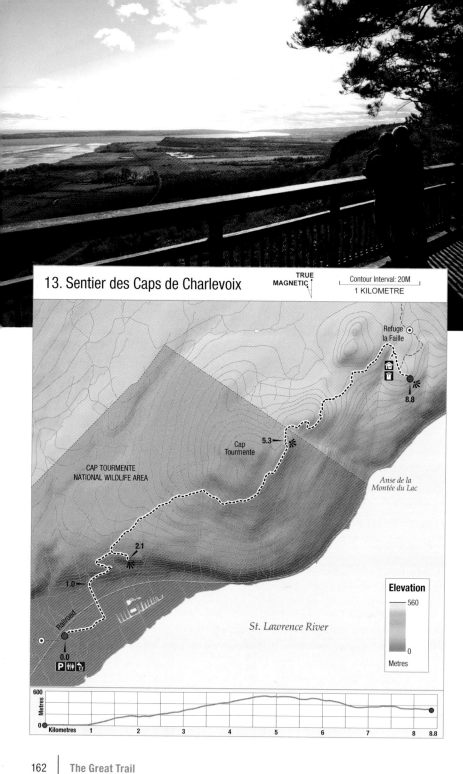

13. Sentier des Caps de Charlevoix

TRUE
MAGNETIC

Contour Interval: 20M
1 KILOMETRE

Refuge
la Faille

8.8

Cap
Tourmente

5.3

CAP TOURMENTE
NATIONAL WILDLIFE AREA

Anse de la
Montée du Lac

2.1

1.0

Railroad

St. Lawrence River

0.0

Elevation

560

0

Metres

600
Metres
0
Kilometres   1   2   3   4   5   6   7   8 8.8

13. Sentier des Caps de Charlevoix

Distance: 8.8 km (5.5 mi) – one way
Ascent: 642 m (2,106 ft)
Descent: 327 m (1,073 ft)

Trail conditions: crushed stone, natural surface
Cellphone coverage: yes
Hazards: railway crossing, rugged terrain, wildlife

Permitted Uses							
Walking	Biking	Horseback Riding	Inline Skating	ATV	Snowshoeing	Cross-country Skiing	Snowmobiling
✔	—	—	—	—	✔	✔*	—

Finding the trailhead: The trail begins from the parking lot inside the Cap Tourmente National Wildlife Area near the Maison des Français, about 1 km (0.6 mi) from the toll kiosk. There are garbage cans and picnic tables nearby, as well as a large information pavilion.

Trailhead: 47°04'37.5" N, 70°46'56.1" W (Start — Cap Tourmente National Wildlife Area)
47°06'30.2" N, 70°43'50.7" W (Finish — Lookout)

Observations: I walked this on a windy, wet, late September day, and low clouds obscured some of the tremendous views available from Cap Tourmente, but even so, it was thrilling. Inside the bird sanctuary, the trail is wide and well maintained. Once you leave their grounds, the track becomes far more rugged and challenging. It really is two different experiences. When wet, those rocks are very slippery, and I skidded more than once during a steep descent. This is a lovely area, however, and even on this cool, wet day, there were plenty of other hikers. Many were surprised that I was walking alone on such a rough track.

Route description: Cross a bridge at the northeast end of the parking lot and follow l'Allée des Ormes. It is marked by a blue sign with white lettering, which states that it is 1.5 km (0.9 mi). The path is wide and clearly intended for vehicle use. Within 150 m/yd on the left is the Pavillon Léon-Provancher, where there is a large picnic area, interpretive panels, a viewing platform — the birds of prey observatory — and washrooms.

Once past the pavilion, the ground on either side is quite open. These fertile lowlands have been farmed for centuries, reputedly since Samuel de Champlain

Sentier des Caps de Charlevoix

The first section of this long-distance hiking trail opened in October 1996. Over the next several years, additional sections were added, including into the National Wildlife Area in 1999. By 2013, the system had grown to a main route of more than 50 km (31 mi), supplemented with more than 20 km (12.4 mi) of side trails. Supporting this are nine overnight shelters, each of which can accommodate ten people.

The trails are managed by Le Sentier des Caps de Charlevoix, a not-for-profit organization established by the local municipalities that maintains an office and welcome centre in the community of Saint-Tite-des-Caps. Fees are charged for use of their trails, whether single day or requiring overnight stays in the shelters.

established a settlement here in 1626. To the right, the St. Lawrence River is visible across the low ground; to the left and ahead, the fearsome-looking cliffs of the escarpment and the towering mass of Cap Tourmente. Should you happen to be in the area in spring or fall during the snow goose migration, you can hear their ceaseless honking, even if you cannot see them.

After 550 m/yd, you reach a well-signed junction where there is a bench and turn left. The wide, grass-covered track crosses the fields and in 250 m/yd reaches a railway track—and stop #7 on the brochure for a self-guided historical tour. Continue straight, entering a forested area filled with gorgeous maples. Less than 100 m/yd further, the path begins to climb and enters a small field. Soon, however, it returns to being under tree cover, where it stays for the remainder of the hike.

⚲ **1 km (0.6 mi)** The easy walking ends at the junction of Le Pierrer and La Falaise Trails. Most of the extensive pathway network in the National Wildlife Area remains below the escarpment, but La Falaise, La Cime, and The Great Trail climb it. There is a bench at this intersection, though you probably do not require it yet.

Continue straight; the sign says that La Falaise—the cliff top observation deck—is 1.1 km (0.7 mi) away. The track is natural surface but wide enough for wheeled maintenance vehicles to climb. As it climbs, the grade keeps increasing. Despite the steepness, there is remarkably little erosion, and mitigation infrastructure, such as ditches and drainage channels, is prominent.

Small creeks run down the hillside; these are all crossed by sturdy bridges. The first bench is at 1.4 km (0.9 mi), just where the trail switches back to the left. The climb continues unrelieved to the turnoff to La Falaise at 1.9 km (1.2 mi). The sign says that it is 500 m/yd to the viewing area; that turns out to be the return distance.

2.1 km (1.3 mi) After a flight of stairs and a boardwalk, you reach La Falaise observation deck, which enjoys a panoramic view of the lower portions of the Wildlife Area, the northern tip of Île d'Orléans, and the St. Lawrence River. You might even be able to spot the towers of Québec City in the distance.

When you return to the main trail, it is 2.4 km (1.5 mi). The section that continues to climb is called "La Cime" (The Top). The sign says that it is 3 km (1.9 mi) long and closes after 3:00 p.m. The path is still wide and free of rock and tree roots, but it continues to climb.

By 2.8 km (1.7 mi), the grade reduces and seems almost easy after the previous steep climb. The slope to the right also lessens, suggesting that you have moved beyond the sharp edge of the escarpment. This is a pleasant walk through attractive hardwoods, including many maples and oaks. There are occasional small bridges or other crossings over wetter areas, but nothing difficult.

Around 3.7 km (2.3 mi), there are a number of mature maple and beech hardwoods, some of the largest I have seen in Quebec. One or two are adjacent to the pathway. About 150 m/yd later, another sign states that 1.5 km (0.9 mi) remain to the lookout.

The path narrows as it ascends, transforming gradually into a footpath. By 4.6 km (2.9 mi), small bridges are frequent, and bare rock intrudes more and more often into the treadway. The trees have also changed, completely to softwoods. Within 100 m/yd, the trail is wholly exposed rock that is criss-crossed with deep, glacial gouges.

At 4.9 km (3 mi), a sign says that 500 m/yd remain to the observation deck, and this remaining section actually descends slightly. As the climb from the trailhead has exceeded 500 m/yd, a little downhill is probably welcome. The ground is also boggy and wet, so sections are surfaced with the plank boardwalks known here as "puncheons."

5.3 km (3.3 mi) A huge sign marks the end of La Cime, but a further 100 m/yd walk is required to reach the viewing platform and return. The view is exceptional even on a rainy day, which it was when I visited. The deck projects out from the hillside, perched more than 500 m/yd above water level. Massive shipping vessels sailing down the St. Lawrence look miniscule from this height, so pack binoculars. Looking along Cap Tourmente to the east, you can even see the railway track, a tiny, steel ribbon hugging the mountain's base.

Returning to the main trail, turn right to continue along the Sentier des Caps de Charlevoix. Affixed to many of the trees are flashes of fading yellow paint and/or the plastic tags marking the Sentier national au Québec, of which this is a part. For the first time, the trail signage is their signature bright red with white lettering. It states that the Refuge La Faille is 2.8 km (1.7 mi) ahead.

Within a very few steps, it becomes clear that the standards of trail construction between the National Wildlife Area and the volunteer trail builders varies considerably. While the ground is quite wet and muddy, there are no more puncheons or bridges. The path is quite narrow with rocks and tree roots in abundance in the treadway. Tree branches brush against your shoulders on either side.

The route soon begins to descend quite significantly, even requiring a staircase at 5.8 km (3.6 mi). Less than 50 m/yd later, there is a sign proclaiming the boundary of the Reserve Cap Tourmente and outlining a lengthy list of prohibited activities. Over the next few hundred metres/yards there are several areas to the right where views are possible from patches of bare rock.

At 6.5 km (4 mi), the trail drops precipitously, and some clambering over rocks is required. There is even a rope to assist. This challenging stretch lasts for about 400 m/yd, after which the trail widens and the downhill grade decreases. Once again, hardwoods are in the majority, providing a welcome leafy canopy in summer. This is a pleasant section, although with occasional short difficult spots. (A rope alongside the route is usually a clue.)

At 8.1 km (5 mi), you reach an extravagantly signed junction with several trails. There is even a TCT marker and an interpretive panel. Keep straight to reach the Refuge La Faille, which is 200 m/yd ahead. Just before you arrive, the path becomes a woods road, and the refuge is to the right. This is an excellent place to overnight; the cabin has room for ten inside and a number of campsites outdoors. There are a water source, picnic tables, a wood stove, and an outhouse.

Return to the main trail and turn right. Follow the easy wide woods road for 250 m/yd to the next junction, where there is another interpretive panel about the black bear — always a comforting thought. A blue-and-white sign says that the lookout is another 175 m/yd.

📍 **8.8 km (5.5 mi)** Arrive at the viewing platform where there are a picnic tables and benches. Once again, there are expansive vistas of the river, its islands, and the opposite shore of the broad St. Lawrence River. This is a delightful place to rest and snack or lunch before retracing your route back to the trailhead at the Cap Tourmente National Wildlife Area.

Further Information:
Cap Tourmente National Wildlife Area: http://www.ec.gc.ca/ap-pa/default.
    asp?lang=En&n=0533BC0A-1#
Sentier des Caps de Charlevoix: http://www.sentierdescaps.com
Tourism Charlevoix: https://www.tourisme-charlevoix.com

Snow Goose

Each spring and fall, tens of thousands of plump, white birds cover a few fields and wetlands along the St. Lawrence River, stopping for a brief rest as they make their way north to their breeding grounds in the Arctic tundra or south to their wintering sites in Mexico and the southern United States.

Conservation efforts have resulted in a substantial increase in snow geese numbers in recent years with the eastern flocks having tripled since the 1970s. So when they appear in local skies, expect to see — and hear — large numbers of these sociable geese congregating in their preferred locations.

Beaver

The many small lakes and wetlands of the Canadian Shield are ideal habitat for beaver, and their dams, lodges, and trails of felled trees may be found throughout Canada. This largest rodent in North America creates dams as protection against predators and to provide easy access to food during winter. Beavers generally work at night and are prolific builders, each gnawing through an average of 216 trees per year.

During the peak of the fur trade era some two hundred thousand beaver pelts were sold each year to the European market, driving the animals almost to extinction. Because of recent conservation measures, their numbers have increased tremendously, and colonizing beavers have returned to many sites where they had disappeared.

14. Sentier Mestachibo

If your tastes run to rugged, you will relish the Sentier Mestachibo. Following the Rivière Sainte-Anne-du-Nord through an impressive canyon, the trail constantly climbs and descends over the rock-strewn terrain. Frequently, only a slender footpath is hacked into a sheer hillside, often augmented by ropes to aid the hiker. Carry plenty of food and water on this one, and if possible, leave a car at both trailheads. (Or the trail website has the number of a taxi service — write it down before you start.)

This path is designed not merely for hiking, but for those who want their exercise to be physically demanding. Although this area of Quebec has been settled from near the beginning of New France, the deep canyon of the Rivière Saint-Anne-du-Nord was largely inaccessible until this trail was developed. And it is scarcely more so now. This sinuous route might be possible to snowshoe but definitely not to cross-country ski.

In addition to being part of The Great Trail, the Sentier Mestachibo is also a section of the Sentier national au Québec (SNQ) and the National Hiking Trail. Most of the trail signage you see on trees and rocks is the SNQ's red-and-white paint flashes.

14. Sentier Mestachibo

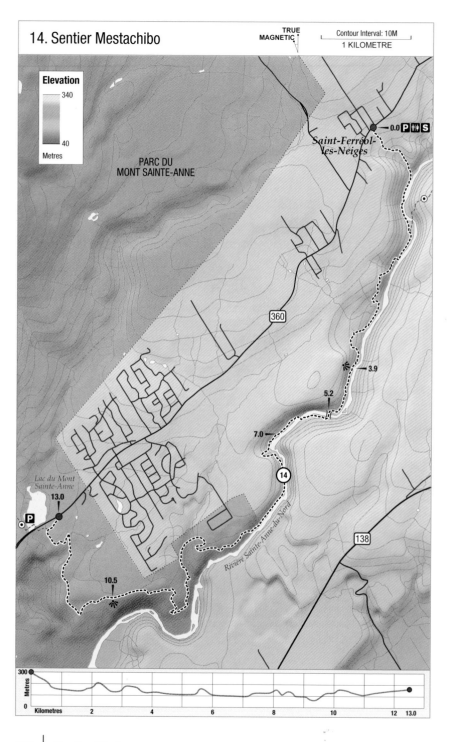

TRUE
MAGNETIC

Contour Interval: 10M
1 KILOMETRE

Elevation

340
40
Metres

PARC DU
MONT SAINTE-ANNE

Saint-Ferréol-
les-Neiges

0.0 P 🚻 S

360

3.9

5.2

7.0

14

138

Lac du Mont
Sainte-Anne

13.0

P

Rivière Sainte-Anne-du-Nord

10.5

300
Metres

0
Kilometres   2   4   6   8   10   12 13.0

14. Sentier Mestachibo

Distance: 13.1 km (8.1 mi) – one way
Ascent: 550 m (1,804 ft)
Descent: 687 m (2,254 ft)

Trail conditions: crushed stone, natural surface
Cellphone coverage: partial
Hazards: rugged terrain, wildlife

Permitted Uses							
Walking	Biking	Horseback Riding	Inline Skating	ATV	Snowshoeing	Cross-country Skiing	Snowmobiling
✔	—	—	—	—	✔	—	—

Finding the trailhead: Start at Saint-Ferréol-les-Neiges. A large road sign indicates the trailhead, and there is ample free parking. (The lot at Mont Sainte-Anne requires payment.) In a small greenspace adjacent to the lot are a shelter, picnic tables, garbage cans, and a bike rack. There are also washrooms, a water source, and a store close by. A large map kiosk is positioned at the edge of the forest with a crushed-stone pathway beckoning beyond it. Affixed to the panel are both a Great Trail TCT marker and one for the National Hiking Trail (Sentier national au Québec) labelled km 13.

Trailhead: 47°07'01.3" N, 70°51'33.1" W (Start — Saint-Ferréol-les-Neiges)
47°04'38.2" N, 70°53'55.1" W (Finish — Mont Sainte-Anne)

Observations: This trail exhausted me. After I descended the steep path from the trailhead to river level, I anticipated a fairly easy amble alongside the water. Instead, the deep ravine frequently forced me to scrabble up steep-sided canyon walls, frequently with ropes to assist to bypass sheer cliff faces – only to descend the other side just as precipitously. After a few such manoeuvres, often over terrain littered with boulders, my legs ran out of gas. It's important to note that there are several dead spots for cellphones at the bottom of the canyon, though coverage is good higher up the slopes.

While wildly scenic and definitely worthwhile, the Sentier Mestachibo requires strength and stamina to complete, and probably more time than you expect. How challenging did I find this trail? When I finished my trek at Mont Sainte-Anne, rather than return to Saint-Ferréol-les-Neiges by the trail, I trudged back on Highway 360. That walk was completely devoid of pleasure, but far, far easier.

Route description: As soon as you enter the trees at the trailhead, the crushed-stone path becomes a rough, naturally surfaced footpath dropping sharply downhill. At first, rough stairs have been cut into the hillside, and when the trail reaches a small creek, there is a bridge. But by the time you reach the Rivière Sainte-Anne, 800 m/yd from the start, it is evident that this is not a hike for the inexperienced or unfit.

Any lingering doubts are dispelled by the last crossing of the small creek as it empties into the river, a single plank flanked by a rope strung between trees on opposite banks. (And I am guessing that the plank may not be there now – or at least, not the same plank.) The river is shallow but fast moving, and the hills on either side are thickly forested and steep sided. Tree roots and rocks intrude into the treadway, and a scramble over boulders and along a sheer hillside – assisted by ropes – is required at 1.4 km (0.9 mi).

Fortunately, the surprisingly difficult terrain ends about 200 m/yd later, where there is an idyllic picnic site in a flat dell beside the river with a table and two interpretive panels. Easy walking continues for the next 400 m/yd, but then the flat ground ends and is followed by an arduous climb on a narrow track over very rough terrain. Small creeks have washed away the treadway in several places, and ropes have been placed to aid crossing these rocky, slippery messes. Both wooden and stone steps have been cut into the hillside in various places, and near the crest of the hill, there is even an elaborate staircase. When you reach the highest point, more than 70 m/yd above the river, you have hiked 2.6 km (1.6 mi).

About 200 m/yd of mostly level walking follows, and you should see a cabin to the right just before a steep descent. It takes you through multiple switchbacks back to river level and a signed junction – an emergency exit – at 3.1 km (1.9 mi). Keep straight and the trail crosses a small creek beside the river, where there appears to be a pool where you might want to swim. This spot is known as "La Tourmente."

Very shortly after, the path begins to climb again on a steep rough track that turns away from the water and cuts behind the next hill. At 3.8 km (2.4 mi), you reach a sign; it is not a junction, but the path turns left 90˚.

3.9 km (2.4 mi) You arrive at two lookouts, each facing a different direction over the river. Visiting both adds about 200 m/yd to your trip, but the views of the river ravine are quite nice. Each has a viewing platform, bench, and guardrail, as they are perched high on a nearly vertical hillside. As soon as you leave the lookouts the trail descends, reaching water level 300 m/yd later at Rapide des Trois Rouleaux.

Although still fairly rugged, the trail remains close to the river and is relatively easy walking. For nearly 800 m/yd, until the river makes a sharp bend right, you are able to relax and enjoy the attractive forest and swift-moving river.

5.2 km (3.2 mi) Just after sighting a sandy beach, the track reaches a suspended bridge. This narrow 70 m/yd-long span bounces and sways when you cross. Hang on tightly to any equipment! On the far side, your route appears to be an old woods road at first and quite easy walking. But after about 250 m/yd, the trail branches off, returning to a narrow footpath. There is a sign and directional arrow to ensure you remain on the correct path. It also states that this is km 8.

You reach the second bridge less than 450 m/yd from the first and cross the river once again. These bouncy crossings were one of the trail highlights for me, and my appreciation for the force of the flowing river was intensified by its appearance from mid-span.

Another comparatively undemanding 650 m/yd follows, with the trail close to the water's edge and a fiercely steep slope crowding on the right. At 6 km (3.7 mi), there is a sign in French only, "Chutes de Pierres Possible," warning of falling rock. Immediately afterwards the trail almost disappears, reduced to a narrow, rock-strewn shelf at the base of an immense, vertical rock face. After scrambling over these rocks, you cross a bridge over a short stretch where even a narrow shelf doesn't exist. The river makes a sharp left turn, squeezed into a narrow funnel beneath the towering cliffs of La Cathédrale.

Once across the bridge, you climb up the hillside directly ahead, picking a way through a wall of rock and boulders. After a tough 450 m/yd, you reach a signed junction where there is another escape trail, this time to Faubourg. A bright red sign warns that you are entering the Sections Les Cathédrales, which is rated "Difficile" (difficult).

Turn left and start dropping back towards the river. After another challenging 400 m/yd, in an area of large fallen rocks, is another junction, this one to a lookout. Turn left and head towards it; there is a new staircase to assist in climbing the difficult ground.

7 km (4.3 mi) You reach the observation deck in narrow La Cathédrale gorge, where there are two interpretive panels. The river is jammed into a channel less than half its previous width, so it pulses through at a ferocious speed, generating a roar that echoes off the high canyon walls. After the demanding last 100 m/yd,

you might wish to rest for a few minutes before continuing.

It is 100 m/yd back to the junction, where the trail remains near water level. Large boulders are strewn everywhere, so the path must work its way around or over them. After 800 m/yd, there is a short (200 m/yd) climb with rope assist. The worst of the rocky rubble ends, and walking becomes much easier. After another short climb, you reach another trail junction at 8.5 km (5.3 mi), again to Faubourg.

The trail is now quite high and out of sight of the river, and the surrounding trees are predominantly hardwoods. It is an easy walk, at times on a former woods road, to the next junction, an exit to Rue de Turin at 9.3 km (5.8 mi). This is followed by another sharp descent with stairs, switchbacks, and puncheons, leading to a small brook where the climb afterward requires rope assists – a difficult 500 m/yd.

10.5 km (6.5 mi) You reach the viewing platform that looks upriver into the Canyon Sainte-Anne private park after some relatively easy walking. You can see the base of the falls, the highest cliffs on the river, and two suspended bridges. About 250 m/yd further is a junction and to the left a beach and picnic area on the river. The main route curves away from the water and undertakes a long, steady climb through a lovely area of hardwoods. At the next junction at 11 km (6.8 mi) and the one following 400 m/yd later, exiting the trail takes you towards a golf course on the right that is close to the trail for the remainder of the walk.

The trail has moved away from the river and turned inland. The treadway becomes much easier, even surfaced with crushed stone at times. The remainder of the trail is fairly uneventful, although there are several small bridges, more clearly signed junctions, and a side trail to Rivière Jean-Larose.

13 km (8 mi) Follow the winding footpath to the junction with Highway 360, where there is a trail map. Those considering the return hike probably should retrace their route now. Otherwise, cross Highway 360, turn left, and cross the highway bridge to the Mont Sainte-Anne parking area, 500 m/yd away.

Further Information:
Resort Mont Sainte-Anne: https://mont-sainte-anne.com
Sentier Mestachibo: http://www.mestachibo.com
Tourism Côte-de-Beaupré: http://cotedebeaupre.com

Sentier national au Québec

In 1984, the Fédération québécoise de la marche, now Rando Québec, took over coordination of the Sentier national au Quebec (SNQ), a long-distance hiking pathway traversing the province. Once completed, present plans call for a 1,600 km (994 mi) route that will pass through nine of Quebec's regions: l'Outaouais, les Laurentides, Lanaudière, la Mauricie, Québec, Charlevoix, Manicouagan, le Bas-Saint-Laurent, and la Gaspésie.

Currently, approximately 1,075 km (668 mi) are completed, and each year new sections are added. Marked with its distinctive red-and-white flashes, the SNQ is an often rugged and challenging footpath that passes through quite remote areas. In addition to connecting various recreational tourism sites, it travels through provincial and regional parks, ZECs (Zones d'Exploitation Contrôlée), and private land. The SNQ is little known outside of Quebec but is one of the best purely hiking trails in Canada.

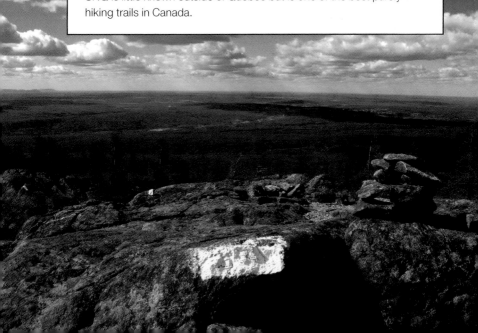

Mosquitoes

Between May and first frost, no hike is entirely free of these annoying tiny blood-sucking pests. Forget bears; mosquitoes are the real threat found on most trails. If you do not take adequate precautions, your walk can easily turn into a running fight where the scenery is forgotten while you slap frantically at biting bugs and flail the air vainly trying to drive them away.

Even though their primary food source is nectar from flowers, mosquitoes prefer blood to develop their eggs. Some species carry diseases such as St. Louis encephalitis and the West Nile virus, which they can transmit to humans. To limit your exposure to this ubiquitous nuisance, wear long sleeves and pants, especially during dawn and dusk (and a hat for those of us hair challenged). Use insect repellents with up to thirty-five percent DEET for adults and twenty percent for children over six months of age.

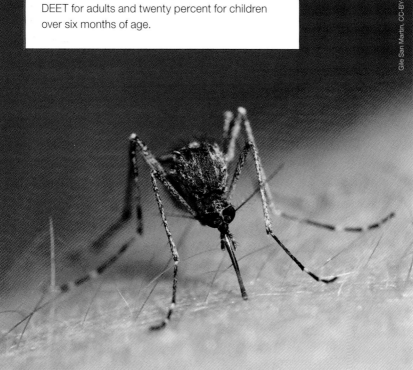

15. Parcours des Anses

Old Québec City is rightly considered one of the most picturesque capitals in North America and is the continent's only walled city. One of the best views of Québec, and particularly of its famous hotel, the Chateau Frontenac, is from the opposite bank of the St. Lawrence River, on the Parcours des Anses. This splendidly constructed and maintained pathway traces the shoreline of the St. Lawrence River, affording an unequalled sight of this remarkable urban vista.

The Parcours des Anses is asphalt surfaced and well appointed with benches, picnic tables, parks, and every facility desired by the walker or biker. The trail follows the route of the former Intercolonial Railway, which was abandoned in 1994. The Parcours des Anses opened in 2001. While not a challenging ride, it is worthwhile entirely for the scenic views available from it.

Confession: only the first 6.7 km (4.2 mi) of the 13 km (8 mi) profiled in this route is actually part of The Great Trail, which crosses the St. Lawrence on the ferry and resumes on the other shore. However, I enjoyed that first section of the Parcours des Anses so much that I followed it to its end and decided to include the additional 6.4 km (4 mi) to its junction with the Parcours Harlaka. Once you ride it, I hope that you agree with my decision.

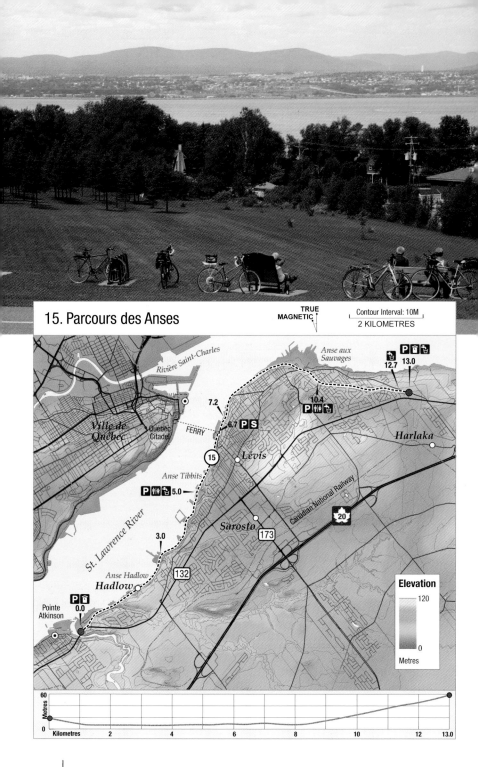

15. Parcours des Anses

TRUE
MAGNETIC

Contour Interval: 10M
2 KILOMETRES

15. Parcours des Anses

Distance: 13 km (8.1 mi) – one way
Ascent: 76 m (250 ft)
Descent: 34 m (112 ft)

Trail conditions: asphalt
Cellphone coverage: yes
Hazards: road crossings, heavy use

Permitted Uses								
Walking	Biking	Horseback Riding	Inline Skating	ATV	Snowshoeing	Cross-country Skiing	Snowmobiling	
✔	✔	—	✔	—	✔	✔	—	

Finding the trailhead: This route begins at Parc du Domaine-Etchemin, where there is a large parking area with picnic tables and an outhouse close by.

Trailhead: 46°45'39" N, 71°13'40.9" W (Start — Saint-Romuald)
46°49'27.4" N, 71°07'18.7" W (Finish — Rue Saint-Joseph)

Observations: This could not have been an easier bike ride. Paved throughout the entire route, with designated pedestrian and cycling lanes, this was smooth and effortless riding. The only obstacle on this sunny July day were the hundreds of other cyclists and walkers enjoying this beautiful trail. This route took me much longer than its modest distance would normally require, simply because there were so many wonderful places to photograph and to sit and enjoy the view. Old Québec City observed from the Parcours des Anses is magnificent, and several of the viewing areas overlooking the St. Lawrence further downstream were almost as appealing. The only challenge was the lack of shade along most of the route, which was uncomfortable at times on a hot July day. To balance against that, there were several places where public water fountains were available.

Route description: From the parking lot of the Parc du Domaine-Etchemin, walkers/cyclists return to the parking lot entrance on Rue St. Laurent, turn left, and continue downhill about 200 m/yd. On the right is a gate, and beyond that is the Parcours des Anses. Once on the main trail, turn left.

The Parcours des Anses is an asphalt-surfaced rail-trail conversion and extremely heavily used. For much of its length, it has a separate lane for walkers and one for cyclists and inline skaters. The cycling lane is marked with a centre line. You can spot signage fairly often for the Route verte, Quebec's provincial cycle path; you are unlikely to see any for The Great Trail.

At first, the broad pathway is lined by housing on both sides, sheltered somewhat by barriers of dense vegetation. At the first road crossing, about 485 m/yd from the start, there are side access trails and benches.

The St. Lawrence River and the first view of Québec City are reached at 700 m/yd. However, there are still some wooded areas between the trail and the river, so the views are fleeting. You cross the first small bridge at 1,000 m/yd, and about 850 m/yd beyond that reach the first park area, which contains benches, garbage cans, bike racks, and even a playground and basketball court.

At 2.2 km (1.4 mi), there is the first unobstructed view of the river when the trail reaches small Hadlow Cove. Several benches face the water – though the view is dominated by a shipping pier – and there are garbage cans, interpretive panels, and a bronze plaque in French only dedicated to "Les Huard," placed by the Association of Huard Families.

Just 300 m/yd further, the trail passes beneath two massive pipes. These are used to transport oil and gas between the nearby jetty and one of eastern Canada's largest oil refineries, located nearby. This pipe parallels the trail for another 450 m/yd, past two oil tanks, until you reach and cross the road entrance to the Quai Ultramar.

3 km (1.9 mi) The trail reaches the Parc de la Jetée d'Ultramar. This is another major trailhead with parking, signage, washrooms, and a large greenspace that extends to the river. There are benches, tables, interpretive panels, and plenty of shade.

Once beyond the Ultramar Jetty, you obtain the first unobstructed views towards Québec's Citadel. The trail runs close to the water's edge and benches are frequent. About 750 m/yd beyond the park, there is an interpretive panel next to the birth home of Louis Fréchette, a famous 19th-century Québec poet. At 4.3 km (2.7 mi), the trail passes the entrance to the Parc Nautique Lévy, the local marina.

Although the land where the trail has been built is virtually at water level, there is a cliff on the right, separating this lower area from most of the city. There are a few houses on the lower ground, including a number of new condominium projects, but there is little space.

5 km (3.1 mi) In an area where the cliff curves inland, a sizable greenspace, Parc de l'Anse-Tibbits, has been created. Along with the usual benches, playgrounds, garbage cans, and picnic tables, it has washrooms, drinking water, and a large shelter, providing cover both for cold rainy and hot sunny days. Next to the large parking area is a map of the trail system. Best of all, there is even a beach.

Here, as at several locations along the trail, the walking and cycling lanes are actually separated by a grass median, although usually only for short distances. Possibly because of the beach and the large, grassy playing areas – busy with ultimate frisbee teams when I passed – the trails here are extremely busy and particular care must be taken to avoid others.

Continuing past this park, the coastal shelf narrows. Road and trail, and occasionally houses, are squeezed together, and often fences line both sides of the trail. However, the views across the river as you approach Old Québec City and the iconic Chateau Frontenac are superb.

6.7 km (4.2 mi) You arrive at the junction for the ferry to Québec City. The trail splits here with the left branch conducting you to an adorable, amateurish-looking plywood ticket booth for cyclists wishing to cross on the ferry. That is the official Great Trail route.

The Parcours des Anses continues straight, passing beneath a long overhead platform, left over from railway days. The route passes in front of the ferry terminal and past a row of restaurants, pubs, B&Bs, and other businesses – a very busy place. When I cycled this, the next several hundred metres/yards were disrupted by construction, and the trail was routed through detours, but by 7.2 km (4.5 mi), I was back on the paved treadway.

7.2 km (4.5 mi) You reach the site of the original A.C. Davie shipyard, which is marked with a National Historic Sites bronze plaque. There is also a small museum on the inland side. This may also be the closest and best view available of Old Québec City and just past the remains of the shipyard are a number of deck chairs with people taking advantage of their prime placement.

Shortly afterwards, the trail heads into a lovely area where it is separated from the city by the cliff, which crowds immediately to the right of the pathway. In the small space remaining, an attractive, linear greenspace with benches, tables, garbage cans, and some shade trees has been developed. There is one elaborate steel staircase, permitting access from the streets above at 8.5 km (5.3 mi). Perhaps because of its relative isolation, this section even features nighttime lighting.

The trail, which has begun a long climbing curve to the right, begins to re-enter an area of houses at 9 km (5.6 mi). At first, these are on the left and are actually below the level of the trail. However, when the trail crosses Rue Jolliet 300 m/yd later, there are residences to the right as well, and the cliff has been left behind.

To the left is the current location of the Davie Shipyards, and this large facility is visible until the trail crosses the second of two steel bridges more than 700 m/yd later. The pathway continues to curve away from the river and climb as it passes through the working-class housing clustered near the shipyard.

10.4 km (6.5 mi) The trail reaches another significant rest area and trailhead. There is a public structure adjacent to the corridor with washrooms and water fountains as well as benches and garbage cans and a large parking area. And for those feeling peckish, visible across Rue du Moulin-Ruel is a Casse-Croute (snack bar), very busy on a warm summer day.

The corridor widens significantly beyond this point, bordered by a wide, mowed greensward. Houses line the passage as well, but are set well back from the trail, particularly once across busy Rue Carron 300 m/yd from the rest area. Benches are common alongside the pathway, and as the trail climbs, views of the St. Lawrence River become possible. At 11.6 km (7.2 mi), the Montmorency Falls are clearly visible, and at 12.2 km (7.6 mi), there is a wonderful rest area over-looking the Île d'Orléans.

This section of trail appears quite new and is very well constructed. At 12.4 km (7.7 mi), there is a roundabout where side trails connect, and 150 m/yd later is a playground on the right. More valuable to walkers and cyclists, at 12.7 km (7.9 mi), there is a water fountain.

13 km (8.1 mi) The trail reaches a junction with Parcours Harlaka, where it crosses Rue Saint-Joseph. Less than 100 m/yd further is a rest area/trailhead with a shel-ter, tables, a garbage can, an outhouse, and a water fountain. There is also a trail map and a bus stop is conveniently located next to it. Although the Parcours des Anses continues further, this is an excellent stopping point. Rest in the shade, refill your water bottle, and retrace the route to return to the start at the Parc du Domaine-Etchemin.

Further Information:
Tourism Chaudière-Appalaches: https://chaudiereappalaches.com
Tourism Lévis: https://levis.chaudiereappalaches.com
Ville de Lévis: https://www.ville.levis.qc.ca/accueil

Route verte

Quebec possesses the longest network of designated cycling routes in North America, the Route verte. Extending more than 5,000 km (3,107 mi), more than forty percent of the Route verte follows off-road shared-use pathways, and it connects all the regions of the province.

Originally conceived in the late 1980s, construction on the system began in 1995 through a unique partnership between the Ministère des Transports du Québec and the not-for-profit cycling organization Vélo Québec. La Route verte was officially opened in 2007, but more portions have been added every year since then. In Quebec, The Great Trail piggybacks on more than 1,000 km (621 mi) of Route verte trails.

16. Eastman — Mont Orford

Quebec's Eastern Townships (Cantons-de-l'Est) are known as a place of cottages and farms. The region is also home to some rugged terrain and mountainous park areas, and none of these is more popular than Parc national du Mont-Orford. Situated just north of Lac Memphrémagog, the park's mountains dominate the skyline.

Since it first opened in 1938, Parc national du Mont-Orford has been one of the most popular and well-visited sites in the Quebec park system. As was common in the earliest parks, recreation – not ecological protection – was the governing influence, so a golf course and ski hill were built, with the ski lodge opening in 1943. In 1951, the Orford Music Academy was established within the park, and each summer more than four hundred university students from around the world come to study with the internationally renowned faculty.

In 1975, the park was expanded to 58 km^2 (22.4 mi^2) to which an additional 1.5 km^2 (0.9 mi^2) has recently been added. Part of the Appalachian mountain chain, the park's highest peak, Mont Orford, rises to 853 m (2,798 ft). Pic de l'Ours climbs to 740 m (2,428 ft), and Mont Chauve to 600 m (1,969 ft). Mature maple forests cover almost seventy-five percent of the park. In addition to campsites, cabins and "huttopia" tents are available.

Passing through the park is La Montagnarde cycling path, part of Vélo Québec's Route verte provincial cycling network, and The Great Trail. Unlike most cycling pathways, which are often built on former railway right of ways, this route is quite hilly. It climbs steadily, though gradually, between Eastman and the park boundary; after that, it becomes hilly, rolling terrain that can be quite taxing, particularly on the return.

Dogs on leash are permitted on La Montagnarde; dogs are not permitted in Parc Mont-Orford at all, except for guide and service animals. Cell coverage is assured only near Eastman and close to Parc Mont-Orford's Le Cerisier Discovery and Visitor Centre.

16. Eastman – Mont Orford

TRUE
MAGNETIC

Contour Interval: 40M

3 KILOMETRES

Lac Parker

6,7

16

8,9

PARC NATIONAL DU MONT-ORFORD

Mont Lily-Butters

Pic de l'Ours

Étang aux Cerises

2.0 P

15.3
P S

Lac d'Argent

Railroad

P S
0.0

Orford Lake

Mont Orford

Eastman

Bolton Forest

Lac Orford

Mont Orford

141

10

400
Metres
200
Kilometres 2   4   6   8   10   12   14   15.3

16. Eastman – Mont Orford

Distance: 15.3 km (9.5 mi) – one way
Ascent: 244 m (801 ft)
Descent: 230 m (755 ft)

Trail conditions: asphalt, crushed stone
Cellphone coverage: partial
Hazards: poison ivy, road crossings, ticks, wildlife

Permitted Uses							
Walking	Biking	Horseback Riding	Inline Skating	ATV	Snowshoeing	Cross-country Skiing	Snowmobiling
✔	✔	—	—	—	✔	✔	—

Finding the trailhead: The trail begins at Highway 112 in Eastman. To the left is a restaurant and to the right, a Home Hardware. A variety of other businesses, including grocery stores, are nearby. A narrow wooden gateway frames the asphalt pathway, and a large map beside it includes everything on this section. Just beyond it are distance markers for Stukely-Sud, Canton Orford, and Magog.

Trailhead: 45°18'04.7" N, 72°18'53.8" W (Start — Eastman)
45°19'48.2" N, 72°11'53.5" W (Finish — Mont Orford Visitor Centre)

Observations: I had originally intended to extend this route as far as the community of Magog, but when I biked through the area, there was both considerable construction inside the park and very poor signage once outside of it. I also thought that too much of the route beyond Parc Mont-Orford was on the road. Perhaps because of the poor signage, I lost track of the route and abandoned the effort once I reached Chemin du Parc.

However, between Eastman and the park Visitor Centre, this was a lovely, startlingly hilly trip through attractive forests. The crushed-stone surface was in excellent condition, providing an easy and enjoyable cycle. The small rolling hills provided a rollercoaster-like ride at times – see my YouTube video – although some were so steep that I had to walk up them. I was not the only one who had to do so.

Route description: The path soon enters a wooded area, instantly insulated from the surrounding community. There are some well-constructed stone benches in this tiny sanctuary and two overhead signs: "Tu m'aimes mais encore" and "Tu

Black-capped Chickadee

If you see tiny energetic birds flitting among the trees, chances are you soon hear the easily identifiable call *chik-a-dee-dee*. Black-capped chickadees are found throughout Canada, and they are quite comfortable around people. Chickadees are curious as well, and a slow steady *pish-pish-pish*, repeated while standing motionless, often can soon result in several of the little birds landing in nearby trees to get a closer look. If you put seeds in your hand and sit very still, they may land momentarily on your fingertips. Chickadees are one of the few bird species that remain in the forest year round, and in winter are often the only birds you encounter.

m'aimais encore." After this enigmatic comment, made famous by chanteuse Celine Dion, the trail emerges from its vegetative shroud at 275 m/yd, passes through metal gates, and briefly follows the road to pass beneath a high steel railway bridge.

Less than 100 m/yd later, the pathway resumes. Gates again restrict vehicle access. It is quite attractive as it passes through Eastman. Houses are often adjacent, and sometimes residents mow their lawns on both sides of the trail right to the edge of the asphalt. At a little bridge at 975 m/yd, flowering bushes have been planted.

Rue Martin is crossed at 1.1 km (0.7 mi), and Lac d'Argent is visible to the left. Several gates must be navigated where driveways cross the trail and Camping du Lac d'Argent is on the left beside the trail at 1.8 km (1.1 mi). Near the campground office are benches, garbage cans, and washrooms. It also sells a few convenience items.

2 km (1.2 mi) After crossing busy Chemin des Diligences, the Eastman spur connects to the main route of La Montagnarde, part of Vélo Québec's Route verte #1 and The Great Trail. There is a parking area here with an outhouse, a picnic table, a map, distance markers, and garbage cans. Unusually, there is also a warning sign indicating no cell coverage for the next 6 km (3.7 mi).

La Montagnarde heads west and follows the roadway, but to the east is a first-rate off-road pathway, surfaced with crushed stone. Although wide and straight like a rail trail, the track undulates like a wavy lake surface and clearly was not built on the route of a former railway. Although a few houses are nearby to the right near the start, thick forest soon edges the trail for most of this route. It feels far away from habitation. At 2.9 km (1.8 mi), there is a road crossing and 800 m/yd beyond that a km 43 marker for La Montagnarde. The dense stands of maple and other hardwoods provide an impenetrable green shroud, concentrating your attention on the view ahead.

At 4.5 km (2.8 mi), the trail turns sharply right and the first modest hill presents itself; from its crest, the mass of Mont Orford can be seen in the distance. The uneven ground persists with the trail making another 90° turn to the left at 5.8 km (3.6 mi). After this, the ground levels out somewhat as the path takes another hard-right turn about 500 m/yd later and continues to the crossing of Chemin George-Bonnallie.

6.7 km (4.2 mi) This is the final place to exit the trail before Parc Mont-Orford. Only a few houses are nearby, and the road does not appear terribly busy, but there is a yellow crosswalk over the highway and cyclists are instructed to dismount. As usual with every road crossing, there are gates.

The trail makes two sharp turns, left and then right, then settles into a gently curving section with only slight elevation changes. Another sign states that there is no cell coverage for the next 4.5 km (2.8 mi) (although mine worked fine). At first there are a few houses to the left and the trail is lined with a cedar-rail fence, but the path is soon enveloped once again by a thick blanket of trees. Two unsigned crushed-stone side trails are encountered on the left at 7.5 km (4.7 mi) and 8.6 km (5.3 mi), but otherwise only the blue-and-white kilometre markers dispute the forest's hegemony.

8.9 km (5.5 mi) The trail reaches the Parc Mont-Orford boundary, gated and with a self-registration station—including a comprehensive list of the various fees—as well as a picnic table. Users of the trail are required to register and pay the daily park fee. Signs indicate that water and washrooms are 6.5 km (4 mi) ahead, and there are the first of the brown park signs with golden lettering.

Immediately, the trail becomes more "sporty," descending rapidly and twisting through a couple of tight turns. For 700 m/yd it drops before rising again almost as steeply. At 1 km (0.6 mi) from the park boundary, the side trail to the

Lac Stukely campground – and beach for those interested – branches left. Keep right; there is a second exit shortly, and it features a park map.

Several interpretive panels have been placed along the trail. At 10.8 km (6.7 mi), Le Ponceau picnic area sits among the trees next to a small creek to the right. This is also the trailhead for the Sentier des Crêtes, one of the park's finest hiking paths. If you have time, try to climb as far as the Pic de l'Ours lookout; the view is outstanding. Be warned: the 3.4 km (2.1 mi) climb is challenging.

Trail junctions occur frequently now as the trail moves deeper into the park. Some are hiking footpaths while others are for mountain biking. All have informational and directional signage; there are infrequent interpretive panels and a few maps posted as well. Remain on the wide crushed-stone pathway of La Montagnarde and watch for its kilometre posts, the Route verte signs, and even an occasional TCT marker.

The path continues over rolling hills, trending generally downward. Often there are tight turns at the bottom of slopes, so keep your speed under control. Applying bike brakes at high velocity suddenly on crushed stone does not always end well! Enjoy several kilometres of such amusement.

At 14 km (8.7 mi), there is a large boulder to the left – almost the first rock seen on this route but only the first of several. There is an interpretive panel at a trail junction 600 m/yd later. Shortly afterwards, the trail emerges from its forest cover to cross the paved Chemin du Camping. There is a gate, crosswalk, and a plethora of cautionary signage, both on the trail and on the road. The vividly blue and enticing Étang aux Cerises lies directly ahead, so the trail curves right and parallels the road, its guardrail a right-side barrier.

15.3 km (9.5 mi) The path turns left away from the road and arrives at the Centre de services Le Cerisier, the principal information centre for Parc Mont-Orford. When open, this building contains park staff, maps and brochures, washrooms, water, a small canteen and equipment store, and first aid. Outside, next to a small beach at the tip of Étang des Cerises, there is a wonderful picnic area where canoe rental is available. This is a lovely location to rest and relax before beginning the hilly return trip to Eastman.

Further Information:
Parc Mont-Orford: http://www.sepaq.com/pq/mor
Tourism Eastern Townships: http://www.easterntownships.org
Vélo Québec: http://www.velo.qc.ca

Great Lakes–St. Lawrence Forest

Canada's second largest forest region, the Great Lakes–St. Lawrence Forest stretches from southeast Manitoba to the Gaspé Peninsula and is a transitional forest between the southern broad-leafed species and the northern conifers. As a result, many boreal species may be found here, especially at higher elevations; the distinguishing conifers are white pine, red pine, and eastern hemlock. Deciduous species such as sugar maple, red maple, red oak, and white elm are common, but the most characteristic hardwood is yellow birch (Quebec's provincial tree).

The yellow birch has been among the most productive and versatile commercial species in the province, valued as much for its splendid yellow-red leaves in the fall as for the furniture made from it. Native to eastern North America, this deciduous tree grows as high as 20 m (66 ft) and is covered in the fine yellow bark that gives it its name. Yellow birches often pass unnoticed in contrast to their conspicuously white-barked cousin.

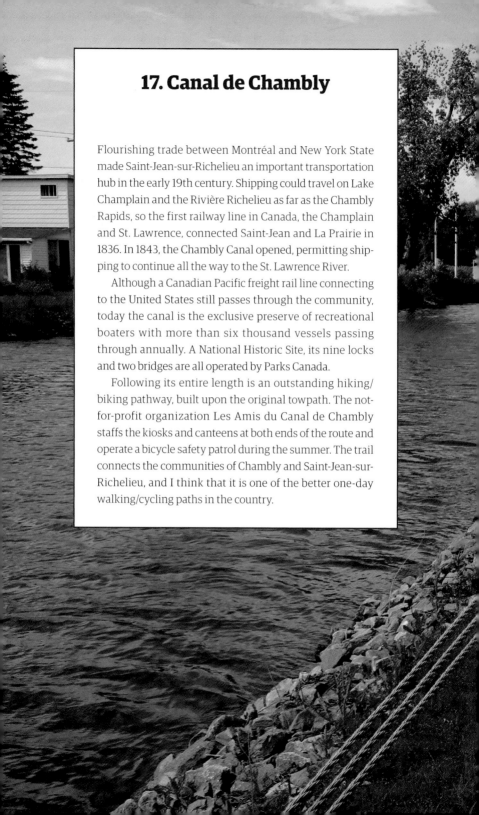

17. Canal de Chambly

Flourishing trade between Montréal and New York State made Saint-Jean-sur-Richelieu an important transportation hub in the early 19th century. Shipping could travel on Lake Champlain and the Rivière Richelieu as far as the Chambly Rapids, so the first railway line in Canada, the Champlain and St. Lawrence, connected Saint-Jean and La Prairie in 1836. In 1843, the Chambly Canal opened, permitting shipping to continue all the way to the St. Lawrence River.

Although a Canadian Pacific freight rail line connecting to the United States still passes through the community, today the canal is the exclusive preserve of recreational boaters with more than six thousand vessels passing through annually. A National Historic Site, its nine locks and two bridges are all operated by Parks Canada.

Following its entire length is an outstanding hiking/biking pathway, built upon the original towpath. The not-for-profit organization Les Amis du Canal de Chambly staffs the kiosks and canteens at both ends of the route and operate a bicycle safety patrol during the summer. The trail connects the communities of Chambly and Saint-Jean-sur-Richelieu, and I think that it is one of the better one-day walking/cycling paths in the country.

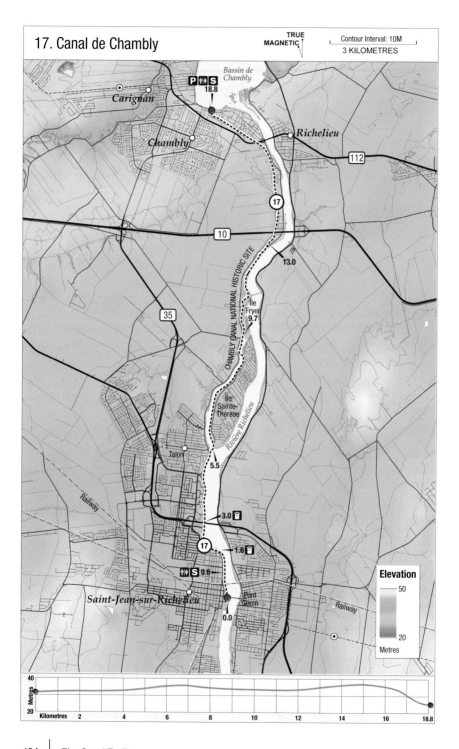

17. Canal de Chambly

TRUE
MAGNETIC

Contour Interval: 10M
3 KILOMETRES

Carignan

Bassin de
Chambly

Chambly

Richelieu

112

10

35

CHAMBLY CANAL NATIONAL HISTORIC SITE

13.0

Île
Fryer
9.7

Île
Sainte-
Thérèse

Rivière Richelieu

Talon

5.5

Railway

3.0

17

1.6

S 0.6

Saint-Jean-sur-Richelieu

Pont
Gouin

0.0

Railway

Elevation
50

20
Metres

40
Metres
20

Kilometres 2 4 6 8 10 12 14 16 18.8

17. Canal de Chambly

Distance: 18.8 km (11.7 mi) – one way
Ascent: 74 m (243 ft)
Descent: 81 m (266 ft)

Trail conditions: asphalt, crushed stone
Cellphone coverage: yes
Hazards: poison ivy, road crossings

Permitted Uses							
Walking	Biking	Horseback Riding	Inline Skating	ATV	Snowshoeing	Cross-country Skiing	Snowmobiling
✔	✔	—	—	—	✔	✔	—

Finding the trailhead: Start your trek on the Pont Gouin, where the Route verte #1 directional sign points down a ramp. This leads to the narrow spit of land separating the canal from the river, a parkland of well-kept lawn, shrubs, and trees. There are numerous benches, tables, and garbage cans for the use of both walkers/bikers and the boaters who moor alongside. On the concrete canal side, there is a sturdy metal railing. On the opposite bank is old Saint-Jean-sur-Richelieu, including some attractive, well-maintained buildings.

Trailhead: 45°18'21.7" N, 73°14'56.2" W (Start — Saint-Jean-sur-Richelieu)
45°26'50.3" N, 73°16'58" W (Finish — Chambly)

Observations: I was not familiar with this area at all, so was very pleasantly surprised with how enjoyable this relatively short pathway was. The trail is in excellent condition, and there are good facilities throughout the route. When it shares the road on Île Sainte-Thérèse, it is on a separate track, and I found this section quite enjoyable. It was helpful to have so many canteens and restaurants at either end, and I particularly enjoyed both the public art and the abundant bird life along the trail.

Route description: About 225 m/yd from the bridge is a Route verte distance marker with Chambly listed as 18 km (11.2 mi) away – although another nearby sign adds another half kilometre. At 490 m/yd, the trail is jammed into a low narrow passageway beneath a railway bridge. A sign instructs cyclists to dismount; you should definitely do so.

The trail reaches Lock #9 after 650 m/yd. This is a very attractive area with flower beds, numerous picnic tables, a water fountain, benches, interpretive panels, garbage cans, and a canteen run by Les Amis du Canal de Chambly. This

group also offers both bicycle and kayak rentals. Free Wi-Fi is even available in the immediate area of the lock building. The canal can be crossed on the lock doors, permitting access to the downtown businesses. In sight of Lock #9 are bars, restaurants, and pizzerias. This area appeared very popular with walkers and families, so cyclists need to be especially cautious here.

Within 100 m/yd, the trail has passed the lock's picnic area and moved onto a charming straight section, flanked on the river side by a stately line of tall hardwoods. The canal is only perhaps 25 m/yd wide, and the narrow strip of land separating river and canal is almost filled by the wide crushed-stone passageway. On the city side, busy Rue Champlain runs parallel.

At 1.6 km (1 mi), there is a wider area, much of it is lawn with large photographic displays of sporting events. There are quite a few panels and a lookout beside the river with side trails connecting them all. Benches and picnic tables are placed among the displays, and there is an outhouse to the side. A solitary TCT interpretive panel is situated on the main trail.

After this sporting display, the trail continues along a slender canal bank all the way to Île-Sainte-Thérèse. About every kilometre, there is a bench or picnic table and a garbage can. And underneath the Highway 35 bridge at 3 km (1.9 mi), there is an outhouse. Otherwise, the wide turbulent river is on the right, the calm narrow canal on the left.

5.5 km (3.4 mi) The trail crosses Rue Sainte-Thérèse on a crosswalk at the end of the bridge connecting the island to the mainland. The route turns right, the crushed-stone path replaced by an asphalt, bi-directional bike lane beside the road.

For all of Île-Sainte-Thérèse, the trail remains alongside the one-lane road. Houses line the entire length of the now much wider canal channel, many having small docks for canoes and swimming. There are a few rest areas on the island, each having benches, garbage cans, and sometimes parking. Street lights are overhead. At Rue Waegener, where there is a rest area, the road becomes two lanes. After a pleasant 3.5 km (2.2 mi) ride on an excellent treadway, the canal narrows again with road and trail curving left towards the opposite shore.

9.7 km (6 mi) The trail reaches a small but impressively sturdy-looking lift bridge where the road must be crossed again. The paved pathway continues another 200 m/yd, to the site of a swing bridge – kept open all the time, apparently – and Rue de L'Île-Sainte-Marie turns right. There is also a trail map here and several informational signs.

Once again, the trail is on crushed stone with no road or houses nearby. The river is not visible to the right, only an area of thick forest. After a few hundred metres/yards, a number of footpaths branch off to the right, and at 10.5 km (6.5 mi), there are interpretive panels about Fort Sainte-Thérèse. This is a very peaceful area; the urban noise has been left behind, and only a few houses dot the opposite bank of the canal. There are many tall trees, mostly hardwoods.

At 11 km (6.8 mi), the trail turns sharply right and for the first time is not alongside water. About 250 m/yd later, there is a junction; straight ahead is the Fryer Dam, a massive structure spanning the river, but the main trail turns left. This part of the trail is known as Île Fryer, and there are several interpretive panels and benches on the small landmass.

The trail returns to the canal at 11.6 km (7.2 mi) and resumes its route alongside. On the right, a large shallow pool is squeezed onto the small island. Watch closely for herons and bitterns – I saw a green heron here, my first ever. At 12.4 km (7.7 mi), there is a small bridge with a picnic table on the far side. About 350 m/yd later, there are houses and a fence to the right.

13 km (8.1 mi) The trail crosses busy Highway 223 at the end of another larger swing bridge. The crossing here is a little tricky, so be very careful. However, road and trail soon separate, and an area of attractive farmland comes into view on the opposite bank. For the first time, the canal is higher than the river, so the land to the right is lower.

Noisy Autoroute 10 passes overhead 700 m/yd later, after which it is a clear ride to the next open bridge at 14.6 km (9.1 mi). It is a very easy and open ride with farmland on the far bank and few trees providing shade or concealment. Houses begin to appear on the right, lower than the canal, until the Rue de Pont 4 bridge and road crossing at 15.6 km (9.7 mi).

More and more houses are on the right though the opposite bank remains farmland. At 16.3 km (10.1 mi), a spillway exits to the right. A helpful interpretive panel explains what a spillway is and why it is important. Just 200 m/yd later is Lock #8, where there is a tempting picnic area on the far side of the canal with benches, picnic tables, washrooms, garbage cans, and interpretive panels.

Barely 100 m/yd beyond the lock, the canal curves quite markedly, and a large factory complex crowds to the edge of the pathway on the right. Another massive bridge, this time carrying Highway 112, crosses overhead at 17 km (10.6 mi).

Once past Highway 112, it is clear that the trail has reached the urban area of Chambly. Lock #7 is 100 m/yd further, almost in the shadow of the bridge. Houses and factories are close on both sides, although a pleasant barrier of trees buffers the trail.

The trail continues for another 550 m/yd before reaching a fascinating spot where three locks – #6, #5, and #4 – are located within 300 m/yd. The loss of elevation is quite apparent, and you can see down a long, straight stretch almost to the canal's end.

The pathway also becomes asphalt and remains so for the remainder of the route. At 18.6 km (11.6 mi), the path reaches the Parc des Ateliers, where the pathway splits. To the right is a Parks Canada parking area, and picnic tables are scattered throughout a large grassy field that is lower than the canal-level pathway.

Continue straight until the path reaches Avenue Bourgogne, 200 m/yd later. Route verte #1 heads left into the town centre where there are restaurants and other businesses. At Avenue Bourgogne, there is a crosswalk.

18.8 km (11.7 mi) Arrive at the Amis du Canal de Chambly kiosk and the end of the canal. The Bassin de Chambly, a small lake, is 50 m/yd further. This is another rest area with washrooms and water, as well as tables, benches, interpretive panels, and other facilities. Refresh yourself before retracing your route back to Saint-Jean-sur-Richelieu.

Further Information:

Chambly Canal National Historic Site: http://www.pc.gc.ca/lhn-nhs/qc/chambly
Fort Saint-Jean National Historic Site of Canada: http://www.historicplaces.ca/
    en/rep-reg/place-lieu.aspx?id=13294
Les Amis du Canal de Chambly: http://lesamisducanalchambly.org
Tourism Montérégie: http://www.tourisme-monteregie.qc.ca

18. Lachine Canal

One of the unusual features of The Great Trail is that it passes through or near almost every major metropolitan area in Canada. When most people contemplate the TCT, they visualize a remote footpath traversing one of the remote corners of the country. In fact, I consider some of its urban elements to be among the most interesting. Of these, none is more remarkable than the section crossing the St. Lawrence River and following the Lachine Canal. From the scenic modern-day skyline of Montréal, to the history found at every step in Old Montréal, to the dynamic urban energy of Atwater Market, this is one trail that everyone should experience.

One warning! Whenever a ship is passing through the Saint-Lambert Locks, the cycling route is inaccessible because it crosses on a lift bridge that opens to allow boats to pass through. There can be a long wait when ships are in transit, sometimes more than one hour, so be prepared. Closure times can be checked on the St. Lawrence Seaway website.

18. Lachine Canal

TRUE
MAGNETIC

Contour Interval: 10M
5 KILOMETRES

Elevation
220
0
Metres

Mont Royal

Petite-Bourgogne

Westmount

Saint-Henri

Montréal-Ouest

Railway

Lachine

Parc René-Lévesque

21.8

18 6.6
Railway

Pont Victoria

0.0 P

10.9

13.3

Côte-Saint-Paul

Verdun

Pont Champlain

Île-des-Soeurs

Saint-Lambert

Bassin de la Prairie

18.2

20.2 P

18. Lachine Canal

Distance: 21.8 km (13.6 mi) – one way
Ascent: 141 m (463 ft)
Descent: 134 m (440 ft)

Trail conditions: asphalt
Cellphone coverage: yes
Hazards: road crossings, heavy use

Permitted Uses							
Walking	Biking	Horseback Riding	Inline Skating	ATV	Snowshoeing	Cross-country Skiing	Snowmobiling
✔	✔	—	—	—	✔	✔	—

Finding the trailhead: This route begins in Saint-Lambert at a parking area on Rue de l'Écluse near the Pont Victoria.

Trailhead: 45°29'33.2"N, 73°30'53.7"W (Start – Saint-Lambert)
45°25'44.4"N, 73°41'17.2"W (Finish – Parc René-Lévesque)

Observations: I rode along this urban Montréal trail with thousands of others, enjoying a brilliant summer day. I stopped for ice cream, had a meal at one of the many vendors, and tarried to admire the public art. It was easy riding, but the sheer number of people on the trails meant that I always needed to be observant and careful. This is a trail to relax on and enjoy, not to rush through. I spent quite a bit of time just watching the Lachine Rapids at Parc René-Lévesque.

Route description: A bike path, signed with both Route verte #1 and TCT or Great Trail markers, climbs onto a steel lift bridge – which fits alongside the road and almost underneath the railway bridge – to cross the canal above the Saint-Lambert locks. On the opposite side, where there are some outhouses, the trail turns left and returns to water level and a well-signed junction. Turn right and immediately there is a sizable rest area with tables, benches, maps of The Great Trail in the Montréal and Montérégie regions, interpretive panels, and a bronze plaque commemorating the "Victoria Tubular Bridge."

The path squeezes through a tunnel underneath the rail bridge then another tunnel beneath the Pont Victoria, about 700 m/yd from your start. Beyond this there is an unobstructed view of the Montréal skyline to the left. About 150 m/yd later, you reach Île Notre-Dame, passing beneath a Parc Jean-Drapeau gateway. This section is known as the South Shore Bike Link and can sometimes be closed because of special events. (Check the Parc Jean-Drapeau website.)

Keep left; there are many directional signs, as there are on the Lachine Canal and in Parc René-Lévesque. In addition, there are more benches and picnic tables; again, these are found everywhere along this busy urban pathway, so this is their final mention.

At 1.2 km (0.7 mi), the path merges with the wide Circuit Gilles Villeneuve, where the recreational walker/cyclist needs to be wary of being run over by more serious, competitive riders that use the circuit for training. Temporary lane markers usually separate the two groups. After 250 m/yd, the trail continues alongside the water while the circuit curves away to the right.

Our path turns right at 2 km (1.2 mi) – watch for the signs – and crosses the Circuit Gilles Villeneuve about 100 m/yd later – watch for the speeding cyclists! The route heads into a busy and complicated system of pathways, the site of Expo 67 and still home to a number of exhibitions. The new and stylish Casino Montréal is conspicuous on your right, but you pass closer to the much more modest Jamaican and Tunisian Pavilions. Watch for the Route verte #1 and TCT markers and follow directional signs to the Pont de la Concorde.

This is an attractive area with numerous shaded groves, flower beds, art displays, and other facilities. At 2.8 km (1.7 mi), you reach a curving ramp that climbs up to the road level of the bridge, which has a bi-directional bicycle lane separated from the roadway by massive concrete blocks.

The view from the bridge, high over the river, is splendid. To the right is the large geodesic dome that was the American Pavilion in Expo 67 and is now home to the Biosphère de Montréal. About 250 m/yd later, there is an exit onto Île Sainte-Hélène, should you wish to explore more of the park.

Once past the exit, the buildings of downtown Montréal fill the skyline, with Mont Royal looming behind them. By 4.2 km (2.6 mi), the bridge curves left and the trail descends to road level. On the left are the architecturally unique apartments of Habitat 67. To the right, you should be able to see Old Montréal, and there might be some ships docked in the piers beside the path.

This delightful pathway, lined with trees and flowers and paralleling Avenue Pierre-Dupuy, reaches parking area #12 at 5.8 km (3.6 mi). From here, it curves right and runs underneath the massive overpass supporting Autoroute 10. Immediately after, it crosses a railway track, then a minor but busy street that features a special traffic signal for cyclists at 6.5 km (4 mi).

6.6 km (4.1 mi) The trail arrives at Peel Basin station and connects with the Lachine Pathway. Turn right and head towards the Old Port of Montréal. There is a park on the left and grain elevators on the right. After 600 m/yd, the pathway passes underneath the Mill Street bridge then curves right to climb and cross it. Once over the bridge, you curve right and pass beneath it again.

As soon as you emerge, you can see a Trail Pavilion. Stop for a moment and view the list of donors, then continue along the canal for another 500 m/yd to

Lachine Canal

Montréal became Canada's most important commercial centre because it was the furthest that ocean-going vessels could sail up the St. Lawrence River. The dangerous Lachine Rapids blocked access to the Great Lakes and the Ottawa River and their extensive watersheds. Primarily for military reasons, the British began construction of the Lachine Canal in 1821, opening it in 1825. However, the new waterway also sparked an industrial boom as companies took advantage of its location near trade and the hydroelectric power it generated. The canal remained an important industrial gateway until the opening of the St. Lawrence Seaway in 1959, gradually decreasing in importance until it closed in 1970.

In 1997, work began to revitalize the canal as a recreational boatway, a massive project of urban renewal that opened in 2002. Instead of the site of factories, its banks became parkland, and just as the original canal transformed Montréal, so has the newly renovated canal encouraged the massive new adjacent housing development. The Lachine Canal is now a 14.5 km (9 mi) long urban park, and its trails are visited by millions of users each year. In 2009, *Time* magazine ranked the canal pathway as the third most beautiful urban circuit in the world.

Blue Flag Iris

Quebec's current provincial flower was adopted only in 1999, when the original choice (the Madonna Lily) was abandoned because it did not actually grow naturally in the province. The blue flag iris, however, blossoms in profusion each spring in wetlands in every region of Quebec — and most of eastern Canada.

Rising nearly 1 m (3.3 ft) above the ground, this colourful flower ranges from light blue to deep violet and frequently grows in clusters of vivid blossoms. It can be found in almost any wet area, including ditches, swamps, sodden meadows, marshes, stream edges, and lakeshores.

return to Peel Basin. Turn right; Autoroute 10 crosses overhead, then in 200 m/ yd, the trail reaches a rail embankment where it turns left. (There is a map and directional signage there.) The path parallels both the embankment and Peel Basin for another 150 m/yd until reaching the canal, where the trail curves right and passes underneath the railway.

This part of Montréal is currently undergoing a massive growth in condominium construction. Normally, it is possible to walk or bike along both sides of the canal in this area, but when I biked it in 2015, the north shore path was closed beyond Rue Wellington. However, the canal can be crossed there to the south bank. Once connected back to the main trail, about 8.6 km (5.3 mi) from the start, a sign indicates that it is 11.5 km (7.1 mi) to the Lachine Lock on the left.

The next part of the trail is one of the busiest — packed with cyclists, walkers, and families with young children— and there is much to see. Former factories have been repurposed as apartments, and there are numerous benches and interpretive panels on the parkland bordering the canal.

About 900 m/yd from Rue Wellington, you reach the Saint-Gabriel Lock, where you may or may not need to cross again to the north (city side) bank because of construction. I did, but only for a few hundred metres/yards before recrossing the canal on the Rue des Seigneurs Bridge. If there is no detour, the path continues on the south bank. The lock grounds are worth a visit, and there are washrooms and drinking water available, as well as a café.

Your easy ride continues along the south bank pathway. About 700 m/yd from the Saint-Gabriel Lock, the trail passes beneath the Rue Charlevoix Bridge and heads into possibly the busiest area you encounter.

10.9 km (6.8 mi) The trail reaches the pedestrian bridge that connects to the Atwater Market. The benches nearby are always full of people and many pedestrians crossing from Rue Saint-Patrick to reach the market. In addition, there are both bicycle and kayak rental services adjacent to the trail and some food wagons. All these make this an area to exercise extreme caution and reduce your speed.

Once safely past Atwater Market, it should be easy riding. The crowds thin somewhat, though the pathway is rarely empty of either walkers or cyclists. The trail passes beneath a railway bridge 350 m/yd later and a pedestrian bridge 500 m/yd after that. From here, there is path on both sides of the canal. For most of its route, the trail has been quite close to the water's edge, but about 100 m/yd from the pedestrian bridge, it shifts to run beside Rue Saint-Patrick; there is a small park area beside the canal.

At 12.8 km (8 mi), you reach the Côte-Saint-Paul Lock. Its rest area is less elaborate; there are picnic tables and washrooms, but no drinking water. The trail continues on the south side of the canal another 350 m/yd before passing beneath another massive bridge, Autoroute 15. Almost immediately after is an old steel bridge where the trail crosses to the north (city side) bank of the canal.

13.3 km (8.3 mi) From the end of the bridge at Avenue de l'Église, the pathway is only on the north bank for the next several kilometres. Once it passes underneath another steel truss bridge – Boulevard Monk – 250 m/yd later, it is a quiet and lovely ride. Walkers have their own crushed-stone path that winds alongside the asphalt cycle track. Yet, there are probably fewer people on the trail here than along any other section of the route. That is because there is almost no housing nearby, only industrial buildings.

Beautiful hardwoods line the path, and there is plenty of grass on which to spread a blanket and picnic. At 15.2 km (9.4 mi), there is a pedestrian bridge crossing the canal and a washroom is situated nearby. If traffic noises seem especially loud around here, it's because Autoroute 20, Rue Notre-Dame Ouest, and several railway tracks now parallel your route and are quite close. Head to the right-hand perimeter of the park.

But the Lachine Canal's slender green corridor through this industrial zone is very pleasant, regardless. Several pieces of public art and a few interpretive panels help. A second pedestrian bridge, very similar to the first, is reached at 16.3 km (10.1 mi). In addition to the tables and benches, there are some barbeque stands.

The pathway continues to the Saint-Pierre parking area at 18 km (11.2 mi), where there are a couple of old railway cars next to the picnic area. Here the trail on the city side of the canal ends, and it crosses the canal on an old lift bridge.

18.2 km (11.3 mi) The path passes underneath the two bridges for Avenue Dollard and begins to follow the southern (St. Lawrence River) side of the canal. It is once again a narrow corridor, with a railway track immediately to the left. Fortunately, the bank is a little higher than the trail, and there is a fairly thick buffer of vegetation.

Another high, massive road bridge – Highway 138 – passes overhead about 500 m/yd later, followed by a railway bridge crossing the canal 500 m/yd after that. Once beyond these bridges, the ground to the left flattens, and Parc Dollier-de-Casson takes the place of the industrial buildings that have dominated the last several kilometres. Single-family homes are visible on the opposite side of the parallel road, Rue Saint-Patrick.

At 19.6 km (12.2 mi), the trail reaches the LaSalle parking area, where there is a water fountain along with picnic tables. After this, the trail runs quite close to the road, reaching Chemin du Musée about 450 m/yd later. The trail navigates this busy street on a crosswalk with a stop sign facing the path. Once across the street, there is a large parking are on the left and the Lachine Canal Visitor Services Centre is visible to the right. Route verte #5 follows Chemin du Musée.

20.2 km (12.6 mi) The trail reaches the Lachine Lock where the Visitor Services Centre is located. To reach it, turn right where the trail crosses Chemin des Iroquois. This is an impressive new building, filled with interpretive and other facilities; it is well worth a visit.

However, before returning to Saint-Lambert, I recommend continuing straight ahead in Parc René-Lévesque. The trail continues another 1.6 km (1 mi) before ending at a lookout where the land ends at 21.8 km (13.6 mi). Along the way, there are benches, tables, and places to swim. There is also a considerable display of public art, definitely a worthwhile addition to the trip.

Further Information:
Biosphère de Montréal: www.ec.gc.ca/biosphere
Lachine Canal National Historic Site: http://www.pc.gc.ca/lhn-nhs/qc/
    canallachine
Parc Jean-Drapeau: http://www.parcjeandrapeau.com
Parc René-Lévesque: http://ville.montreal.qc.ca/portal/page?_
    pageid=7377,94551572&_dad=portal&_schema=PORTAL&id=84&sc=5
Tourism Montréal: https://www.mtl.org

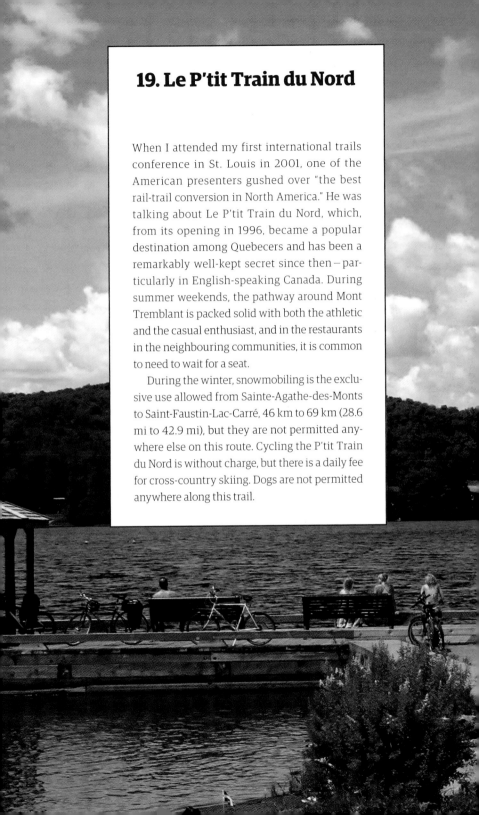

19. Le P'tit Train du Nord

When I attended my first international trails conference in St. Louis in 2001, one of the American presenters gushed over "the best rail-trail conversion in North America." He was talking about Le P'tit Train du Nord, which, from its opening in 1996, became a popular destination among Quebecers and has been a remarkably well-kept secret since then – particularly in English-speaking Canada. During summer weekends, the pathway around Mont Tremblant is packed solid with both the athletic and the casual enthusiast, and in the restaurants in the neighbouring communities, it is common to need to wait for a seat.

During the winter, snowmobiling is the exclusive use allowed from Sainte-Agathe-des-Monts to Saint-Faustin-Lac-Carré, 46 km to 69 km (28.6 mi to 42.9 mi), but they are not permitted anywhere else on this route. Cycling the P'tit Train du Nord is without charge, but there is a daily fee for cross-country skiing. Dogs are not permitted anywhere along this trail.

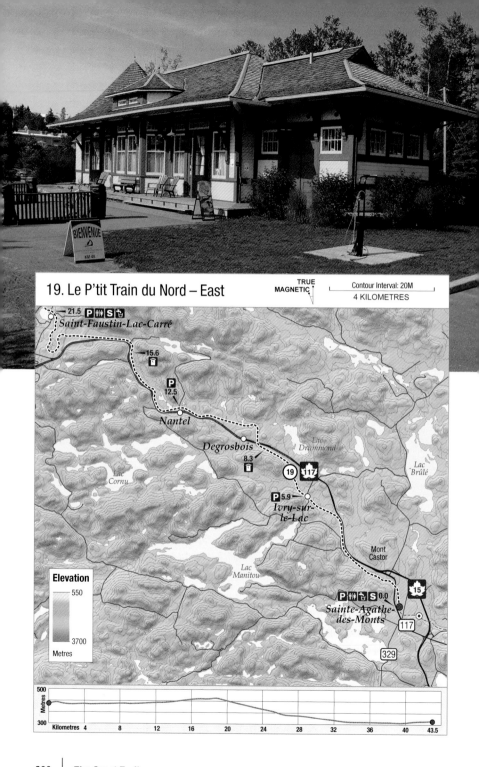

19. Le P'tit Train du Nord – East

TRUE
MAGNETIC

Contour Interval: 20M
4 KILOMETRES

21.5 **P** ⚏ **S** ⚐
Saint-Faustin-Lac-Carré

15.6 🛈

P 12.5

Nantel

Degrosbois
8.3 🛈

Lac Drummond

Lac Brûlé

19 **117**

P 5.9
Ivry-sur-le-Lac

Lac Cornu

Lac Manitou

Mont Castor

Elevation

550

3700

Metres

P ⚏ 🚻 **S** 0.0
Sainte-Agathe-des-Monts

15

117

329

19. Le P'tit Train du Nord

Distance: 43.5 km (27 mi) – one way
Ascent: 231 m (758 ft)
Descent: 351 m (1,152 ft)

Trail conditions: asphalt, crushed stone
Cellphone coverage: yes
Hazards: road crossings, wildlife

Permitted Uses							
Walking	Biking	Horseback Riding	Inline Skating	ATV	Snowshoeing	Cross-country Skiing	Snowmobiling
✔	✔	—	✔*	—	✔*	✔*	✔*

Finding the trailhead: Your route begins at the former train station, which is now the town's tourist bureau. There are a wide range of services available here: parking, tables, water, and washrooms. In addition, there is an air pump for cyclists and a small café. This is also a shuttle bus stop that runs up and down the P'tit Train du Nord for both bikes and their riders. Numerous signs direct you to various services in the community.

Trailhead: 46°03'07.3" N, 74°16'56.4" W (Start — Sainte-Agathe-des-Monts)
46°11'39.5" N, 74°37'52.5" W (Finish — La Villageoise-de-Mont-Tremblant)

Observations: This route was two distinctly different experiences: the crushed-stone surfaced and relatively remote portion beginning at Sainte-Agathe-des-Monts and the busy paved trail within the Mont-Tremblant municipality. Both were enjoyable, but the latter was far busier. So busy, in fact, that I skipped lunch in the various villages because every restaurant and café seemed packed with hungry cyclists and walkers. I really enjoyed riding the several-kilometre-long downhill section near Saint-Faustin as I approached Mont-Tremblant; I did not like it nearly so much on the return when I had to climb back up. For a rail trail, this is startlingly hilly.

Route description: The trail has a Route verte #2 marker and a sign stating that Mont-Tremblant is 42 km (26.1 mi) distant. About 400 m/yd from the start is the km 49 marker. At first, the trail passes through the community, though there is a fairly thick buffer of vegetation. About 800 m/yd from the start, Highway 117 passes overhead, and once on the other side, thick forest crowds in on both sides.

The first of many small brooks and wetlands is crossed at 2.2 km (1.4 mi), and 500 m/yd after that is the first road crossing at Chemin Renaud. Gates have been installed to prevent vehicle access on the wide, crushed-stone pathway. Once across Chemin Renaud, the trail and Highway 117– a very busy multi-lane road – run quite closely side by side and until 4.5 km (2.8 mi), where the path curves away and back into thick forest.

Almost immediately, the houses disappear and the traffic noises fade. The low, rounded, tree-covered hills of the Laurentians quickly shelter the trail and provide an attractive backdrop for your ride. About 250 m/yd later, there is a large wetland cut through by a brook that must be crossed. Although it soon disappears among the trees, it and the pathway keep reconnecting as you continue.

5.9 km (3.7 mi) The trail crosses Chemin de la Gare, where there is a small parking area with no facilities except a garbage can and a map. This is the town of Ivry-sur-le-Lac, the first opportunity to gauge your progress and at approximately 6 km (3.7 mi) a convenient spot to turn around if hiking.

After the road crossing, wetlands are frequent, and the brook makes an occasional appearance. At 6.8 km (4.2 mi), there is an attractive, open area where the trail crosses beneath a powerline and bridges the stream. Most of the trees are softwoods, so there is little overhead shade. However, many are tall enough to provide some cover, except when the sun is directly overhead.

This relatively secluded section continues with traffic noises intruding intermittently, especially by the time you reach the first rest area at 8.3 km (5.2 mi). Almost hidden among the trees on the right, this small refuge has a table, outhouse, and bike rack. Just 500 m/yd beyond that, Highway 117 passes above the pathway again on a large concrete bridge.

The busy road and its noises are quickly left behind as the trail heads directly away from it for 500 m/yd before curving left again. This area is so thickly forested that the km 58 Route verte marker stands out at about 9.6 km (6 mi). But shortly afterwards, the first of several private roads crosses the trail. The most significant of these is the paved road for the Camping du Domaine Lausanne at 10.8 km (6.7 mi). In sight on the right is the campground's casse-croûte (snack shack), in case you want some poutine.

Beyond the campground, houses with driveway crossings become much more common, and the sound of Highway 117 notifies you that it and the trail are converging. One highlight comes at 12.3 km (7.6 mi), where there is a side trail to the Fromagerie Mont-Tremblant. Their sign, facing the trail, advertises fresh ice cream, and I can say from personal experience that it is worth a stop.

12.5 km (7.8 mi) The trail emerges into an open area and crosses paved Chemin du Lac-Nantel S where there is a rest area with a parking lot and shelter. To the right for the next several hundred metres/yards are the very attractive grounds of the Royal Laurentien resort with golf course and chalets. On the left, Highway 117 is quite close again, and except for a short area where it is hidden by a rock face, remains so for several kilometres.

The pathway curves around the lake and golf course, with excellent views. At 14 km (8.7 mi), a side trail leads to the chalet area. The trail finally moves away from the resort, passing a "gîte" (guesthouse/B&B) at 15.1 km (9.4 mi). About 500 m/yd later, there is another rest stop in a wooded area with tables, an out-house, and a garbage can.

At 16.3 km (10.1 mi), the trail crosses Chemin du Lac-Nantel N, turns left, and snuggles up close beside the highway again. There is no buffer of vegetation, and it is quite loud – but you are able to read the road signs. There is a long, straight stretch with the trail climbing noticeably.

A very large, wood-products plant, Groupe Crête, comes into view to the right, and the trail crosses the busy plant entrance at 17.8 km (11.1 mi). There are no gates on the trail here, so exercise extreme caution since large trucks cross. Much less hectic Rue du Sommet is crossed about 500 m/yd later, but this is followed by a quite large gravel pit on both sides of the trail. Cross its very busy entrance road at 18.8 km (11.7 mi) cautiously. The excavated pit continues alongside the trail for another 400 m/yd.

Then very suddenly, the trail is transformed. Barely 200 m/yd from the gravel pit, the trail begins a long, curving descent to the left. The houses and industry alongside a busy highway change to mature hardwoods, including many maples. What follows is my favourite section of this route; you barely need to peddle for the next 2.5 km (1.6 mi). This steep serpentine drop – by rail trail standards – to the community of Saint-Faustin-Lac-Carré is a lot of fun, at least in this direction. The woods are lush, and there are several good views as you descend.

21.5 km (13.4 mi) You arrive at the former train station and the parc de la gare in Saint-Faustin-Lac-Carré. There is a large parking area, and the station has water, washrooms, and other services. On the wide, trimmed lawns of the park sit several tables and benches, as well as a considerable collection of public art. There is a large playground on the right. Blue signs direct you to nearby restaurants and cafés.

The park continues until the trail crosses Rue Principale 200 m/yd later. Restaurants, coffee shops, a grocery store, and an SAQ (government liquor outlet) are all in sight from here. There is a side trail 100 m/yd past the road (complete with stairs and crosswalk) to a very pleasant viewing platform overlooking Lac-Carré.

This is a small community, however, and once you cross Chemin du Moulin David at 22.3 km (13.9 mi), the trail is back into forest. The rapid descent continues with the trail curving and passing through a deep rock cut. The ground to the right is much lower, and the hillside is quite steep. At the km 72 marker, about

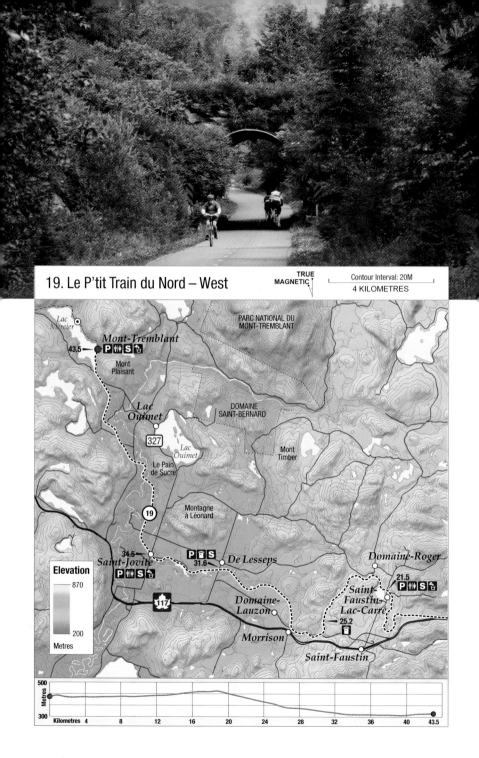

19. Le P'tit Train du Nord – West

TRUE
MAGNETIC

Contour Interval: 20M

4 KILOMETRES

PARC NATIONAL DU
MONT-TREMBLANT

Lac
Mercier

Mont-Tremblant

43.5

Mont
Plaisant

DOMAINE
SAINT-BERNARD

Lac
Ouimet

327

Lac
Ouimet

Mont
Timber

Le Pain
de Sucre

19

Montagne
à Léonard

34.5

Saint-Jovite

31.6

De Lesseps

Domaine-Roger

21.5

Elevation

870

Saint-
Faustin-
Lac-Carré

117

200

Metres

Domaine-
Lauzon

25.2

Morrison

Saint-Faustin

500

Metres

300

Kilometres 4   8   12   16   20   24   28   32   36   40   43.5

24 km (15 mi), there are some picnic tables. There is another rest area at 25.2 km (15.7 mi), where a narrow footpath leads down to an old dam.

The winding path descends through thick forest, including many tall pines, until it reaches Rue de la Pisciculture at 26.1 km (16.2 mi). The trail becomes deep sand – that can bring a speeding bike to a stop very quickly – just before the road crossing. There were quite a few "Danger" signs and a warning barrier when I was there.

A sign at the road indicates that there is a gîte to the right, which has an entrance on the trail 200 m/yd later. The trail crosses the road again at 26.7 km (16.6 mi), but this time on an overpass. There are a few houses nearby, but after a gated private driveway 700 m/yd further, it is back into a thickly forested area for another 1.2 km (0.7 mi), until the trail crosses Rue Raymond.

Very soon, there is a large, sandy area to the right almost devoid of vegetation, which is deeply rutted and carved with ATV tracks. At 29.1 km (18.1 mi), the km 77 marker welcomes you to Mont-Tremblant – but you are still a long way from the village. There is another large, sandy field to the left, just beyond this sign.

As you continue, you can probably glimpse some houses to the left, depending upon the thickness of the leaf cover. On the right, the trail appears as if it was previously quarried but is growing in. At 30.4 km (19 mi), two large powerlines intersect, and the trail passes through the large clearing this has created. One of the powerlines parallels the trail on the right, then crosses overhead about 800 m/yd later, just before the bridge crossing the Ruisseau Noir. From there, another 400 m/yd of crushed-stone pathway remains.

⚐31.6 km (19.6 mi) The trail crosses Montée Kavanagh, which is a major access point with a rest area, maps, and a store beside the parking lot. From here to Mont-Tremblant, the trail is paved and in excellent condition.

The trail continues to descend, but so gradually that only your legs detect it. Rue de Ruisseau is crossed about 700 m/yd later; on the left are several pieces of old mill machinery on display. A paved side trail to the arena and stadium branches left at 34 km (21.1 mi). The brook is on the left and is quite lively as it funnels into a narrow ravine. It has been dammed in several places, creating small lakes alongside the trail.

⚐34.5 km (21.4 mi) The trail arrives in Saint-Jovite, where there is an elaborate rest area. There are sheltered tables, benches, outhouses, interpretive panels, maps – everything a hiker or biker might require. If you did not bring your lunch, there are numerous restaurants within sight. (When I passed through, there were so many cyclists stopping for lunch that there was a 20-minute wait for a table!)

From here to La Villageoise-de-Mont-Tremblant is the busiest section of the trail. This is the heart of the resort area that has built up around the ski hill. In

summer, users of the golf courses and many small lakes fill the cottages, and the trail is packed with walkers, cyclists, and inline skaters.

The 2.1 km (1.3 mi) from Saint-Jovite to the Pont du P'tit-Train-du-Nord, the large bridge crossing the Rivière du Diable, pass mostly next to a golf course. At the river is a small rest area with a side trail down to the water, the lowest elevation on this route and more than 200 m (656 ft) lower than it was at 19 km (11.9 mi).

From here, it is a relatively uneventful ride to the village of Mont-Tremblant. One exception is a dangerous crossing at Montée Ryan at 38.6 km (24 mi). This is a 90 kph (55 mph) highway, so stopping before crossing is essential.

After that, the pathway remains mostly in forested areas, although it crosses a few small streets where there is usually a parking area before reaching Lac Mercier at 42.6 km (26.5 mi). The small lake, enfolded on all sides by low wooded hills, looks especially inviting after a long ride. To your right are cottages, and their canoe docks are on the left. After following the lakeshore for about 700 m/ yd, the Plage municipale du Lac Mercier on the left provides an opportunity for a swim and just beyond that is the community.

43.5 km (27 mi) The trail arrives at the former train station in Mont-Tremblant. Once again, this is a well-serviced rest area with umbrellas shading many of the benches. In addition to the services at the station, there are cafés and restaurants within sight and numerous bike racks.

The P'tit Train du Nord continues another 109 km (67.7 mi) to Mont-Laurier, but I suggest that you stop here. Enjoy the community and the beach, then retrace your route – or take the shuttle bus – back to Sainte-Agathe-des-Monts.

Further Information:
P'tit Train du Nord: http://www.laurentides.com/en/linearpark
Tourism Laurentides: http://www.laurentides.com

Laurentian Highlands

The rugged hills north of Montréal look like a different world from the flatlands near the St. Lawrence River. They are, in fact, part of the Canadian Shield, a portion of that landmass called the Laurentian Highlands that extends from the Gatineau and Ottawa Rivers in the west to beyond the Saguenay River in the east.

Unlike the lowlands around Montréal that are made up of sedimentary rock, the Laurentian Highlands are composed of frequent intrusions of tough igneous and metamorphic rocks. The many south-facing escarpments give the area a mountainous appearance, and its rolling terrain is full of lakes, surrounded by hills ranging in elevation from 400 to 800 m (1,312 ft to 2,625 ft).

20. Wakefield – Gatineau Park

Although home to only a few more than a thousand people, Wakefield is a fascinating and diverse community. Close to Ottawa-Gatineau and nestled on the shores of the Rivière Gatineau, Wakefield boasts nearby ski hills, golf courses, and even bungee jumping. Its restaurants include traditional French and Québécois cuisine (poutine!), and German and Asian fusion, as well as artisan bakeries, cafés, pubs, and markets. But Wakefield is perhaps best known for its dynamic arts scene, particularly the famous Black Sheep Inn, known for constantly discovering new musical acts and introducing them to the Canadian public.

Gatineau Park, which borders Wakefield and extends into urban Gatineau, is a 36 km^2 (13.9 mi^2) triangle of protected forest and lakes administered by the National Capital Commission of Canada. Created in 1938, it is the only federal park that is not controlled by Parks Canada. Within its boundaries are more than 165 km (102.5 mi) of hiking paths and many more for mountain biking. In winter almost 200 km (124.3 mi) of trails are available for cross-country skiing and snowshoeing. Because of its proximity to a major urban centre, the striking scenery, and its excellent facilities, Gatineau Park receives nearly three million visitors every year.

From its start to the boundary of Gatineau Park, this route is walking only, although cyclists can ride alongside on the road for all but a small section. Inside the park, only Trail 53 and Trail 51 are open to cyclists. In the winter, the park trails are reserved for cross-country skiers.

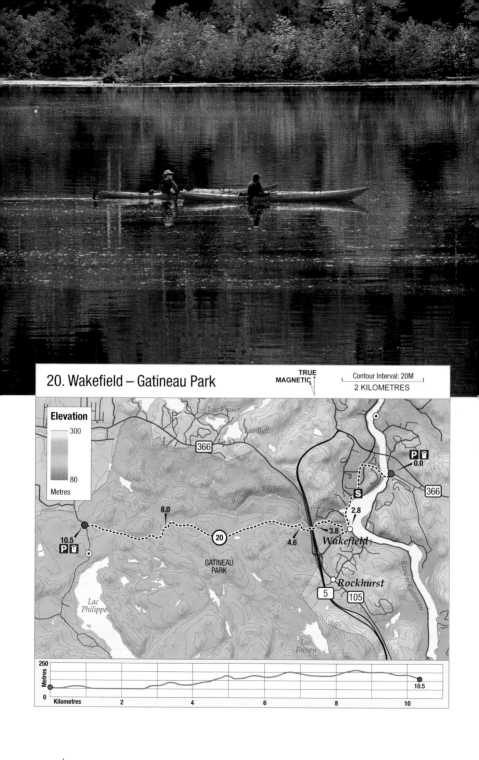

20. Wakefield – Gatineau Park

TRUE
MAGNETIC

Contour Interval: 20M

2 KILOMETRES

Elevation

300

80

Metres

20. Wakefield-Gatineau Park

Distance: 10.5 km (6.5 mi) – one way
Ascent: 214 m (702 ft)
Descent: 132 m (433 ft)

Trail conditions: crushed stone, asphalt, natural surface
Cellphone coverage: yes
Hazards: poison ivy, road crossings, ticks, wildlife

Permitted Uses							
Walking	Biking	Horseback Riding	Inline Skating	ATV	Snowshoeing	Cross-country Skiing	Snowmobiling
✔	✔*	—	—	—	✔*	✔*	—

Finding the trailhead: This hike begins on the delightful grounds of the Fairburn House Heritage Centre, a local museum located in one of Wakefield's oldest houses, carefully restored. There is a considerable picnic area on the Centre grounds with outhouses, and they even boast their own small trail system. There also is drinking water when the Centre is open.

Trailhead: 45°38'47" N, 75°55'04.9" W (Start — Wakefield)
45°37'28.1" N, 76°00'36.4" W (Finish — Gatineau Park P19)

Observations: This was a pleasant woodland stroll, prefaced by an interesting walk through a scenic village. It was lovely to stroll through Wakefield along the Rivière Gatineau, especially on the return when the opportunity to purchase a cold drink and an ice cream cone on a stifling July afternoon was quite welcome. The short, steep, wooded interlude between the community and Gatineau Park surprised me, but it might have been my favourite of the entire route.

Once inside the park, there are no dramatic views, but I enjoyed the wildly flowering meadows in the former fields of abandoned farms. I also appreciated how few people I met along the way, even though Gatineau Park is so close to Ottawa-Gatineau. Because Trail 51 ends at a roadside, not near anything of particular interest, it is not very busy in summer. I treasured those tranquil moments alone on the trail.

Route description: From the parking area, follow a short path back to the road, where a crosswalk delivers you to the entrance of a covered bridge after about 75 m/yd. This bridge is the pride of Wakefield, and its grounds are lavishly

Wakefield Covered Bridge

The Gendron Covered Bridge was constructed over the Gatineau River in 1914 and remained there until destroyed in a bizarre act of arson — involving a car with all its serial numbers removed being set ablaze in the middle of the span — on July 11, 1984. It was a popular tourist attraction, and for photographers such as Malak Karsh, it had been a favourite subject. The community quickly recognized how central this modest structure had become to Wakefield's identity and undertook a challenging thirteen-year long effort to raise the funds for its reconstruction.

Despite limited support from the provincial and federal governments, the local community ultimately succeeded, and the Wakefield Covered Bridge was finished, except for siding and painting, in November 1996. An exact replica of the 1914 Gendron Bridge, it officially opened for walking and cycling in 1997, with a party that boasted the largest dance ever held on a covered bridge. This covered bridge is the pride of Wakefield, and they maintain it in excellent condition.

adorned with flowering plants, benches, and interpretive panels. There is even a TCT marker affixed to the bright-red covered structure. Sadly, it is only 125 m/yd across the Gatineau River on this beautiful replica.

Gates prevent vehicle access to the trail, which is restricted to pedestrian and cycling use. On the opposite bank, you must walk for nearly 700 m/yd along quiet Chemin du Pont Gendron to rejoin the trail, which parallels Chemin Riverside.

Turn left and follow the asphalt pathway. It continues for 700 m/yd, passing a new school and running alongside some old railway tracks until it crosses Chemin Manse (dirt). Keep left on a gravel path, which skirts the edge of a parking area. Restaurants, cafés, and markets are visible to the right. At the end of the parking lot sits a gigantic turntable, on which the engine of the former Wakefield Steam Train was manually turned around at the end of its run to head back to the city of Gatineau.

The crushed-stone path lasts for another 100 to 150 m/yd until it reaches the parking lot of the Wakefield General Store, where the trail rejoins the Rivière Gatineau. From here, cross Chemin Riverside and continue on the sidewalk. You should notice TCT signs on some of the power poles.

Not long after crossing Chemin Burnside, there is a small riverside park in the narrow strip of land between road and river. There are viewing platforms, interpretive panels, benches, and an outhouse. If you wish, cross Chemin Riverside and walk on this little path until you reach the bridge across Mill Pond at 2.3 km (1.4 mi). The views of the river, which is as wide as a small lake here, are gorgeous.

To cross the Mill Pond bridge, you must return to the sidewalk and proceed past a number of houses and small businesses – including the famous Auberge Le Mouton Noir (Black Sheep Inn) – until you reach Valley Road.

2.8 km (1.7 mi) At the intersection of Chemin Riverside and Valley Road – officially Chemin de la Vallée-de-Wakefield – a TCT marker and directional arrow are conveniently positioned on the Arrêt (Stop) sign. Turn right and follow the sidewalk on Valley Road past more shops and cafés for 250 m/yd to the entrance to the Wakefield Community Centre.

Another TCT arrow directs you right, where you proceed through the parking area to the forest edge, keeping to the right of the skateboard park and outdoor rink. There, if you are in the correct spot, are oodles of trail signs and a little bridge.

Once in the forest, this becomes a quite different experience. The narrow, crushed-stone footpath quickly heads uphill, climbing 50 m (164 ft) in the next 400 m/yd. The area is thickly forested with a mix of mostly hardwoods, and the trees deaden any community noises. Near the top of the hill, the trail passes some quite large rock outcroppings. However, the footing is never difficult; although the climb may be slightly challenging, it is still fairly easy.

After this short – and probably unexpected – climb, the path curves left and drops down the hillside. Along the way, a small sign announces that you are entering Gatineau Park. The footpath emerges from the trees and onto Mill Road within sight of the Mill Inn and Spa, where another small bridge spans the final few steps.

3.8 km (2.3 mi) At this junction, there are numerous regulatory and directional signs and a map. Turn left and follow the wide dirt road. Although still open for vehicle use, and with at least one house on the riverbank, this portion of Mill Road is also Gatineau Park Trail 52. From this point, the trail is open to cyclists.

A small stream, which is considered part of the Rivière Gatineau, is on the right and a wooded hill to the left. About 300 m/yd from the junction, the road is gated, barring vehicles. Once beyond this, the trail continues to be wide, but there is a high wooden fence on the water side. As you continue, you can see that a retaining wall has also been added to stabilize the trail. This was done when the Autoroute 105 was twinned in the area in 2013.

The work done to preserve the trail was quite elaborate; the fence runs for several hundred metres/yards, as does the retaining wall; the treadway is wide and covered in an excellent layer of crushed stone; and the path passes beneath three road bridges within about 200 m/yd: both lanes of Autoroute 105 and Highway 366.

After passing beneath the final road bridge, the trail swings left then right in a climbing switchback before re-entering the trees. Once it does, the new stone surface ends, and the path gradually narrows, though it still retains the look of a one-lane forestry road.

4.6 km (2.9 mi) You reach a well-signed four-way junction. Trail 52 continues straight, and for those wishing to camp, the Lac Brown area is only 2.5 km (1.6 mi) further along that route. Parking area P17, a very large and popular trailhead in Gatineau Park, is 500 m/yd to the left. To the right is Trail 53, your route, marked with one sign for The Great Trail and another for the National Hiking Trail.

Trail 53 still resembles the settlement road that it originally was, wide enough for side-by-side walking (watch for cyclists) and naturally surfaced. Over the years, the bordering trees have grown quite tall, so there is shade along much of this route, which is very welcome on hot, humid, summer days. A considerable proportion of the trees are deciduous beech, birch, maple, and even oak, so fall hikes here are colourful.

For most of its remaining length, your route is a forested meander with few views. The terrain is rolling, though it climbs steadily until near the end. With the exception of a few former fields and some wetlands adjacent to the path, there are few breaks in the tree cover and little to observe.

At 5.8 km (3.6 mi), you might notice the remains of an old stone wall on the right. About 800 m/yd later, the only bench along this trail overlooks one of the larger clearings and wetlands. Otherwise, let the sounds of the forest relax you as you amble towards the next, and final, junction.

8 km (5 mi) Another well-labelled signpost indicates that P19 is 1.5 km (0.9 mi) away to the left on Trail 51. (As you undoubtedly discover, this is short by about 1 km (0.6 mi).) TCT markers also show the turn left, while Trail 53 (Chemin Kennedy) continues straight.

Though not really steep, a noticeable climb follows for the next 800 m/yd, after which there is an even sharper descent for about 300 m/yd. Where the grade nearly levels, there is a wet area and hidden in the thick vegetation a small creek that parallels the route for the remaining distance.

The path gently descends the rest of the way to P19, often emerging from the trees onto a grass-covered track with wetland to the left and forested higher ground on the right. Only occasionally is the brush low enough to see the brook that floods this pathway every spring.

10.5 km (6.5 mi) About 100 m/yd further, before the parking lot, a wooden gate that blocks vehicle access onto Trail 51 is visible from the trail. Once you reach it, you can see P19 just to the right, where there are a map, the usual regulatory signage, an outhouse, and garbage cans.

I ended this route at P19, where the off-road path ends. However, Lac Philippe is only 800 m/yd to the left, with its very large picnic area, and a beach (Plage Breton) is another 700 m/yd further. This is a beautiful location to rest and eat lunch, although extremely busy in the summer. Follow the road — which is also the marked TCT route — to reach it. Otherwise, retrace your route back to Wakefield.

Further Information:

Fairburn House Heritage Centre: www.fairbairn.ca
Gatineau Park: http://ncc-ccn.gc.ca/places-to-visit/gatineau-park
Tourism Outaouais: www.tourismeoutaouais.com

25. Toronto Waterfront

SOUTHERN ONTARIO

21. Ottawa River Pathway - West

One of the most interesting features of The Great Trail is that it attempts to pass through every major metropolitan area in the country. It truly is intended to be a voyage of discovery of the entire nation, from its peripheries through its heartlands, its wilderness to its urban centres. Perhaps nowhere did I appreciate that design concept more than when I followed its route through the City of Ottawa.

Fortunately, the National Capital Region possesses what is arguably the best urban trail network in North America. Thanks to the policies of the National Capital Commission, nearly the entire shoreline of the Ottawa River is protected parkland, and an exceptional path system has been developed through it. The Great Trail follows the western section of the Ottawa River Pathway, which passes close to some of the most important civic structures and museums in the country. Leaving the river, it follows other pathways through the Greenbelt to connect to the route continuing deeper into Ontario.

This is one section that every Canadian should hike or bike and experience, taking time to stop and visit the many fascinating sights along the way. This is one trail that you should not be in a hurry to complete.

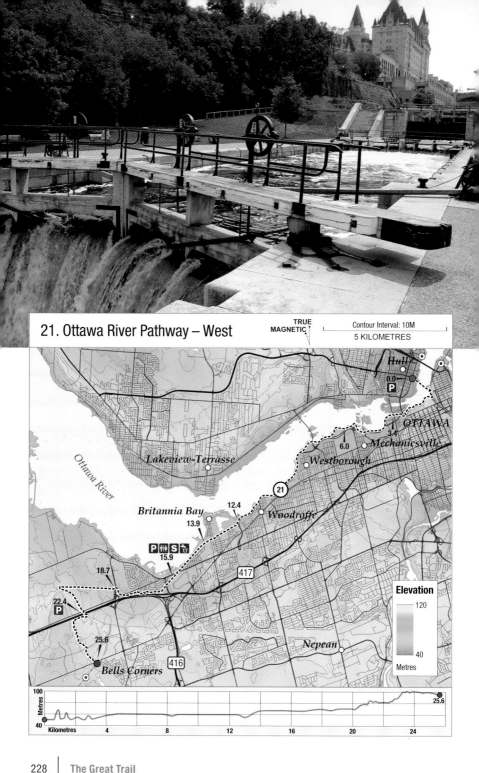

21. Ottawa River Pathway – West

TRUE
MAGNETIC

Contour Interval: 10M

5 KILOMETRES

Hull

0.0
P

OTTAWA

3.4
Mechanicsville

6.0

Westborough

Lakeview-Terrasse

Ottawa River

21

Britannia Bay

12.4

13.9

Woodroffe

P S
15.9

18.7

417

22.4
P

Elevation

120

25.6

Nepean

40

Metres

Bells Corners

416

100
Metres
40
Kilometres   4   8   12   16   20   24

25.6

21. Ottawa River Pathway – West

Distance: 25.6 km (16 mi) – one way
Ascent: 129 m (423 ft)
Descent: 83 m (272 ft)

Trail conditions: asphalt, crushed stone, natural surface
Cellphone coverage: yes
Hazards: high usage, poison ivy, road crossings

Permitted Uses								
Walking	Biking	Horseback Riding	Inline Skating	ATV	Snowshoeing	Cross-country Skiing	Snowmobiling
✔	✔	—	✔*	—	✔	✔	—

Finding the trailhead: Begin at the Quebec side of the Alexandria Bridge, next to the Canadian Museum of History. Parallel cycling and walking tracks cross the bridge.

Trailhead: 45°25'54.4" N, 75°42'34" W (Start — Canadian Museum of History)
45°19'00.7" N, 75°50'44.3" W (Finish — Bells Corners)

Observations: I had intended to end this section at Britannia Beach, only about 14 km (8.7 mi) in total length, but the riding was so enjoyable that I kept going until I reached the western end of the Greenbelt. I did stop at Britannia Beach to eat my lunch and dip my toes in the river, but the excellent paved pathway made cycling so effortless that I continued onto the Greenbelt and its slightly rougher tracks. There, the wooded areas within the protected ring around the urban core were so appealing and so varied from the earlier portion of the ride, that I continued until I reached the end of this section of The Great Trail. Ottawa contains so many landmarks, particularly near the Parliament Buildings, that walking my bike was the most comfortable option. You need to slow down and enjoy the scenery. I loved this ride!

Route description: Enjoy the exceptional views of the Parliament Buildings and many other iconic national landmarks from the Alexandria Bridge. Do not hurry this first part of the route; the vista is superb, the best of the day. After 650 m/yd you have reached the Ontario shore. Your route continues alongside the road for another 300 m/yd with the imposing glass towers of the National Art Gallery on the left before turning sharply right and heading steeply downhill to the mouth of the Rideau Canal at 1.3 km (0.8 mi). To the left, the turreted castle-like Chateau

Laurier looms. On the right, the East Block of Parliament Hill sits atop one of the wooded cliffs that ring the cleared space around the locks. Interpretive panels and monuments of various description are scattered everywhere, so take time to explore this historic area.

Expect hundreds of others to be in the area as well. Patience is required to navigate safely through the groups of gawking and excited tourists and family groups, especially if you are cycling this route. To cross the canal, cyclists must dismount and make their way across the narrow plank walkways built over top of the canal lock doors; consider staying dismounted until well past this busy area.

For hikers, one of interpretive panels is of particular interest. The mouth of the canal is kilometre zero of the 387 km (240 mi) Rideau Trail that, like the canal, eventually makes its way to Kingston at the eastern end of Lake Ontario. The eight locks also enable recreational boaters to proceed uphill 24 m (79 ft) on the Rideau Canal and go all the way to Kingston.

Attempting to describe every landmark visible in the next several kilometres is difficult; this area is rich in museums, monuments, and nationally significant buildings. From the canal, the paved pathway traces the riverbank, working its way around Parliament Hill. Should you wish to visit, long staircases disappear in that direction up the wooded hillside – excellent exercise. And there are innumerable benches lining the path, should you want to rest afterwards.

The path continues past and below the Supreme Court and Library and Archives Canada. As it comes level with the tip of Victoria Island, about 2.5 km (1.6 mi), the trail begins to climb. There are many side paths in this busy area, so follow the gold centreline.

At 2.8 km (1.7 mi), there is a junction where a map is posted; keep left, going under a tunnel beneath the road a few metres/yards later. This is Bronson Park, where a Trail Pavilion sits nestled among the shrubbery. The path curves right and passes through a second short tunnel. After skirting a parking area – with a pub, should you wish a break – there follows a lovely stretch alongside an overflow spillway for the Chaudière Falls dam, its sides bordered by wild roses.

3.4 km (2.1 mi) You arrive at the first road crossing at Booth Street, opposite the Canadian War Museum. Street lights regulate this busy crossing; be attentive. The trail curves to the right, around the massive museum structure, past the dam, and over a bridge at 4.1 km (2.5 mi). Just before the bridge, there is a side trail connecting to Wellington Street.

The downtown core with its many tourist attractions is finally behind you. From this point, it is more like riding through parkland, with the Ottawa River to the right much wider now above the Chaudière Falls. On the left the busy Ottawa River Parkway is a constant companion.

Benches, picnic tables, and interpretive panels are too common to mention. At 4.6 km (2.9 mi), the trail passes beneath the Prince of Wales railway bridge and

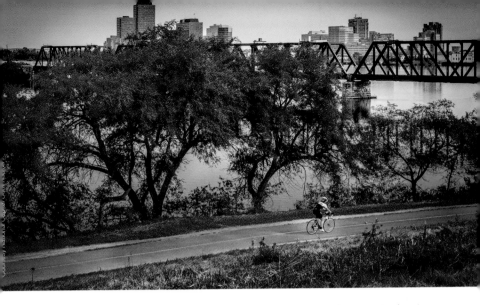

crosses River Street, passing the exit to the Lemieux Island Water Purification Plant 300 m/yd later. Exits to the city are frequent.

6 km (3.7 mi) Just past one of these junctions, there is a sheltered rocky area of the river where people build inukshuks, and there are hundreds of inukshuks and similar rock constructions. Originally an artist named John Ceprano created free-standing, balanced, natural-rock sculptures at Remic Rapids Park. Since then, members of the public have added their own contributions beside his.

Although I am not in favour of building inukshuks on most trails, something which has become quite popular in recent years, it works here. If the flocks of grazing geese permit it – they can be quite aggressive, especially when they have young – find a grass-covered seat and enjoy the view.

The trail continues its sinuous path beside the river. There are always benches and picnic tables, and interpretive panels are frequent. So too are maps. Washrooms are often available at parking areas and picnic grounds, and sometimes water fountains are nearby. That is true at the large parking area just before the trail crosses beneath Island Park Drive, at 7.6 km (4.7 mi).

The path continues alongside the Ottawa River, which slowly widens. Curving left, the trail crosses the entrance to the Kitchissippi Lookout at 8.7 km (5.4 mi) and cozy Westboro Beach, where there is a café open much of the year. On a summer day, this is a very busy spot.

After the beach, road and trail run side by side with very little space between them and the river, although occasionally side paths branch off towards the water's edge where there is more room. There are occasional benches, but no more picnic areas until the Deschênes Rapids parking area, at 11.4 km (7.1 mi). At 12.1 km (7.5 mi), both road and trail curve left, away from the river.

12.4 km (7.7 mi) Arrive at a major junction, the turnoff to the Central Experimental Farm. Keep right, heading towards the Greenbelt, also keeping right at the next junction just 100 m/yd later. The trail settles into an arrow-straight section. Additional side trails, such as the one for Lincoln Heights, connect to the adjacent neighbourhoods, which are now much closer to the edge of the pathway.

To the right is the thickly wooded Britannia, or Mud Lake, Conservation Area. Several footpaths branch off into the low swampy ground. If you have good footwear on, or are a big fan of amphibians, this is worth a visit. Have on good mosquito protection, however!

At 13.5 km (8.4 mi), the trail crosses Britannia Road at the crosswalk at a road intersection. Houses are all around, and there is a bus stop here. Once across the street, you are again in parkland with large lawn areas to the right. Benches, picnic tables, and people are everywhere, and this might be the busiest section of pathway since the Rideau Canal

13.9 km (8.6 mi) You arrive at the Ron Kolbus Lakeside Centre at Britannia Park and Beach. There are several large parking areas on both sides of the trail, so be watchful for people and vehicles. Again, Britannia Beach can be extremely busy, so be prepared to slow to a walk. To the left is an interesting, protected picnic area that uses the former long, slender railway shelter as its roof. Several buses stop on Greenview Avenue, which the trail crosses.

From Britannia Beach, the trail soon narrows to a narrow pathway with houses quite close on the left, while the Ottawa River almost laps against the treadway in an area known as Britannia Bay in Lac Deschênes. I found this one of my favourite sections of this trail, a tranquil path in the middle of the city.

15.9 km (9.9 mi) The Ottawa River Pathway ends at the extremely busy Carling Avenue, where the trees of Andrew Haydon Park hide all sight of the water. The pathway continues on the other side of the road after an extremely elaborate signalized crosswalk. Wait to cross when advised to do so, as this four-lane road is a main thoroughfare.

Once across, the straight track of a former rail line continues as the Watts Creek Pathway. Housing lines both sides of the path but is often hidden by the lush vegetation. The trail turns away from the river, moving inland. At 16 km (10 mi), there is a bridge crossing the small Graham Brook, and 200 m/yd later, you reach another busy wide street.

This is Holly Acres Road, where there is a slightly unusual road crossing because, once across the crosswalk, walkers and cyclists must briefly use Aero Drive to continue on the off-road pathway. It is to the left on the other side of Aero Drive but less than 100 m/yd from the crosswalk.

Once back on the path, the trail meanders into an area of thick forest. Though houses are actually quite close on the right, they cannot be seen. To the left, noisy

Highway 417 disrupts the tranquil mood. Twisting and turning, the trail crosses Stillwater Creek at 17.5 km (10.9 mi) and again 450 m/yd later.

Emerging from the forest, the trail crosses Corkstown Road at 18.2 km (11.3 mi) and changes to a crushed-stone surface. It works around the edge of several soccer fields, arriving at Moodie Drive 500 m/yd later. This is another extremely dangerous road crossing; use the crosswalk and traffic signals.

18.7 km (11.6 mi) The trail enters the Ottawa Greenbelt, a verdant oasis amid the urban sprawl of one of Canada's largest cities. Once past a gate, the trail is a straight ride along a wide paved track. To the right, through the trees, is a modern-looking glass-turreted structure that was once the home to one of Ottawa's high-tech giants. On the left is the sprawling Wesley Clover Parks Equestrian Centre and outdoor learning hub.

We are far now from either housing or highway, so this area feels remarkably separate from the city. The easy ride continues until 20.9 km (13 mi), where it intersects with the Greenbelt pathway. This is not particularly well signed, although there was a TCT marker mounted on a fence beside the National Capital Commission (NCC) sign.

Turn left; the trail surface is now crushed stone, and the pathway enters an area of hardwoods with a high overhead canopy. Within a short time, railway tracks can be seen to the right, and once the path emerges from the forest, the equestrian centre stretches out in fields to the left slightly below.

22.4 km (13.9 mi) The trail crosses Corkstown Road, where parking area P3 is in sight to the right. Almost immediately, it passes beneath the twin overpasses of Highway 417 and in 250 m/yd turns right and crosses the railway tracks. This is lovely area, complete with farm fields. Both Great Trail and NCC interpretive panels provide information.

Your route makes another 90° turn to the left when it intersects Trail #20 at 23.2 km (14.4 mi). Now back in forest, the wide pathway undulates over small hills and meanders among the trees, emerging to pass beneath some powerlines 500 m/yd from Trail #20. This is lovely forest, including dense stands of cedar.

There is another intersection with Trail #20 shortly before reaching Timm Drive at 24.6 km (15.3 mi). On the far side, Trail #21 branches right then connects to the main path again less than 300 m/yd later. Coming out of the woods for a final time, the trail continues alongside cropland for 200 m/yd to reach Robertson Road. Although there is an exit here, the pathway turns left and continues parallel to the highway for an additional 250 m/yd, where it connects to a former railway line. Turn right, and cross above Robertson Road on the old railway bridge.

25.6 km (15.9 mi) Arrive at the end of the Greenbelt western pathway at Bells Corners. The Rideau Trail, marked by a large wooden sign, heads left back into the

Canada Goose

Canada geese are easy to identify; they are large, plump birds with black heads and necks and contrasting white throats. They are noisy, constantly making low honking sounds that rise in volume considerably when they become airborne. Their long V-formations, often heard before seen, forever evoke in me a sense of awe.

Eastern Ontario and western Quebec lie in some of North America's main migratory flyways, and every spring and fall, watercourses and farmers' fields are dimpled with tens of thousands of these raucous, and often unwelcome, visitors. In many cities, Canada geese have become comfortable with humans, and some even remain year round. They are sometimes a hazard, either because of their violent territorial defensiveness when approached, especially when there are young birds, or their extravagant and large droppings — cyclists beware!

forest. The Great Trail continues along the former rail line, heading to Stittsville and Carleton Place.

There is a map here and some benches but no parking area nearby. Retrace this route to return to the start at the Canadian Museum of History.

Further Information:
National Capital Commission (Pathways): http://ncc-ccn.gc.ca/places-to-visit/
    parks-paths-and-parkways
Ottawa Tourism: www.ottawatourism.ca
Rideau Trail Association: www.rideautrail.org

The Ottawa Greenbelt

Surrounding the urban core of Ottawa, the 20,600 ha (50,904 ac) Greenbelt is as large as the city it envelops. Originally proposed by Parisian architect-planner Jacques Gréber in 1950, acquisition of land did not begin until 1958, and the majority of property was not purchased until 1966. Gréber's proposal to the National Capital Commission envisioned this protected space as the key component of "an organic system of parks and uninterrupted network of verdure within the entire region."

Though unsuccessful in limiting the urban growth of the Capital — as many people now live in surrounding suburbs such as Kanata and Orleans as do in the metropolitan core — and constantly having bits nibbled away for "essential" services, Ottawa's National Capital Greenbelt remains one of the largest and most continuous greenbelts in the world. It has become an increasingly popular and valuable recreational resource with hundreds of kilometres of managed and informal paths within its boundaries. The Greenbelt is one of the National Capital's most distinctive features.

Snapping Turtle

The first time you see a snapping turtle, you may be forgiven if you think you have encountered a small dinosaur. With its sawtooth back ridge, armoured claws, and long tail, the snapping turtle looks as if it is a living remnant from a long-past age.

Snapping turtles venture from the water only from late June to early July to lay their eggs. Because they cannot run or hide, the turtles defend themselves aggressively. Don't be fooled by this turtle's withdrawn head; its neck extends to over half its body length, so if you are unwary — well, there's a reason it's named "snapping." Leave these turtles alone and give them plenty of room.

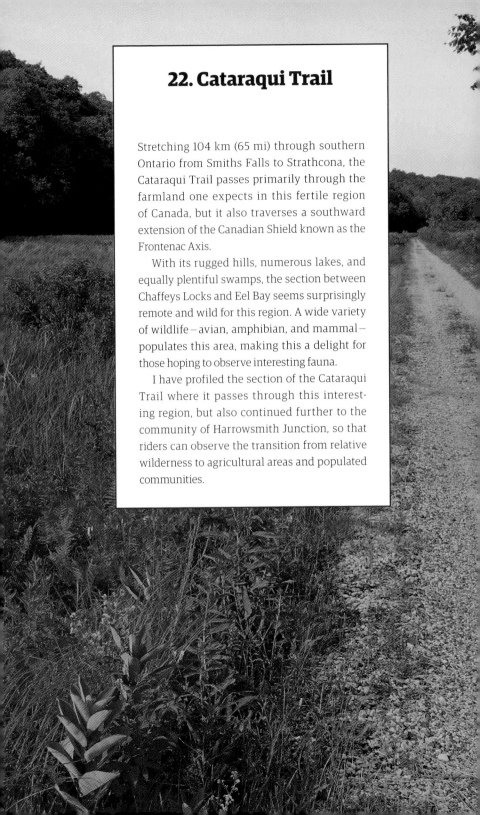

22. Cataraqui Trail

Stretching 104 km (65 mi) through southern Ontario from Smiths Falls to Strathcona, the Cataraqui Trail passes primarily through the farmland one expects in this fertile region of Canada, but it also traverses a southward extension of the Canadian Shield known as the Frontenac Axis.

With its rugged hills, numerous lakes, and equally plentiful swamps, the section between Chaffeys Locks and Eel Bay seems surprisingly remote and wild for this region. A wide variety of wildlife – avian, amphibian, and mammal – populates this area, making this a delight for those hoping to observe interesting fauna.

I have profiled the section of the Cataraqui Trail where it passes through this interesting region, but also continued further to the community of Harrowsmith Junction, so that riders can observe the transition from relative wilderness to agricultural areas and populated communities.

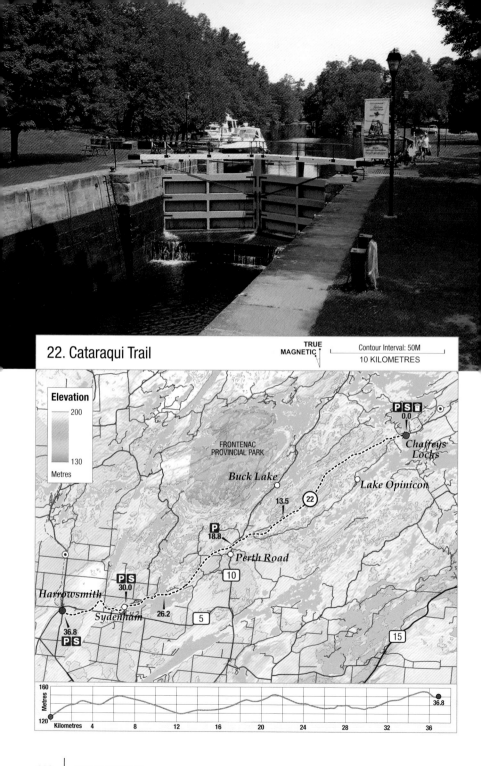

22. Cataraqui Trail

TRUE
MAGNETIC

Contour Interval: 50M

10 KILOMETRES

Elevation

200

130

Metres

FRONTENAC
PROVINCIAL PARK

Buck Lake

13.5

22

Lake Opinicon

P S 🗑 ✕
0.0

*Chaffeys
Locks*

P
18.8

Perth Road

10

P S
30.0

Harrowsmith

Sydenham

26.2

5

15

36.8
P S

160

Metres

120

Kilometres   4   8   12   16   20   24   28   32   36

36.8

22. Cataraqui Trail

Distance: 36.8 km (23 mi) – one way
Ascent: 187 m (614 ft)
Descent: 159 m (522 ft)

Trail conditions: crushed stone, natural surface
Cellphone coverage: partial
Hazards: poison ivy, road crossings, ticks, wildlife

Permitted Uses							
Walking	Biking	Horseback Riding	Inline Skating	ATV	Snowshoeing	Cross-country Skiing	Snowmobiling
✔	✔	✔	—	—	✔	✔	✔

Finding the trailhead: Start this route from a parking area on the Opinicon Road, to the left just across the bridge over the Rideau Canal.

Trailhead: 44°34'45.4"N, 76°19'14.2"W (Start – Chaffeys Locks)
44°24'07.1"N, 76°39'53.6"W (Finish – Harrowsmith Junction)

Observations: This was the roughest pathway I experienced in southern Ontario, with some parts of the trail wet and nearly grown over in vegetation. It felt isolated throughout most of the route, except near Sydenham and Harrowsmith, and I saw very few other walkers or cyclists during the entire day. The long rows of poison ivy I could see growing at both sides of the trail in some places made me nervous, so I rarely stopped except at benches, road crossings, and clearings. I had no cellphone reception from 2.5 km (1.6 mi) to 24 km (15 mi).

However, I quite liked this remote passage through the Canadian Shield terrain. Sydenham Lake was a delight and so very welcome on a hot July afternoon. I also saw more wildlife on this trail than nearly any other in eastern Canada: deer, turtles (three species), hare, fox, coyote, and many birds – including an owl. Each of the many small lakes seemed to have some animal, bird, or amphibian of interest nearby.

Route description: Continue along the narrow, paved road for 400 m/yd, turning right onto a wide, grass-covered path where indicated by a Cataraqui Trail sign. It is also marked with the blue triangle used to sign a side path of the Rideau Trail. About 100 m/yd after the sign, you reach a former railbed, a straight sand-and-gravel track bisected by a centre strip of grass. A rock embankment borders the opposite edge. No houses, other than one abandoned structure among the trees, are in sight. The forest is thick, and it instantly feels remote.

Turn left; in 500 m/yd the trail crosses Indian Lake Road, where there is a small parking area and gates restrict access to the trail. Very quickly, the ruggedness of the terrain becomes apparent. By 1.5 km (0.9 mi), the railbed sits much higher than the ground on the left, and 800 m/yd from the road, there is an excellent view of a small lake, left and far below. A nearby interpretive panel profiles the snapping turtle. Just beyond, on the right, is the Cataraqui Trail km 44 marker.

Throughout this rugged terrain, the trail alternates between sitting above the nearby ground or passing through cuts in the rock. Swamps and marshy ground are frequent, as are the birds and other wildlife that live in them. Turtles and frogs sun themselves on semi-submerged logs, and kingfishers scold you as you cycle past. Some of these bogs are quite large.

At 2.5 km (1.6 mi), the main Rideau Trail connects to the Cataraqui, and they continue together in the direction of Kingston until 4.1 km (2.5 mi) where it separates to the left. This is a very isolated section with no human structures visible, except for the trail itself.

The next distinctive feature is when Round Lake appears on the left at 7.7 km (4.8 mi). The trail curves behind another rocky hill, and when you next see water at 8.9 km (5.5 mi), it is long slender Garter Lake. The path continues alongside for some distance, and the Rideau Trail rejoins the Cataraqui at the far end.

Once past this lake, there are several large swamps that may look more like lakes after heavy rainfalls. Beyond the swamps, there is an extended area with high cliffs on the right; at several places there are "falling rock" warning signs.

At 11.5 km (7.1 mi), Stonehouse Lake comes into view on the left, and the trail is almost at water level. About 200 m/yd later, there is a bench facing the water, the first structure other than signs encountered so far. From here, the crushed stone on the trail makes cycling much easier. Some of the higher rock faces are along here as well, consisting of attractive, pink granite.

The trail begins to follow a small creek about 12.3 km (7.6 mi). This is on the right and grows into an extensive wet area. In spring, this often spills over into the treadway. As the swamp widens, houses become visible far ahead.

13.5 km (8.4 mi) The trail crosses the gravel-surfaced Macgillivray Lane. There are several houses to the right and probably a few horses grazing in nearby fields. There are also several informational signs, both for the Cataraqui Trail and the Ontario Federation of Snowmobile Clubs (OFSC).

The crushed stone ends here, with the treadway mostly grass covered afterwards. There are open areas on the right while the hills on the left are tree covered. At 14.9 km (9.3 mi), the trail crosses a short causeway, traversing wetlands on both sides. The trail also begins to curve away from the road and the houses along it.

At 16 km (10 mi), there is an interpretive panel about the white pine in an open area where the treed ridge on the left is covered in these trees. The trail curves lazily right, still alongside wetlands for a considerable distance. The trail crosses Maple Leaf Road (gravel) 800 m/yd later, where the Rideau Trail branches away again, and then, just 400 m/yd later, it crosses the paved Opinicon Road. The first road crossing is minor, but the second is quite tricky, as the road turns sharply on both sides of the crossing.

Just before reaching this, there is an uncharacteristically – for a rail trail – short, steep hill. The next section is rough. It is almost completely grass covered and appears to be sinking into the boggy ground surrounding it. This is the least pleasant section of this route.

18.8 km (11.7 mi) Arrive at the Perth Road, where there is a trailhead parking area on the opposite side. This features a large map but no tables, garbage cans, or benches. The pathway returns to the thick forest, crossing a small driveway about 1 km (0.6 mi) later, just after a lake to the left.

A larger lake bordered by cottages becomes visible on the right, and the trail crosses Spring Mill Lane at 20.4 km (12.7 mi). Quite high above the surrounding land now, the treadway is fairly dry. With a thick, overhead canopy of leaves, this is very pleasant cycling – even if it is still climbing slightly.

Norway Road (paved) is crossed 600 m/yd later, then the McFadden Road at 22.4 km (14 mi). By now you can sense that you are moving out of the Canadian Shield terrain. The path is quite straight and descending gently. Surrounding hills are not as high; the neighbouring ground is not nearly as rough. There are still plenty of swampy areas, but they are smaller.

At 24.4 km (15.2 mi), an appealing, little rest stop of two benches overlooks tiny Hogan Lake. There is even a cedar-rail fence on which to lean your bicycle. You should finally have good cell coverage here. Soon afterwards, several houses are visible on the left, and the trail crosses Hogan Road at 25 km (15.6 mi).

Once again, crushed stone surfaces the treadway, and within 150 m/yd, the trees give way to views of the very large Sydenham Lake on the left. After the hours spent in thick forest, the wide, blue vista is fantastic. Suddenly there are numerous side tracks, connecting to the main trail, and even a few driveway crossings. It is almost as if a switch has been flipped: before Hogan Road wilderness, after it, people.

At 25.9 km (16.1 mi), there is an exquisitely positioned bench overlooking a small cove. Several painted turtles basked on logs a few metres away. Water lilies, their delicate white blossoms punctuating a carpet of circular green pads, bob serenely. The setting begs you to stop and absorb the beauty, even if only for a few moments.

📍**26.2 km (16.3 mi)** The trail crosses a causeway and bridge, traversing a wide arm of Sydenham Lake known as Eel Bay. It connects to small Boyce Island, on which there is another TCT interpretive panel, and crosses a longer causeway 500 m/ yd later. There are gates on both bridges that require cyclists to dismount and lift their bikes over. The water is deep and clear, making either causeway a great place for a swim.

Once across the second bridge, human habitations become much more common. The trail remains close to the lake edge, though sometimes it is hidden by thick vegetation. Driveways and even dirt-road crossings are frequent.

At 27.2 km (17 mi), the trail diverts from the former rail track and unusually climbs very steeply. At the top of this short hill is a stop sign and a directional arrow pointing left into Connally Lane. Your route follows this dirt road back downhill for 200 m/yd, where it rejoins the original rail line.

From here there is a plentiful collection of boat docks and cottages along the water, and staircases lead up the hillside to unseen residences. At 29.5 km (18.3 mi), the trail crosses another causeway, traversing a tiny bay. Ahead, the houses of Sydenham appear quite close.

📍**30 km (18.6 mi)** Emerging from the forest, you quickly reach the community of Sydenham and a challenging road crossing. It is a busy road junction where the main road, George Street, curves past the parking lots of large businesses; a grocery store and a hardware store are on the immediate left.

On the opposite side of this tricky crossing is a welcome greenspace with benches, shade trees, and a trailhead kiosk, including a map for the Cataraqui Trail. Another large sign announces that the Rideau Trail has reconnected with this one. The small Sydenham Dam, from which Millhaven Creek flows, lies across a comfortable, grass-covered clearing.

The Cataraqui Trail continues, a pleasant ride with overhead shade through the village. Although many residences are near, few are visible through the lush

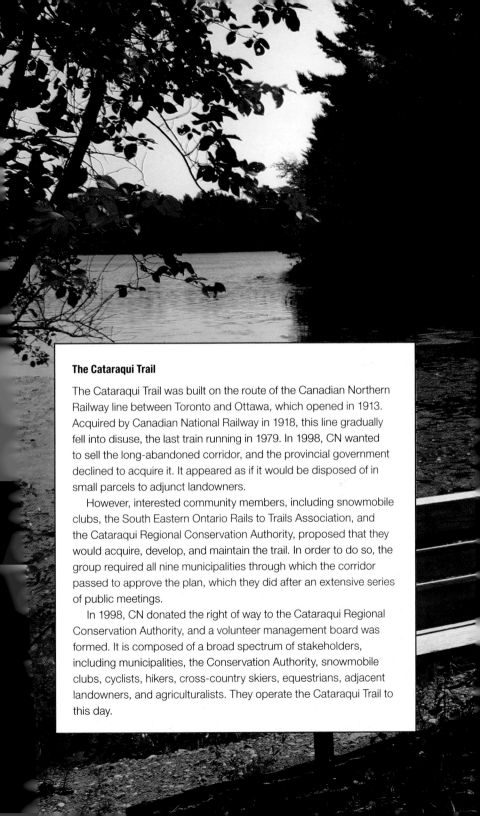

The Cataraqui Trail

The Cataraqui Trail was built on the route of the Canadian Northern Railway line between Toronto and Ottawa, which opened in 1913. Acquired by Canadian National Railway in 1918, this line gradually fell into disuse, the last train running in 1979. In 1998, CN wanted to sell the long-abandoned corridor, and the provincial government declined to acquire it. It appeared as if it would be disposed of in small parcels to adjunct landowners.

However, interested community members, including snowmobile clubs, the South Eastern Ontario Rails to Trails Association, and the Cataraqui Regional Conservation Authority, proposed that they would acquire, develop, and maintain the trail. In order to do so, the group required all nine municipalities through which the corridor passed to approve the plan, which they did after an extensive series of public meetings.

In 1998, CN donated the right of way to the Cataraqui Regional Conservation Authority, and a volunteer management board was formed. It is composed of a broad spectrum of stakeholders, including municipalities, the Conservation Authority, snowmobile clubs, cyclists, hikers, cross-country skiers, equestrians, adjacent landowners, and agriculturalists. They operate the Cataraqui Trail to this day.

foliage. At 31 km (19.3 mi), the trail crosses Church Street then enters a rail cut. The rock now includes some limestone mixed in with the gneiss.

This is a gentle, easy cycle. The route is climbing again as you leave Sydenham Lake behind, but the grade is gentle. Houses are occasionally visible, and there are even views to the left as the trail slowly gains altitude. At 32.3 km (20.1 mi), the pathway crosses the paved Loughborough-Portland Road.

From here, the trail makes a long curve left, almost 180°, as it winds around a former quarry. On your right, there is a rock face. You might notice farmland to the right and above. At 34 km (21.1 mi), there is the signed Escarpment Rest Stop, where a stone staircase ascends to a bench overlooking the valley.

Just 300 m/yd further, the path crosses above Highway 5 as it passes through a deep cut in the hillside. The trail crosses beneath three massive powerlines 400 m/yd beyond that. For the remainder of the route, cultivated fields line both sides of the trail, making an attractive pastoral setting.

At 35.2 km (22 mi), the Cataraqui Trail connects to the K&P Trail, a crushed-stone pathway that extends 26 km (16.2 mi) to Kingston and Lake Ontario. For the last time, the Rideau Trail separates from the Cataraqui, now following the K&P. Your gentle ride through lush farmland continues until Regional Road 38 at 36.7 km (22.4 mi).

36.8 km (22.9 mi) You arrive at the end of the ride in Harrowsmith Junction. A single bench sits in a grass field, flanked by interpretive panels. Beside them sits a trailhead kiosk with a map of the Cataraqui Trail. It continues an additional 20 km (12.4 mi) plus to the community of Strathcona. It's a pleasant and tranquil trek through farming lands, but I recommend that you begin your return to Chaffeys Locks from here.

Further Information:
Cataraqui Region Conservation Authority: https://crca.ca
Cataraqui Trail: http://cataraquitrail.ca
Rideau Canal National Historic Site: www.pc.gc.ca/en/lhn-nhs/on/rideau
Trans Canada Trail Ontario: www.tctontario.ca

Poison ivy

These skin-irritating plants are increasingly found along the edges of many trails and fields. Managed trails usually post warning signs, but as both poison ivy and other noxious plants such as giant hogweed are spreading and extending their range, they could be growing anywhere alongside the pathway. The best way to avoid poison? Stay on the path.

23. Kawartha Trans Canada Trail

With its 220,000 population, the Greater Peterborough area is the largest urban centre north of Lake Ontario between Ottawa and Toronto. Although known as a manufacturing centre, Peterborough is also considered the "Gateway to the Kawarthas," and one of Ontario's principal cottage regions. The Trent-Severn Waterway, a National Historic Site that is a 386 km (240 mi) navigable route connecting Lake Ontario and Lake Huron, also runs through the city.

Though it boasts a population of less than fifteen hundred, the community of Omemee is the largest single population centre and the administrative hub of the City of Kawartha Lakes region. It is most well known for being the childhood home of Canadian folk singer Neil Young. The Kawartha Trans Canada Trail begins at the Peterborough/City of Kawartha Lakes municipal boundary and continues for nearly 54 km (33.6 mi). It only officially opened in 2014, and it may have the most comprehensive website of any trail in Canada. Check out their podcasts – amazing work.

This route is a pleasant and easy ride through a mix of urban, rural, and agricultural landscapes. There are no dramatic views with the single exception of Doube's Trestle, a long steel bridge more than 25 m (82 ft) above the swampy Buttermilk Valley. At Omemee, you find a grocery store, restaurant, and other businesses. There is also a charming little municipal beach park on the Pigeon River, where you can enjoy a meal break.

23. Kawartha Trans Canada Trail

TRUE
MAGNETIC

Contour Interval: 10M
5 KILOMETRES

Elevation

360

180

Metres

Fowlers
Corners

Omemee

Jackson
Heights

1.8

21.1
P S

13.8

Orange
Corners

23

5.8

P S
0.0

Peterborough

Pigeon River

300

Metres

150

Kilometres   4   8   12   16   20

21.1

23. Kawartha Trans Canada Trail

Distance: 21.1 km (13.1 mi) – one way
Ascent: 132 m (433 ft)
Descent: 77 m (253 ft)

Trail conditions: asphalt, crushed stone, natural surface
Cellphone coverage: yes
Hazards: hunting (in fall), poison ivy, road crossings

Permitted Uses							
Walking	Biking	Horseback Riding	Inline Skating	ATV	Snowshoeing	Cross-country Skiing	Snowmobiling
✔	✔	✔*	✔*	—	✔	✔	✔*

Finding the trailhead: Start this route at the corner of Brock and Bethune Streets in Peterborough, beside the Hutchison House Museum and almost where the off-road path begins. There is no trailhead, but there is plenty of free parking nearby. The asphalt-surfaced trail sits in a little greenspace and is well signed.

Trailhead: 44°18'25.3"N, 78°19'28.9"W (Start — Peterborough)
44°17'58.8"N, 78°33'24.8"W (Finish — Omemee)

Observations: This was an easy trail to ride, being very well done both within the City of Peterborough and along the Kawartha Trail. It is a relaxing bike ride and passes through some beautiful country. My only regrets are that I did not continue as far as Lindsay, where Sir Sandford Fleming College offers a Sustainable Trails Certificate program, and that I was unable to include the section in Peterborough on the east side of the Otonabee River.

The trail around Little Lake, which crosses the Trent Canal, is worth exploring as well. However, the connecting route through busy streets in downtown Peterborough prevented me from including it. It might be easier to make the connection now because a new trail bridge over the Otonabee was almost completed in 2015, and the only challenging section would be 950 m/yd downtown, mostly on Simcoe Street.

Route description: Travel towards Jackson Park, away from the downtown, where mature tall trees provide shade in a narrow green corridor. At 200 m/yd, the path crosses Jackson Creek and then crosses the first road 150 m/yd later. Trail users initially cross Rubidge Street, then are funneled to the right by a fence, leading to

The Missing Link

In Canada, the middle and late decades of the 19th century were filled with ambitious railway construction. As the farmland and forests north of Lake Ontario developed, so did the competition to get their products to market more quickly.

For many years, no connection was possible between Omemee and Peterborough, even though connecting these communities would significantly shorten the travel time between Ottawa and Toronto. Engineering challenges with sinkholes at Tully's and Doube's Valleys stymied its completion, and this area became known as "the missing link."

Work began in 1882 to bridge, quite literally, this gap. In order to make the connection, Doube's required a wooden trestle 460 m/yd long and more than 25 m (82 ft) above the valley, and Tully's was filled. The first train crossed on October 8, 1883, moving at a cautious 6.5 kph (4 mph)! In 1923, earthen embankments were extended at either end, and the wooden bridge was replaced by the 175 m/yd long steel span, which is in place now.

an immediate second crossing at Reid Street. This is quite a well done and elaborate construction for a difficult junction.

After this, the trail returns to the trees, passing behind housing with Jackson Creek to the left. It crosses quiet Donegal Street before arriving at the extremely busy intersection of Park and McDonnel Streets after another 750 m/yd. Cyclists should dismount and cross this signalized intersection on the crosswalks. The trail resumes on the north side of McDonnel, 50 m/yd along the sidewalk from the road crossing.

A tall signpost with a TCT marker sits beside the trail entrance. At 1.2 km (0.7 mi), after crossing Bonaccord Street, where there is a trail map, you leave the urban core behind. For the remainder of its route through Peterborough, the trail passes through parkland. The trail surface also changes here to crushed stone.

Just 150 m/yd further, the trail passes beneath Parkhill Road and enters Jackson Park. As it curves left, the pathway passes a small pond with benches and picnic tables.

1.8 km (1.1 mi) You arrive at a major trail junction with paths splitting into several directions. A sign indicates that Omemee is 19.3 km (12 mi) straight ahead. Once past the junction, urban structures are no longer visible and connecting side trails are frequent. Jackson Creek parallels on the left initially, although the trail crosses over it at 2.9 km (1.8 mi) and again 800 m/yd later.

Few views are possible through the thick, surrounding vegetation, but when there are, you can see that the pathway is at the bottom of a small valley created by the creek. After crossing it the second time, the trail curves sharply – for a rail trail – right, reaching a junction on the left where there is a large steel bridge, at 4.5 km (2.8 mi). The main path then curves left, crossing a small bridge 100 m/yd later; on the right sits small Lily Lake and a sizable wetland.

Once across the bridge, the trail is arrow straight with low wetlands and a meandering slough on both sides of the path. Don't stop unless you want to feed the mosquitoes, although this is an excellent observation area for waterfowl, beavers, and muskrats.

5.8 km (3.6 mi) You reach Ackison Road, where the municipal trail ends and the Kawartha Trans Canada Trail (KTCT) begins. Metal posts narrow an elaborate gateway arching above the trail access. Oddly, there is no parking area, and cars line the busy road, but there are a large map and multiple informational signs. There are other large signs indicating that what you were on previously is the Peterborough Rotary Greenway Trail.

The city is far behind you now with the exception of a large electric generating station on the right. At first, the Jackson Creek wetland is to the left, but very quickly, nothing but farmland is visible in every direction – although small wetlands are common.

At 7.9 km (4.9 mi), the trail crosses Lily Lake Road at a diagonal, so be particularly cautious. Look closely at the KTCT signs; these are the best I have seen on any Canadian Trail. They name your current location, provide its GPS coordinates, and show the name of and distance to both the next and the previous road crossings.

The trail continues to climb gently, passing through a forested area and bridging a small brook 400 m/yd from Lily Lake Road. At 9.5 km (5.9 mi), Highway 7 passes overhead, where a sign says that the next road crossing is 2 km (1.2 mi) further.

After a relaxing passage through forest and field, the trail arrives at Cottingham Road at 12.3 km (7.6 mi). At almost the same time, it shifts from the ongoing climb that it has been doing since the start to begin a gentle descent. The pathway curves left, reaching Orange Corners Road just 500 m/yd later.

13.8 km (8.6 mi) You arrive at the start of Doube's Trestle, a 175 m/yd steel bridge standing more than 25 m (82 ft) above the marshy Buttermilk Valley. Considering how gentle the remainder of this route is, the panoramic views from this startlingly high bridge stand in greater dramatic contrast.

Once across, the trail returns to a pastoral tranquility that it retains for the remainder of its course. At 16.3 km (10.1 mi), it once again passes underneath Highway 7, and at 17.1 km (10.6 mi), there is a challenging crossing of the high-speed Emily Park Road. There is a trail map and a large "K" sculpture, shaped to resemble an inukshuk, located here.

After this tricky road crossing, an unchallenging ride through cultivated fields, forest glades, and small wetlands resumes. There is one more minor road crossing before reaching Omemee at the end of Emily Street, 20.6 km (12.8 mi). Continue straight; the pathway reaches the Pigeon River, which is spanned by a sturdy steel bridge, just 100 m/yd later.

At 20.8 km (12.9 mi), the trail intersects with Colborne Street. Turn left off the trail and continue along the quiet residential street towards King Street and Omemee's business centre.

21.1 km (13.1 mi) You arrive at King Street, where grocery stores and diners are to your right. Continue straight ahead to reach Omemee Municipal Park and beach. Have lunch or take a rest stop in the village, then retrace your route back to Peterborough.

Further Information:
City of Peterborough Parks & Trails: www.peterborough.ca/Living/Recreation/
Free_in_Peterborough/Parks___Trails.htm
Kawartha Trans Canada Trail: https://ktct.ca
Peterborough/Kawartha Tourism: http://thekawarthas.ca

24. Uxbridge Township

Uxbridge Township was named as "Canada's Trail Capital" by Industry Canada in 2009. With more than 220 km (137 mi) of trail within the 32 km² (12.4 mi²) of protected greenspace, this relatively small community on the eastern edge of Toronto's urban sprawl certainly deserves to be recognized for its commitment to outdoor recreation. The municipality plans to add many more kilometres of pathway in the coming years.

This route passes through three separate, but physically connected, tracts of protected lands: the Durham Forest, Walker Woods, and the Glen Major Forest. Viewed on a map, they look like pieces of a jigsaw puzzle that have been put together, but with holes left where other pieces are missing.

Each forested area is criss-crossed by a maze of footpaths and mountain biking tracks, found in much greater density than is usual anywhere but in urban parks. Fortunately, the signage is excellent and finding the correct path should be straightforward, though you need to be attentive at each intersection.

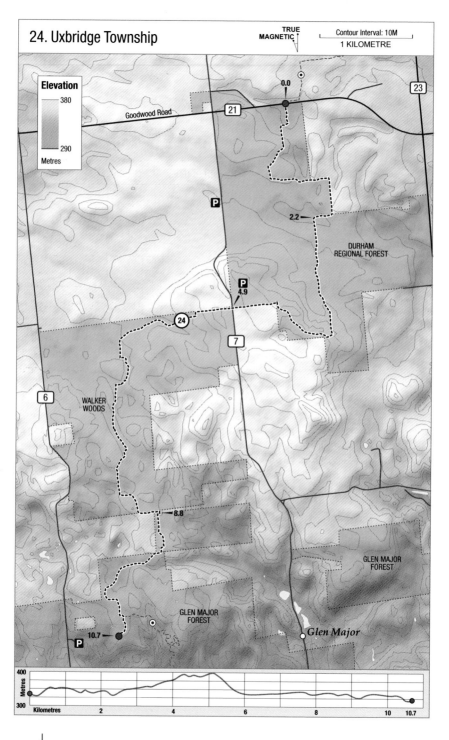

24. Uxbridge Township

TRUE
MAGNETIC

Contour Interval: 10M
1 KILOMETRE

Elevation

380

290

Metres

Goodwood Road

0.0

21

23

P

2.2

DURHAM
REGIONAL FOREST

P
4.9

24

7

6

WALKER
WOODS

8.8

GLEN MAJOR
FOREST

10.7

P

GLEN MAJOR
FOREST

Glen Major

400

Metres

300

Kilometres 2 4 6 8 10 10.7

24. Uxbridge Township

Distance: 10.7 km (6.6 mi) – one way
Ascent: 238 m (781 ft)
Descent: 211 m (692 ft)

Trail conditions: crushed stone,
natural surface
Cellphone coverage: yes
Hazards: poison ivy, road crossings,
wildlife

Permitted Uses							
Walking	Biking	Horseback Riding	Inline Skating	ATV	Snowshoeing	Cross-country Skiing	Snowmobiling
✔	✔	✔	—	—	✔	✔	—

Finding the trailhead: This route begins at the north gate of the Durham Regional Forest on Goodwood Road, officially at #749 Regional Road 21. There is no trailhead parking, and the road is an 80 kph (50 mph) zone, so use caution if you must cross it. An old iron gate prevents vehicle access to a wide grass-covered track with signs for Durham Trails and the TCT posted on a fence next to the gate.

Trailhead: 44°03'33.2" N, 79°05'15" W (Start — Goodwood Road)
44°00'26.5" N, 79°05'43.5" W (Finish — Glen Major Forest reclaimed aggregate pit)

Observations: This was the only wooded footpath of the ten routes recommended by Trans Canada Trail Ontario, so I was naturally eager to walk it. I quite enjoyed it, even though the maze-like collection of paths in these well-trodden woodlands requires constant attention to navigation. The forest is magnificent, with many mature trees in areas that are regenerating from farmland.

Ultimately, I hiked considerably more trail on both ends of this route than I profiled in this description. I decided to finish at the Glen Major Forest reclaimed aggregate pit because this was the only spot with any extended view. All the other trailheads were at road junctions, where there are numbered posts throughout the forest; take a picture of the trailhead map for reference.

Unfortunately, despite nearly half a day spent wandering around the parks and streets of Uxbridge, I was unable to locate the connection between its trail pavilion and the Durham Forest. I wanted to include the town, and I recommend that you include it in your explorations.

Route description: The start seems like on old forest road with a thin strip of gravel in the centre. Tall trees border the path, including towering white pines. Almost immediately you reach a small clearing, where there is a weather monitoring station. The first junction is little more than 200 m/yd from the road; the signs direct you to the right. Turn left less than 100 m/yd later at another intersection. Most of this walk is similarly short segments of path between junctions with frequent changes of direction. Fortunately, there is good signage; watch closely for the TCT markers at every intersection.

The forest is strikingly attractive with tall trees and an overhead canopy of branches and leaves. The main track is wide, and unsigned side trails frequently intersect. Various types of signs are common: interpretive signage about the various tree species, orienteering markers, brightly coloured Durham Forest Trail markers, and TCT markers with directional arrows.

The route is a meandering one, turning left and right every few hundred metres. The one constant is the trees, which line the trail edges and rise high overhead. Except for the occasional overgrown stone wall and private property signs, there is little evidence of people.

2.2 km (1.4 mi) Assuming you took all the correct turns, you arrive at Coyote Junction, where there is a trailhead kiosk with a map. The route turns left and continues past the pavilion on what is the longest straight section of this walk.

Numerous mountain bike tracks cross the trail, and there are still many intersections with walking paths. Continue more or less straight until 3.6 km (2.2 mi), where you turn right. You should also notice the occasional white (or blue), painted blazes and the plastic signs of the Oak Ridges Trail Association (ORTA). Their 250 km (155 mi) plus of hiking trails shares much of this route.

At this intersection, the paths and parking are all to the right. A more winding path climbs between two small knolls, topped by the most attractive hardwoods seen thus far. There are several minor junctions, and at 4.3 km (2.7 mi), there is another trailhead kiosk and a dirt road that allows automobile access. A fiesta of signage decorates this intersection.

Turn left and walk along the dirt track that is Houston Road. There is a gate across it 300 m/yd from the kiosk, and a fenced compound encircles two communication towers on the left. Keep going 200 m/yd to the intersection with Concession Road 7 (paved).

4.9 km (3 mi) You arrive at the trailhead parking area for the Walker Woods east loop on the opposite side of Concession Road 7. There are a large map on a kiosk and plenty of signs for the various users, hikers and mountain bikers in particular.

Once again, the route enters a forest, although this is more of a footpath than a former woods road. It more or less parallels the dirt Albright Road for the first

400 m/yd. Then, at junction post #7, you turn sharply left. Vegetation near the trail is young and thick as the path descends noticeably for the next 700 m/yd. There are TCT markers, but the ORTA's blue paint blazes appear more frequently. The path continues over the rolling terrain.

At a multi-path junction at 6.3 km (3.9 mi) is post #9 and a bench, the first seen on this walk. Continue straight until the next junction 200 m/yd later, where you turn left, then right barely 50 m/yd later. The next little bit is lovely, with tall hardwoods and no understorey. Sunlight filtering through the leafy canopy high overhead suffuses everything with a green aura. There is a map at 6.6 km (4.1 mi), Post #10.

Your walk through a delightful forest continues past posts #13 and #14, negotiating numerous junctions as it winds its way onward. Although the TCT markers are not always easily visible, you can see them if you look carefully. The walking is gentle and restful with one or two small clearings and even one wet area.

8.8 km (5.5 mi) After 200 m/yd past a fence on the right and private-property signs, you arrive at Post #16, where there is a bench. This is also where you leave the Walker Woods and enter the Glen Major Forest. As you continue, the trail is actually on a small parcel of public land, surrounded by private property. Please keep closely to the trail. When you reach post #21 at 9.2 km (5.7 mi), you are at the corner of the conservation lands

The vegetation bordering the trail changes somewhat as the mature trees give way to younger saplings that are more densely packed together. The long views that were possible through the tall trees have been lost, and you can see little but the footpath ahead and behind.

Do not be surprised when the next post you encounter at 10.2 km (6.3 mi) is #38 since the numbering system is not sequential. Turn sharply right, and in 200 m/yd, you reach the edge of a large, open field. Turn off the main trail here and head into the clearing.

You are at the top of a large, grass-covered pit. The path to the right heads to the low ground and eventually leads to a trailhead parking area on Concession Road 6. You keep left and follow a footpath along the lip of the pit. This is the first extended view you have had since entering the Durham Forest, and it is quite a contrast to the thick forest through which you have been walking

10.7 km (6.6 mi) You arrive at a lookout with flat stones arrayed as seats, where an interpretive panel explains that the shallow bowl of the pit was where gravel was quarried for construction. It also mentions that further information panels may be found on the 3 km (1.9 mi) loop trail around the pit.

However, I recommend stopping here and having a break before returning to the start. There is comfortable seating, from which you can even see Lake Ontario. The route through Uxbridge Township may lack other breathtaking views, but it is a delightful natural preserve, especially so close to Toronto's millions of people.

Further Information:

Durham Forest Trail map: https://www.lsrca.on.ca/Shared%20Documents/ca_maps/durham-forest.pdf
Lake Simcoe Region Conservation Authority: www.lsrca.on.ca
Oak Ridges Trail Association: www.oakridgestrail.org
Toronto and Region Conservation: www.trca.on.ca
Town of Uxbridge (Trails): http://town.uxbridge.on.ca/canada_trail_capital
Walker Woods/Glen Major Forest Trail map: www.trca.on.ca/dotAsset/47411.pdf

Ontario's Conservation Authorities

A unique feature of Ontario is the network of thirty-six Conservation Authorities. Created in 1946 to address the extensive damage to southern Ontario's environment from unsustainable farming methods and the overcutting of forests, these community-based management agencies are mandated to conserve and protect Ontario's natural resources within the area of particular river watersheds.

Although primarily interested in ensuring that the province's rivers, lakes, and streams are properly safeguarded, managed, and restored, the conservation authorities have to provide opportunities for the public to respect and enjoy the natural environment as part of their mandate. Methods to do so vary across the different authorities, which are managed by boards made up of elected municipal officials. Increasingly, they have come to include the creation and management of non-motorized recreational trails on their properties.

Within Uxbridge Township, several tracts of forested land are protected by two of these agencies: the Toronto and Region Conservation Authority and the Lake Simcoe Region Conservation Authority. The former manages the trails in Walker Woods and the Glen Major Forest, the latter the Durham Forest.

Wild Turkey

One of the newest wildlife residents in Ontario and Quebec, the wild turkey, is returning to where it once was common. Having almost vanished across North America because of deforestation and unregulated hunting, turkeys have been reintroduced in many regions of the continent — and populations have grown quickly. In eastern Canada, wild turkeys have spread north from New York State and rapidly expanded their range throughout Ontario and Québec. By 2005, the local population was considered secure enough to permit regular hunting in the spring during breeding season. Turkeys are the largest game bird in North America.

25. Toronto Waterfront

Toronto is Canada's largest city and, with a population of more than 2.7 million, is also the fourth largest in North America. It is also the capital of the province of Ontario, though another Ontario city, Ottawa, is the capital of Canada. Toronto's waterfront with its protected harbour on Lake Ontario has always been important to the community, one of the principal reasons for its founding. The city's first industrial developments were concentrated on its lakeshore with freight access to the rest of Ontario by railway and to US markets by water.

With an increase in trucking freight overland, industries abandoned the waterfront, leaving a vast area of "brownlands" to be reclaimed. By the late 1980s, their future was a source of heated public debate, leading to the creation of the Waterfront Regeneration Trust. Since then, Toronto's lakeshore has undergone a remarkable transformation, revitalizing the former industrial wasteland with new shopping areas, hotels, condominiums, and trails.

Today, it is possible to walk, cycle, or inline skate across the entire length of the city – except for one tiny section – on a dedicated off-road pathway. Users can enjoy both the Lake Ontario shoreline and some of Toronto's most iconic landmarks. Variously named the Martin Goodwin Trail (Toronto), the Great Lakes Waterfront Trail (Ontario), and The Great Trail (Canada), this is a marvellous route.

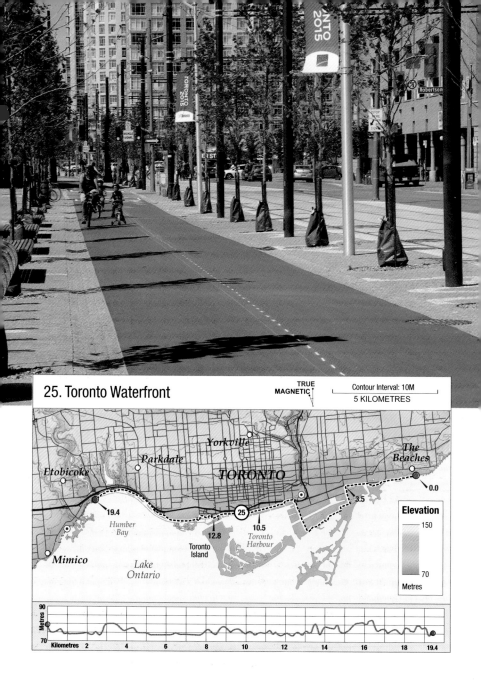

25. Toronto Waterfront

TRUE
MAGNETIC

Contour Interval: 10M

5 KILOMETRES

Yorkville

The Beaches

Parkdale

Etobicoke

TORONTO

0.0

19.4

Humber Bay

25

3.5

Mimico

12.8

10.5

Toronto Island

Toronto Harbour

Lake Ontario

Elevation

150

70

Metres

Metres 90

70

Kilometres 2 4 6 8 10 12 14 16 18 19.4

25. Toronto Waterfront

Distance: 19.4 km (12.1 mi) – one way
Ascent: 73 m (240 ft)
Descent: 77 m (253 ft)

Trail conditions: asphalt
Cellphone coverage: yes
Hazards: high usage, road crossings

Permitted Uses							
Walking	Biking	Horseback Riding	Inline Skating	ATV	Snowshoeing	Cross-country Skiing	Snowmobiling
✔	✔	—	✔	—	✔	✔	—

Finding the trailhead: Starting at the bottom of Fernwood Avenue, the paved Martin Goodwin Trail runs parallel to the Lake Ontario shoreline through Balmy Beach Park. There is no dedicated parking area, but plenty of on-street spaces. To the left is a boardwalk, running along the edge of a lovely wide sandy beach. Benches are distributed widely throughout this greenspace, as well as garbage cans. Even early in the morning, expect to share this trail with joggers and people walking their dogs.

Trailhead: 43°40'10.4"N, 79°17'16.7"W (Start — The Beaches)
43°37'53.3"N, 79°28'17.9"W (Finish — Humber River)

Observations: When this route was suggested by the Ontario representative, I was skeptical. As a person who enjoys wilderness hiking, I could not imagine cycling through the downtown of the largest urban centre of the country. However, when I began riding through the attractive parkland of The Beaches, I was pleased by how pleasant the lakeshore appeared and how relaxing it was to cycle. Even when the trail moved into busy urban areas, I was impressed that the city maintained so much off-road pathway. By the time I reached the Harbourfront Centre, I was captivated by the new and elaborate pathway that permitted riding across the whole city.

I had a wonderful day cycling across Toronto. My most difficult decision was deciding where to stop, but the bridge spanning the Humber River is so impressive and the view of the Toronto Waterfront from the mouth of the river so striking, that I made this the point at which to end the ride.

Route description: At 750 m/yd from the start on Fernwood Avenue, there is a sign for the three trails sharing this passageway: Martin Goodwin Trail, Great Lakes

Waterfront Trail, and The Great Trail. To the right are a lawn-bowling facility and just beyond that the Kew Gardens Tennis Club.

This section is lovely and very pleasant, with only quiet residential streets adjacent to the parkland. At 1.4 km (0.9 mi), the beach broadens and curves out into the lake. This area is known as Woodbine Beach, and you pass its large public parking area 400 m/yd later. There are canteens nearby and so many other facilities that it is difficult to mention them all.

The first road crossing is Ashbridge's Bay Park Road at 2.2 km (1.4 mi). The trail then turns left and follows this street to reach multi-lane Lake Shore Boulevard within 250 m/yd. Fortunately, the broad trail turns left and parallels the busy roadway rather than crossing it. However, the quiet parkland is now a distant memory. With the high-rise buildings of the downtown directly ahead, the route heads into an industrial zone.

3.5 km (2.2 mi) After passing the massive new Leslie Barns streetcar maintenance facility, the trail turns left at the intersection of Lake Shore Boulevard and Leslie Street. While still a distinct pathway, the trail now runs alongside the street like a sidewalk. The area is starkly industrial; several streetcar tracks must be crossed, and there are street crossings at North Service Road and South Service Road.

After the latter road crossing at 4.2 km (2.6 mi), you continue alongside community gardens on your left side until the trail arrives at the entrance to Tommy Thompson Park 200 m/yd later. Often called "Toronto's Accidental Wilderness," this is a completely man-made series of islands, created from concrete, earth, and sand, that now extends almost 5 km (3.1 mi) into Lake Ontario.

Although these are well worth exploring, your route turns right, leaving the dedicated pathway and following relatively quiet Unwin Avenue. There is no bike lane or sidewalk here; you must share the road with automobiles. The next 800 m/yd are the only on-road portion of entire route, and the trail reconnects at the entrance to the Outer Harbour Marina with a bridge visible on the left. Once across this bridge, the trail enters its most remote section, passing through an area of thick vegetation, which hides views of the nearby industrial plants—except for one very tall smokestack. This area, North Shore Park, is actually a fairly narrow strip of greenspace between the Outer Harbour Channel and the Port Lands.

At 6.1 km (3.8 mi), the trail passes some sailing clubs and 400 m/yd later crosses Regatta Road. There is a massive parking area 200 m/yd beyond on the left for the patrons of Cherry Beach. When the trail reaches the entrance road at 7 km (4.3 mi), it curves right and heads back towards more industrial areas.

At Unwin Avenue, the greenspace is left behind 300 m/yd later, and the trail once more runs beside Cherry Street like a sidewalk. At 7.5 km (4.7 mi), it crosses the lift bridge over Sunfish Cut, where cyclists are directed to dismount before crossing. The trail continues alongside this very busy and noisy street until the intersection of Cherry and Commissioners Streets at 8.1 km (5 mi). Turn left and cross Cherry Street; the trail resumes on the opposite side. After a further 400 m/yd, the pathway once again reaches Lake Shore Boulevard.

From here, the path curves left, almost – but not quite – passing beneath the elevated Gardiner Expressway. At 9.1 km (5.7 mi), the pathway curves left again when it reaches Parliament Street, running alongside this road as it changes into Queens Quay East.

You are now riding on a beautiful, new, dedicated, bi-directional pathway and heading into the very heart of the city. From industrial grey lands, the properties adjacent to the trail transition into towering new condominiums, hotels, and commercial centres. To your left, the waterfront quickly shifts from a scruffy industrial zone into a sanitized tourism mecca.

◉ 10.5 km (6.5 mi) You arrive at the intersection of Queens Quay and Yonge Street. Towering buildings now surround you, but the dedicated pathway continues. At these busy intersections, crossing is regulated by signal lights, and the pathway is almost certain to be crowded with other users.

Just 150 m/yd further at Bay Street, Harbour Square Park and the ferry terminal are on the left. You pass the Westin Harbour Castle Conference Centre and continue alongside Queens Quay, passing innumerable businesses and attractions. Should you wish to stop, there are hundreds of benches, restaurants, and other services in the next kilometre. On the right, it appears as if you could touch the CN Tower, which sits on the other side of the Gardiner Expressway 500 m/yd away.

The magnificent pathway continues to parallel the recently rebuilt Queens Quay past dozens of new condominium developments. A streetcar line is to the right, the sidewalk to the left. At 11.6 km (7.2 mi), there is the first of several small parks next to the lake. There are an almost infinite number of stopping options available, and many gorgeous places to sit and view the water.

◉ 12.8 km (8 mi) Queens Quay ends at Stadium Road. The off-road trail continues straight ahead, weaving behind some buildings before entering Coronation Park. To the left is HMCS *York*, a Canadian Forces Naval Reserve facility, nicknamed "the stone frigate." The trail continues through the park, connecting once more to Lake Shore Boulevard at 13.5 km (8.4 mi), opposite the Princes' Gate entrance to Exhibition Park, home of the Canadian National Exhibition.

Turn left and follow Remembrance Drive for 300 m/yd, once again beside the lake. At Inukshuk Park, next to its – unsurprisingly – really large inukshuk, turn right again onto an off-road pathway; this junction is well signed. In just 200 m/yd, the path returns to Lake Shore Boulevard at the entranceway to Ontario Place.

From this point onward, the trail enjoys an almost unrestricted passage to the Humber River through parklands along the shoreline of Lake Ontario. There is still quite a bit to see. It is more than 1 km (0.6 mi) to pass the various buildings and pavilions of Ontario Place, which occupy several small islands. Several pedestrian bridges cross over both Lake Shore Boulevard and the pathway.

Shortly after that, upon entering Marilyn Bell Park, a boardwalk separates from the asphalt pathway. The former follows the shoreline; the latter remains quite close to the road. In between the two is a lovely greenspace with picnic tables, benches, and other facilities.

A few minor road crossings remain, and there are a number of recreational structures along the lakeshore. Oarsman Drive, the entrance to the Argonaut Rowing Club, is crossed at 16.1 km (10 mi) and Net Drive 200 m/yd later. About 100 m/yd after that, the trail passes directly in front of Royal Canadian Legion Branch 344, and the next small greenspace is named Vimy Ridge Parkette.

Next are the Boulevard Club at 16.8 km (10.4 mi) and Palais Royale 400 m/yd further, where another long pedestrian bridge connects to the trail. Budapest Park follows with its very large parking lot, and at 17.9 km (11.1 mi), the Sunnyside Pavilion has cafés, an outdoor pool, and a beach.

There is a particularly interesting monument at 18.4 km (11.4 mi) that is dedicated to Sir Casimir Gzowski, an extremely important 19th-century railroad engineer – and the great-great-grandfather of past CBC radio personality Peter Gzowski. The trail continues through the park named in his honour, but as the lake curves, the width of the greenspace diminishes.

By the time the pathway reaches a Trail Pavilion with interpretive panels at 19 km (11.8 mi), the water and boardwalk are just to the left with pathway and parking lot squeezed in on the right. The asphalt track and boardwalk run parallel for the next 150 m/yd until they converge at the Humber River.

♀ 19.4 km (12 mi) Continue to the far end of the impressive Humber Bay Arch Bridge, 139 m/yd long. This dramatic structure, the winner of several architectural awards, was completed in 1994 and is a major reason why this route is one of the most popular cycling paths in Toronto.

The views from the bridge to Humber Bay are quite good, but if you turn left from the bridge onto a tiny spit of land known as Sheldon Lookout, the view back towards downtown Toronto is even more impressive. This is another delightful location for a break before beginning your return ride to The Beaches.

Further Information:
Tommy Thompson Park: https://tommythompsonpark.ca
Toronto Tourism: www.seetorontonow.com
Waterfront Trail: https://waterfronttrail.org/the-trail/

The Great Lakes Waterfront Trail

In 1992, the same year as the concept of creating the Trans Canada Trail was launched, the province of Ontario created the Waterfront Regeneration Trust to oversee the future of the Toronto Waterfront. One of the recommendations from public consultations was to create a connected recreational pathway along the entire length of Lake Ontario.

In 1995, a 350 km (217 mi) route was opened, providing a signed route on roads and trails between Stoney Creek (Hamilton) and Trenton. Almost as soon as it was opened, nearby communities requested that the new pathway be extended, and plans have been revised to lengthen the Waterfront Trail to 740 km (460 mi).

In 2007, the trail was connected to the Quebec border, and in 2010, work began to add a section along the Lake Erie shore, adding an additional 600 km (373 mi). In 2013, the Lake Erie section was officially added, extending as far as Lake St. Clair. By 2015, with plans underway to extend the pathway to include Georgian Bay on Lake Huron, the Waterfront Regeneration Trust amended the name of the trail, adding "Great Lakes" to more accurately reflect its expanded areas of operation.

Today, the Great Lakes Waterfront Trail signed route is more than 3,000 km (1,864 mi) long, with new connections being added continuously. Some of its newest routes are between Sudbury and Sault Ste. Marie, almost connecting with Lake Superior. Although only twenty-one percent of its total is currently on off-road pathways, every year community partners improve and upgrade their sections, adding more pathways. The Great Lakes Waterfront Trail is truly one of Canada's greatest Great Trail projects.

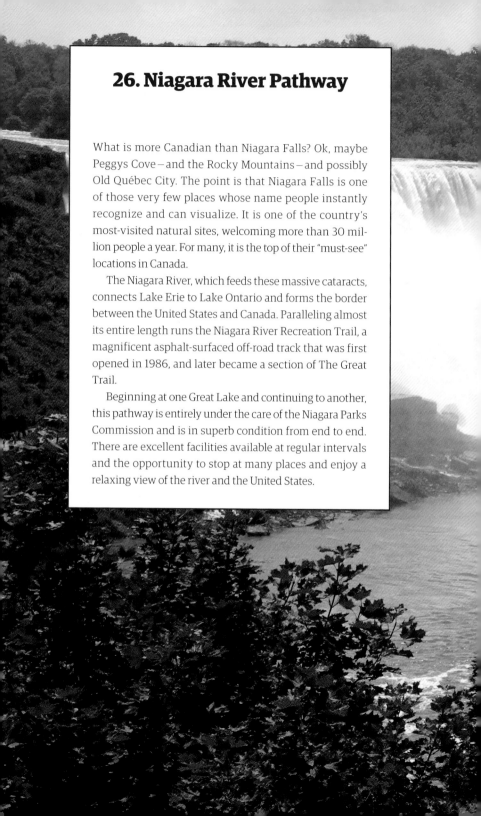

26. Niagara River Pathway

What is more Canadian than Niagara Falls? Ok, maybe Peggys Cove – and the Rocky Mountains – and possibly Old Québec City. The point is that Niagara Falls is one of those very few places whose name people instantly recognize and can visualize. It is one of the country's most-visited natural sites, welcoming more than 30 million people a year. For many, it is the top of their "must-see" locations in Canada.

The Niagara River, which feeds these massive cataracts, connects Lake Erie to Lake Ontario and forms the border between the United States and Canada. Paralleling almost its entire length runs the Niagara River Recreation Trail, a magnificent asphalt-surfaced off-road track that was first opened in 1986, and later became a section of The Great Trail.

Beginning at one Great Lake and continuing to another, this pathway is entirely under the care of the Niagara Parks Commission and is in superb condition from end to end. There are excellent facilities available at regular intervals and the opportunity to stop at many places and enjoy a relaxing view of the river and the United States.

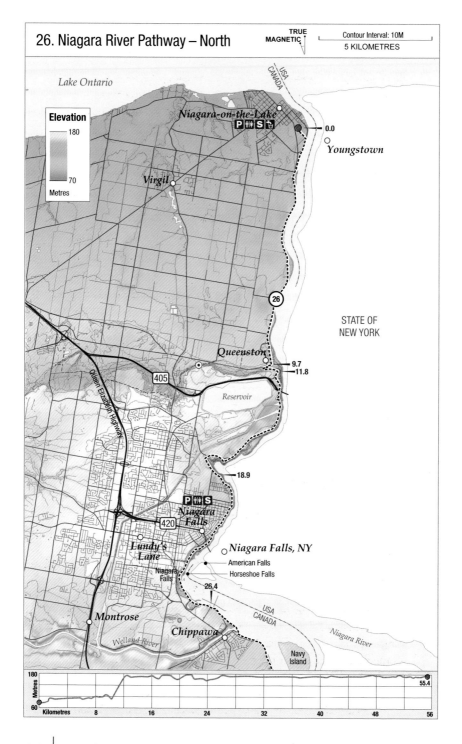

26. Niagara River Pathway – North

TRUE MAGNETIC

Contour Interval: 10M
5 KILOMETRES

Lake Ontario

Elevation

180

70

Metres

Niagara-on-the-Lake

P ♿ S ⚓

0.0

Youngstown

Virgil

26

STATE OF
NEW YORK

Queenston

9.7
11.8

Reservoir

Queen Elizabeth Highway

405

18.9

P ♿ S

Niagara
Falls

420

Lundy's
Lane

Niagara Falls, NY

American Falls

Horseshoe Falls

Niagara
Falls

26.4

USA
CANADA

Montrose

Chippawa

Welland River

Navy
Island

Niagara River

180
Metres
60
Kilometres   8   16   24   32   40   48   56

55.4

26. Niagara River Pathway

Distance: 55.4 km (34.4 mi) – one way
Ascent: 399 m (1,309 ft)
Descent: 307 m (1,007 ft)

Trail conditions: asphalt
Cellphone coverage: yes
Hazards: high usage, poison ivy, road crossings, ticks

Permitted Uses							
Walking	Biking	Horseback Riding	Inline Skating	ATV	Snowshoeing	Cross-country Skiing	Snowmobiling
✔	✔	—	✔*	—	✔	✔	—

Finding the trailhead: You begin this trip at the corner of the Fort George National Historic Site parking area where it comes closest to the asphalt pathway. The wooden ramparts of the fort are directly ahead; to the right is a large modern-looking picnic pavilion with washrooms and water.

Trailhead: 43°15'04.3"N, 79°03'49"W (Start — Fort George)
42°53'31.9"N, 78°55'21.4"W (Finish — Fort Erie)

Observations: I rode this route on one of the hottest days of the year, when the humidex reading was above 40°C. There is very little shade, and I roasted in the hot sun. I could never have completed this ride without having the Niagara River nearby to stick my head in and cool off. Based on my experience, I recommend riding this route when the temperature is more moderate.

It also takes much longer to complete than its distance suggests. Because of the crowds at Niagara Falls, you must walk for a considerable distance, and slowly at that. I required the entire, long, summer day for the return ride, and I did not linger in any spot for long. This might best be undertaken as a two-day trip; I would have enjoyed it more if I had had the time to relax and explore more of the sights.

Route description: The path crosses through a large field for about 500 m/yd before crossing Ricardo Street. Once across, it curves right, and there is the Niagara River with some picnic tables overlooking it. There are excellent views as the trail remains near the river. Tables and benches are frequent in this well-maintained area, which resembles an urban park with large, individual trees scattered through an area of closely clipped, grass-covered lawn.

At 1.3 km (0.8 mi), near a large parking area at McFarland Point, there is a

trail junction featuring a large map. There is also a sign indicating that this is an access point for the Bruce Trail, a more than 890 km (553 mi) hiking trail that follows the Niagara Escarpment to the shores of Lake Huron. The Bruce's blue rectangle navigation markers join with Niagara River Pathway and Waterfront Trail markers on signposts along the route.

The paved Niagara River Pathway continues straight ahead, joined shortly by the Niagara River Parkway to the right. Parking areas are frequent, as are picnic tables, barbeque pits, and benches to accommodate visitors. At 2.1 km (1.3 mi), there is a bicycle rental shop, and 300 m/yd later, the path crosses its first bridge. About 150 m/yd beyond that is a very large parking area and the McFarland House Historical Landmark. On the far side of the road, perhaps of more interest to some, is the entrance to a winery.

At this point, trail and road parallel each other with the park a slender edge of land beside the river. Many large houses line the road, and the occasional farm market and winery provide opportunities for diversion. There are excellent views of the river, with wooden fences along the viewing areas.

At 5.9 km (3.7 mi), the trail briefly connects to and follows Service Road 60. For the first time, there are houses on your left, but this populated interval is brief, and the off-road path resumes 200 m/yd later. Shortly after this, the trail reaches an enormous picnic ground – Browns Point – with two parking areas. Once past this larger area of parkland, the narrow path resumes, remaining close to the road.

Houses, almost palatial in size, resume on the left at 8.4 km (5.2 mi) with driveways to be crossed. Within 200 m/yd, the pathway seems more like a sidewalk with no greenspace remaining between road and residences.

9.7 km (6 mi) The off-road pathway ends at the intersection with Queenston Street. Turn left on this well-signed, quiet, residential street and follow as it descends then begins to climb quite markedly. Queenston Street is lined with attractive, old, stone residences, and historic plaques are frequent.

The route continues straight, crossing several other streets before turning right at the Mackenzie Printery (and Museum) at 10.6 km (6.6 mi). Just before Queenston Street reconnects to the Parkway, 200 m/yd later, an off-road path turns left. This continues uphill another 100 m/yd, crossing York Street then the Parkway. Oddly, there are no crosswalks.

Once across the Niagara Parkway, the path/sidewalk continues along York Road for less than 100 m/yd before turning left into a thickly forested area. The trail continues to ascend steeply, winding left in a tight curve up the hillside. It emerges from the forest at a traffic circle where you should stop.

11.8 km (7.3 mi) A plaque identifies this spot on the lip of the Niagara Escarpment as Roy Terrace. To the left, across the Parkway, is a viewing platform overlooking the river from high above. To the right, higher still and somewhat distant but tastefully framed by flanking trees, is the columnar Brock's Monument. This is Queenston Heights, scene of one of the most well-known battles of the War of 1812. Roy Terrace also marks the southernmost point of the Bruce Trail, the beginning – or end – of its long journey.

The pathway continues, crossing the Niagara Parkway 150 m/yd later and the entrance to the Locust Grove Picnic Area in another 150 m/yd. Parkway and pathway resume their parallel journey, though now through parkland edged with towering oaks. At 12.7 km (7.9 mi), both pass underneath the massive Lewiston-Queenston Bridge, after which the pathway enters a large parking lot. For a bit more than 350 m/yd, trail becomes parking area before the pathway resumes.

To the right, considerable electrical infrastructure is visible, and when you reach the top of a large dam at 13.3 km (8.3 mi), banks of electrical wires pass overhead. For 700 m/yd, your route passes the industrial behemoths of the Sir Adam Beck Generating Stations before rejoining the world of nature. This is a fascinating area, where the trail runs along the lip of the river gorge. Below the escarpment lies the river, hemmed in by steep cliffs and lined on both banks by enormous dams and generating stations.

Briefly traversing another parking lot next to a picnic viewpoint, the trail meanders through what is signed as a "remnant Chinquapin Oak savanna." This tree species (*Quercus muehlenbergii*) is common in the eastern and southern US, but in Canada is only found in a few sites in southern Ontario. There are occasional views of the deep gorge to the left.

At 15.1 km (9.4 mi), the trail crosses the Parkway into a busy large parking lot. The path turns left, crossing the entrance to the Butterfly Conservancy and passing the resplendent grounds of the Niagara Commission's School of Horticulture

and Botanical Gardens. The trail is more like a sidewalk through here and is quite busy with pedestrian traffic. There are substantial areas of flowering plants, fountains, and . . . mini-golf!

At 16.2 km (10 mi), the trail crosses the Parkway once again. To the left, for those who wish to hike, is the Niagara Glen Nature Reserve with its maze of footpaths descending the gorge to the river below. On the rim of the ravine, the pathway continues to Thompson's Point, 700 m/yd away. This busy viewpoint, situated at a bend in the river, has so many people milling about that it likely reduces your speed to a crawl. From here, the trail winds around the river with numerous side paths disappearing into the woods to the left.

18.9 km (11.7 mi) The pathway reaches the parking area for the Whirlpool Aero Car—an antique cable car that travels over the river above the Niagara Whirlpool. The pathway essentially ends here, although a short connection resumes on the opposite end of this busy site. Within 300 m/yd, the bicycle path connects to the sidewalk and also ends.

Your route must now pass through the community of Niagara Falls, quite possibly the busiest tourism site in Canada. To quote the Niagara Falls Tourism website: "sidewalks are present for the entire distance, so it is possible to walk your bicycle from the Whirlpool Aero Car crossing right past Niagara Falls and resume active cycling in Chippawa. Cycling along the roadway on the Niagara Parkway is also possible, but not recommended for inexperienced cyclists or children."

I cycled on the road until passing beneath the Rainbow Bridge at 22.4 km (13.9 mi). After that, I found the traffic was too dangerous and walked my bicycle through thickening crowds until I was well past Horseshoe Falls. In fact, to reach the prime viewing site at the falls, I had to leave my bicycle chained to a tree because there were too many people to wheel it on the sidewalk.

Everyone, pedestrians and motorists alike, is distracted here. Cycling on the road through this frenzied and chaotic area is challenging, to say the least, and probably unwise. Take your time in this section because there is much to see, including both sets of waterfalls.

26.4 km (16.4 mi) At the International Control Dam, I resumed cycling on the pathway. Before this point, a walkway made of paving stones traces the shoreline and is usually busy. However, by the time I reached the dam, there were few people walking, so I felt comfortable bicycling again.

The trail continues alongside the Niagara River, which is far wider above than it was below the falls. At 27.8 km (17.3 mi), the pathway crosses a bridge atop a water-control dam across the mouth of the Welland River. When you reach the far side 300 m/yd later, you have reached the community of Chippawa.

After crossing the Parkway, the trail turns left and resumes its interrupted passage through parkland. This is a lovely, tranquil section, the gently curving pathway now at river level and with much more greenspace, bordered by cedar-rail fences.

At 30.4 km (18.9 mi), the trail reaches the site of the Battle of Chippawa, where there are interpretive panels, benches, flags, and monuments. The relaxing ride continues on a virtually flat pathway, placidly following the Niagara River through pleasant parkland. There are occasional road crossings and several places where the pathway merges with a service road for a short distance. Every few kilometres, there is a picnic site alongside the river, providing an opportunity to access the water.

After crossing Weaver Road at 32.6 km (20.1 mi), the trail passes the tiny Willoughby Historical Museum, which features cold drinks – and an air-conditioned washroom! That, plus several picnic tables strategically placed below leafy, shade trees, encourages stopping.

Once past Weaver Road, the sections on service roads lengthen, but this rarely detracts from the ride. Houses are always to the right, and the quiet service roads only access these residences. Sluggish Boyer Creek is spanned by an attractive bridge at 36.5 km (22.7 mi). At 38.5 km (23.9 mi), the trail passes large Riverside Campground with its playground, motel, and mini-golf.

At 39 km (24.2 mi), the trail shares the road bridge over Black Creek, but on its own dedicated portion. At Baker Creek, 1.7 km (1.1 mi) further on, there is a separate bridge for the trail that provides an excellent view of the creek. I saw two species of turtle, leopard frogs, and bullfrogs. Neither road nor trail is very busy.

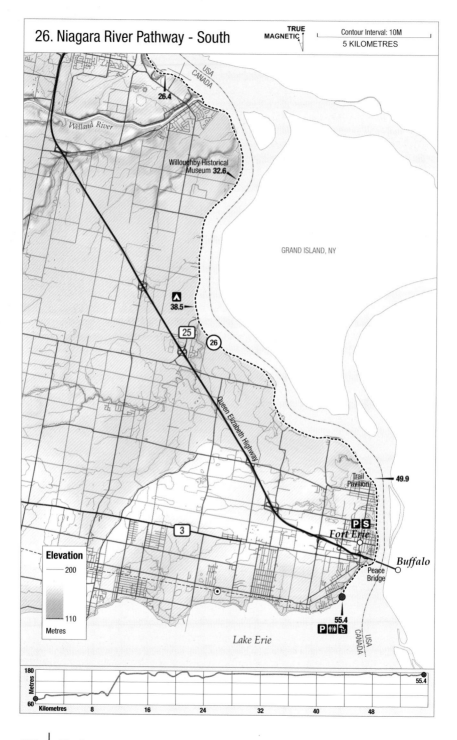

26. Niagara River Pathway - South

TRUE
MAGNETIC

Contour Interval: 10M
5 KILOMETRES

USA
CANADA

26.4

Welland River

Willoughby Historical
Museum 32.6

GRAND ISLAND, NY

38.5

25

26

Queen Elizabeth Highway

Trail
Pavilion

49.9

P S
Fort Erie

Buffalo

Peace
Bridge

3

Elevation
200

110
Metres

55.4
P

Lake Erie

USA
CANADA

180
Metres
55.4

60
Kilometres   8   16   24   32   40   48

One kilometre blends into the next as the trail follows the gently curving Chippawa Channel of the Niagara River, with the rural or wooded shoreline of Grand Island on the far shore. At 44.1 km (27.4 mi), the pathway reaches the bucolic grounds of the Niagara Christian Collegiate, crossing Miller Creek 300 m/yd later. Just 500 m/yd beyond that, the small Miller's Creek Marina, where there is a restaurant/store, is across the Parkway on the left.

As the trail climbs above Grand Island, the high-rises of Buffalo come into view. After 45.3 km (28.1 mi), the trail begins sharing space with Service Road 4-N and the sections of pure off-road pathway become less frequent. After crossing Thompson Road at 47.1 km (29.3 mi), the next stretch follows Frenchman's Road, where you see massive industrial buildings dominating the Buffalo shoreline.

Frenchman's Creek is crossed at 48.7 km (30.1 mi), and Anger Avenue is 350 m/yd later. From here, the trail alternates between travelling off-road and running beside the road like a sidewalk. After crossing Central Avenue, another 650 m/yd further, the pathway has clearly reached the community of Fort Erie. Here, the Niagara Parkway changes its name to Niagara Boulevard.

49.9 km (31 mi) The trail reaches a small park where there is a full-size trail pavilion, flanked by benches and a discovery panel. From here, your route continues alongside Niagara Boulevard, with the wide pathway/sidewalk continuing for an additional 900 m/yd. However, once you pass beneath the railway bridge that crosses into the US, the dedicated pathway ends.

Continue along Niagara Boulevard as it passes through downtown Fort Erie. Walkers may use the sidewalk; cyclists remain on the road. At the intersection of Queen Street and Niagara Boulevard at 53 km (32.9 mi), the off-road pathway resumes on the left. There is a map here and another large area of well-trimmed greenspace.

This lovely area is called Mather Park. The asphalt pathway weaves through the grass towards the river, crossing beneath the Peace Bridge after 250 m/yd. A charming, stone wall lines the riverbank, with the buildings of Buffalo on the opposite shore. Directly ahead, the river widens as it merges with Lake Erie. Benches are positioned to view the water, usually in the shade of a towering hardwood.

♀ 55.4 km (34.4 mi) You arrive at the junction of the Niagara River Recreation Trail and the Friendship Trail, just across the road from Fort Erie, where there is sign marking the transition. At the fort, there are a parking area, benches, and a Visitor's Centre where you can refill your water bottle. You probably want a rest before you begin the long return to Fort George at Niagara-on-the-Lake.

Further Information:
Bruce Trail: http://brucetrail.org
Fort George National Historic Site: www.pc.gc.ca/en/lhn-nhs/on/fortgeorge
Niagara Falls Tourism: www.niagarafallstourism.com
Niagara Parks Commission: www.niagaraparks.com

A Military Frontier

Though currently peaceful neighbours and international allies for more than a century, Canada and the United States were not always friends. During the War of Independence, 1776-1783, and the War of 1812, they were on opposite sides, as Canada chose to remain loyal to the British Crown.

During the War of 1812, no part of the common frontier was more bitterly contested than the Niagara Peninsula. Several times during the conflict, American invasion forces attempted to seize this important area, control of which would have permitted them to dominate trade and settlement of the upper Great Lakes. Significant battles were fought at Queenston Heights, Stoney Creek, and Lundy's Lane, and both Fort George and Fort Erie changed hands more than once.

National Historic Sites and monuments related to the War of 1812 can be found throughout the Niagara Peninsula, and at many points along the recreational trail. They add an additional dimension to the natural wonders found along this route and are worth stopping for and exploring.

Her Majesty's Royal Chapel of the Mohawks

After the American War of Independence, many of the displaced Iroquois or Haudenosaunee peoples, who had been allies of the British, chose to be resettled near present-day Brantford. Their community, the Six Nations of the Grand River, is the most populous First Nations Reserve in Canada today.

By the 1780s, many Haudenosaunee had become Christians. To minister to their needs, the British built a chapel for the new community in what was, at that time, land unsettled by Europeans. Originally named St. Paul's, it became the first Protestant church in Upper Canada and is now the oldest surviving church in Ontario. It is one of two Royal Chapels in North America but the only one located on a First Nation Territory. In 1850, the remains of Joseph Brant or Thayendanegea, for whom the City of Brantford is named, were moved to a tomb located next to the Chapel. In 1999, the site became a National Historic Site of Canada.

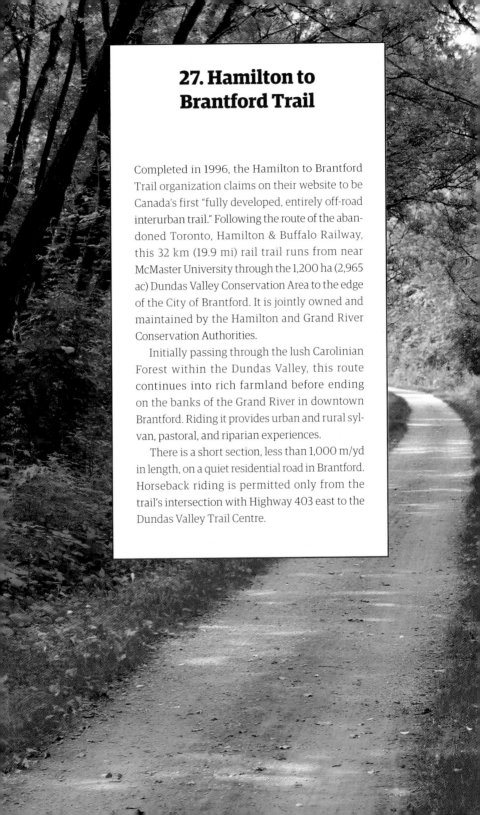

27. Hamilton to Brantford Trail

Completed in 1996, the Hamilton to Brantford Trail organization claims on their website to be Canada's first "fully developed, entirely off-road interurban trail." Following the route of the abandoned Toronto, Hamilton & Buffalo Railway, this 32 km (19.9 mi) rail trail runs from near McMaster University through the 1,200 ha (2,965 ac) Dundas Valley Conservation Area to the edge of the City of Brantford. It is jointly owned and maintained by the Hamilton and Grand River Conservation Authorities.

Initially passing through the lush Carolinian Forest within the Dundas Valley, this route continues into rich farmland before ending on the banks of the Grand River in downtown Brantford. Riding it provides urban and rural sylvan, pastoral, and riparian experiences.

There is a short section, less than 1,000 m/yd in length, on a quiet residential road in Brantford. Horseback riding is permitted only from the trail's intersection with Highway 403 east to the Dundas Valley Trail Centre.

27. Hamilton to Brantford Trail

TRUE
MAGNETIC

Contour Interval: 30M
10 KILOMETRES

Elevation
280
60
Metres

27. Hamilton to Brantford Trail

Distance: 39.1 km (24.3 mi) – one way
Ascent: 278 m (912 ft)
Descent: 175 m (574 ft)

Trail conditions: crushed stone
Cellphone coverage: yes
Hazards: poison ivy, road crossings, ticks

Permitted Uses							
Walking	Biking	Horseback Riding	Inline Skating	ATV	Snowshoeing	Cross-country Skiing	Snowmobiling
✔	✔	✔*	—	—	✔	✔	—

Finding the trailhead: The Hamilton to Brantford Rail Trail begins at Ewan Road, where there is a "km 0" sign. Although there is no parking here, 100 m/yd further on the left is a side track to a large dedicated trailhead parking area beneath several overhead powerlines.

Trailhead: 43°15'22" N, 79°55'54.8" W (Start — Hamilton)
43°08'10.7" N, 80°16'02.9" W (Finish — Brant's Crossing)

Observations: This was a delightful, easy ride along a well-maintained rail trail. I experienced no difficulties anywhere along the route, except for deciding where to end it. When I arrived in Brantford, at the trailhead of the Hamilton to Brantford Trail, I thought that it appeared to be neither near services nor close to anything particularly interesting, so I continued riding.

It is rather uncomfortable to deviate from your plan and to ride into the unknown, even if that unknown is a Canadian city. I had no idea at that point where the trail might lead me because I had not researched it in advance. But I continued, looking for a "destination." I found it – after an additional 7 km (4.3 mi) – at Brant's Crossing, with its trail pavilion and nearby facilities.

Route description: Because of the thick vegetation bordering the pathway, it is difficult to see the adjacent buildings, even though this is a heavily urbanized area. At 350 m/yd, where the trail crosses above busy Main Street, they become more apparent. However, there is an interesting ravine crossing, where a pedestrian bridge remains at grade and a parallel bike path dips low to cross tiny Coldwater Creek before climbing up the far bank. Called Powers Crossing, this is the steepest climb of the entire route.

Though a large shopping centre is just to the right, little can be seen through the trees when you pass through a gate at 750 m/yd. Shortly afterwards, houses can be seen on both sides of the path through a buffer of dense vegetation. Just after the km 1 signpost is Little John Park with benches, tennis courts, and open space.

The first road crossing is at 1.5 km (0.9 mi) at Lynden Avenue. At each crossing, there are elaborate gates and trail signs designed to resemble railway crossing signals. Old Ancaster Road is crossed 400 m/yd later. By this point, it is clear that the trail is very gently ascending, although it is likely only your legs notice.

Benches are scattered along the route, and informal footpaths connect from the neighbouring residential areas. By 2.3 km (1.4 mi), however, there is only the deep, wooded ravine of Spring Creek to the right. The trees bordering the pathway are often very tall and spread a welcome, shady canopy overhead.

The first map is at the km 3 signpost, which indicates that the adjacent lands belong to the Dundas Valley Conservation Area (DVCA) and that maintained footpaths connect. Just beyond this, Sanctuary Park is to the right, with playgrounds and washrooms; the vehicle access road crosses the trail at 3.3 km (2.1 mi). After this small greenspace, the deep ravine resumes along the trail to the right. Within

sight of the km 4 marker, a large sign announces your entry into the DVCA. The trail is visibly climbing by this point, and the adjacent benches begin to look more appealing.

⚲ 5.5 km (3.4 mi) You arrive at the Dundas Valley Trail Centre with its replica Victorian-era railway station, complete with a section of railway track on which there are two old railway cars. The centre is the hub for trail activities within the conservation area and features interpretive panels and displays, washrooms, maps, and even a seasonal canteen. Horseback riding is permitted on the rail trail from this location as far as 26 km (16.2 mi). Benches and picnic tables are scattered throughout the grounds, and a veritable labyrinth of trails head into the forest in every direction.

Nearly straight since its start, the trail begins the first of a series of long curves as it climbs the steepest part of the Niagara Escarpment. Sulphur Springs Road is crossed at 6.1 km (3.8 mi), and there are a few houses nearby, but the trail very quickly enters another isolated area full of small hills and gullies.

Mineral Springs Road is crossed – for the first time – at 7.4 km (4.6 mi) and 500 m/yd later on a bridge above the Gravel Pit Road (dirt). After making a broad curve to the right, the trail again recrosses Mineral Springs Road at 8.2 km (5.1 mi). Fortunately, there is a map at the road with the road name of each crossing prominently displayed on the trail signs.

After paralleling Mineral Springs Road for several hundred metres/yards, Binkley Road is crossed at a diagonal intersection at 9 km (5.6 mi). A bench sits on the far side. As you ride through this lovely, wooded area, which reminded me of an English country lane, the trail begins to curve left rather languidly. About 350 m/yd later, just before crossing Old Route 99, it reaches the first dedicated parking area since the trailhead.

The long, climbing curve continues with farmland visible on the left. Another of the infrequent benches is passed, as is the km10 marker. Turning almost 180°, the trail recrosses Old Route 99 at 10.6 km (6.6 mi). Still climbing through some wet areas, the pathway crosses dirt-covered Slote Road in sight of Mineral Springs Road on the left at 11.7 km (7.3 mi).

The path shifts to a gradual right turn with the uphill grade significantly lessening. At 12.3 km (7.6 mi), you reach the summit of the long climb from Hamilton and Lake Ontario. There are several interpretive panels and an observation deck which overlooks . . . nothing, really, but thickly vegetated bog. However, this was the site of the historic Summit Station, though, today, only the foundations of the water tower remain.

9 12.9 km (8 mi) You arrive at a large trailhead parking area off a dirt road where there is a map in an interpretive information kiosk. Oddly, when the trail crosses busy Highway 52 only 150 m/yd further, there is a second parking area – though no kiosk.

The climb is over, and instead of solid forests, farmland borders both sides of the trail corridor, transforming the scenery into something more pastoral. At 14.8 km (9.2 mi), the grounds of a large golf course begin on the left and are adjacent to the trail for more than 500 m/yd.

A copse of gorgeous, tall hardwoods follows, but only for about 400 m/yd, ending where there is another bench. Large areas of cultivated fields stretch away on both sides as the trail makes a slight turn right and enters into another long straightaway.

The pathway arrives at Field Road at 18.2 km (11.3 mi). To the left is the small community of Jerseyville, with a convenience store and a sidewalk that ends at the trail. The pathway continues along the edge of the community until it reaches the next road 600 m/yd later.

9 18.8 km (11.2 mi) The trail crosses the Jerseyville Road, and the trail management changes to the Grand River Conservation Authority. The signage, kilometre markers, and even the gates at road crossings are different. Just after crossing the road, there is a large parking area to the right.

For the first time, significant portions of the route are without any vegetative cover as the route passes through sizable fields, many of which are cultivated almost to the edge of the trail. Gravel-surfaced Parsonage Road is crossed at 21.1 km (13.1 mi) and equally modest Ranch Road at 22.9 km (14.2 mi). Fortunately, there are several shady sections on this flat, straight stretch. There are also numerous crossings for farm equipment.

About 700 m/yd later, you reach a large lawn area with a pond. This is not a park but the private grounds of a large house visible beyond the pond; do not trespass. The trail crosses the Jerseyville Road once again after 300 m/yd. A large greenhouse facility is on the left.

The trail curves left, descending until the barrier blocking Highway 403 at 25.7 km (16 mi). This new highway is built over the former railbed, so the trail is forced to turn right and drop down almost into Fairchild Creek, where a sign warns that the trail is closed when flooded (seems rather obvious). The route passes beneath Highway 403 then curves sharply left and climbs back uphill.

26.1 km (16.2 mi) The diverted path reconnects to the original route of the rail-bed, where there is a bench. This is the end of the section where horseback riders are permitted. Immediately afterwards, the path briefly becomes a gorgeous laneway flanked by tall trees, which provide excellent shade. But farmland soon reappears, and it seems that farm machinery uses the rickety bridge 900 m/yd later.

There is a small parking area at the Papple Road at 27.8 km (17.3 mi) and more houses nearby. The trail crosses a small wetland, after which it passes beneath another road 850 m/yd later. A "Welcome to Brantford" sign is found almost immediately on the other side. New houses are located quite close to the trail, which then passes beneath a railroad bridge and another road – almost a tun-nel – at 29.6 km (18.4 mi).

From here, the path is actually alongside the Grand River on the left, but it is invisible through the thick vegetation. After manoeuvring around some new houses and their access roads, and down a surprisingly abrupt descent – caused when a 1986 landslide wiped out the railway embankment – the trail crosses Beach Road at 31 km (19.3 mi). The road and houses are now all on the right with river and floodplains to the left.

31.2 km (19.4 mi) You arrive at the Brantford terminus of the Hamilton to Brantford Rail Trail. There is a parking area, a substantial trailhead kiosk with maps, and several interpretive panels. Continue straight, crossing Mohawk Street in the crosswalk, then turning left and following the sidewalk over the bridge.

On the opposite side of the bridge, the off-road path resumes to the right, par-alleling the stream. This is also known as the Tom Longboat section. At 32.1 km (20 mi), it crosses Greenwich Street, after which it moves away from the water. Curving left, the trail reaches Mohawk Road – next to an appallingly malodour-ous sewage-treatment facility – in another 700 m/yd.

The path turns right and parallels the road for another 250 m/yd before cross-ing. It then climbs up and onto the top of a grass-covered dike, where it turns right again. This is a lovely section, open with sweeping views of agricultural lands adjacent to the Grand River.

33.4 km (20.8 mi) The trail arrives at the Mohawk Chapel, where there is an entrance from the path. There are large grounds surrounding the small chapel with picnic tables, benches, and interpretive panels. The pathway continues on top of its earthen berm, crossing Birkett Lane twice, with Bellview Park and the large John Wright Soccer Complex in between.

The trail continues atop the embankment while it passes alongside cultivated fields. At Erie Avenue, 35.3 km (21.9 mi), the signage is excellent, including num-erous interpretive panels and particularly a large map of the City of Brantford

Trails. The dike-top trail continues its constantly veering route, crossing Birkett Lane a final time before ending at River Road at 37 km (23 mi).

The off-road path ends here. Turn right and either cycle along the quiet street or walk on the sidewalk on the river side of the road, which is lined with a waist-high concrete wall. At Baldwin Avenue, 150 m/yd later, a steel guardrail lines the street side of the sidewalk, so it might be possible to bike. The city map indicates that you follow River Road until its intersection with Strathcona Avenue at 37.8 km (23.5 mi). At this point, the off-road pathway obviously separates from the street next to a couple of benches.

At a trail junction 300 m/yd later, just after the km 38 marker, turn left. Rivergreen Park is to the right, and after crossing beneath the Veterans Memorial Parkway through a 1.9 m (6.2 ft) high passage, you reach Earl Haig Family Fun Park with its pool and waterslides. It must be packed with families on a hot summer day. At the next junction, where there is brightly coloured exercise equipment, turn right; the sign indicates that Brant's Crossing is only 500 m/yd distant.

Downtown Brantford does not have many tall buildings, so you really are not certain you are there until 100 m/yd further, when your route turns left and crosses a railway track. Though it looks long unused, this elaborate gated rail crossing requires dismounting your bike and carrying it across. From here, the asphalt path continues alongside the river, passing the Civic Centre, which is a parking area for the trail, and Casino Brantford.

39.1 km (24.3 mi) The trail reaches Brant's Crossing. Sitting slightly below the trail on the right is a full-size Trail Pavilion and directly ahead stands a large building surrounded by gardens where several trails converge. At the large building are washrooms and a water fountain. A skatepark is beside it, and restaurants can be found nearby. If you turn left and walk past the flowers, you can walk onto a bridge that spans the Grand River that has nice views. This is an excellent place to have lunch or even just a short break before returning to Hamilton – on a route which is mostly downhill.

Further Information:
City of Brantford Trails: www.brantford.ca/residents/leisurerecreation/parkstrails
Grand River Conservation Authority: www.grandriver.ca
Hamilton Conservation Authority: https://conservationhamilton.ca
Mohawk Chapel: http://mohawkchapel.ca

Monarchs and Milkweed

Probably the most well-known North American butterfly, the monarch also undertakes the continent's longest insect migration. Starting in the spring from northern Mexico and the southern United States, these fragile 0.5 g (0.02 oz) butterflies travel thousands of kilometres to Canada where several generations reproduce in the summer and early fall.

The health of this beautiful butterfly's population depends on the availability of milkweed plants. The monarch caterpillars eat only milkweed because it produces a toxin that defends them from predators, and adult monarchs lay their eggs on the underside of milkweed leaves.

Turkey Vulture

If you sight a large bird circling overhead, seemingly floating on the wind currents with only minimal beating of its wings, the chances are good that this is a turkey vulture. If so, a quick glance through binoculars reveals its conspicuous bald and bright-red head. Even if you cannot see its head, the shallow V-shape of the vulture's wings as it soars — sometimes for hours — is almost as distinctive.

One of the few birds in North America with a highly developed sense of smell, the turkey vulture relies both on its powerful nose and its keen eyesight to search out food. Contrary to popular belief, however, circling vultures do not necessarily indicate the presence of a dead or dying animal.

28. Chrysler Canada Greenway

The Chrysler Canada Greenway, named after the donor that made its development possible, is the southernmost section of The Great Trail, extending from the southern outskirts of Windsor to Ruthven, near Leamington, Ontario. Owned and maintained by the Essex Region Conservation Authority, the Greenway opened in 1997. It initially was 42 km (26.1 mi) long, but in recent years, additional pieces and connections have been added so that more than 50 km (31.1 mi) of pathway is available. As a connective corridor, the Greenway links 25 separate natural areas and passes through 3 watersheds.

The trail is surfaced with crushed stone throughout its length and has excellent signposting at every road crossing. Benches are scattered at irregular intervals along the entire route. Hikers and bikers have unrestricted access, but horseback riding is only permitted between South Talbot Road and Concession Road 4 on the north-south section, Ferris Side Road, and McCain Road between Harrow and Kingsville.

28. Chrysler Canada Greenway

TRUE MAGNETIC

Contour Interval: 5M
5 KILOMETRES

P S 35.8

McGregor

Essex

New Canaan

12

Marshfield

3

Elevation
225
170
Metres

P S i 21.9

23

20

Harrow

28

Cedar Creek

P i 14.1

P 0.0

Road 3 E

Arner

Kingsville

Ruthven

New California

6.3
P S

Lake Erie

220
Metres
160
Kilometres   4   8   12   16   20   24   28   32   35.8

28. Chrysler Canada Greenway

Distance: 35.8 km (22.2 mi)
– one way
Ascent: 45 m (148 ft)
Descent: 68 m (223 ft)

Trail conditions: crushed stone
Cellphone coverage: yes
Hazards: poison ivy, road crossings, ticks

Permitted Uses							
Walking	Biking	Horseback Riding	Inline Skating	ATV	Snowshoeing	Cross-country Skiing	Snowmobiling
✔	✔	✔*	—	—	✔	✔	—

Finding the trailhead: The path begins from the southwest corner of the parking lot of Colasanti's Tropical Gardens — a year-round restaurant, greenhouse, arcade, zoo, garden, and all-round family-friendly activity centre. The trailhead is not well marked; in fact, the sign was knocked down and leaning on a rock next to the dumpster when I was there. (I am confident that was only a temporary issue.) A km 43 marker is beside the short laneway that connects to the road.

Trailhead: 42°03'45.8" N, 82°40'39.8" W (Start — Colasanti's)
42°08'33.9" N, 82°58'11.5" W (Finish — McGregor)

Observations: This was a remarkably easy ride, nearly flat and on a treadway in excellent condition. Unfortunately, I enjoyed this trail the least of any of the eastern Canadian routes because it is essentially a long ride through a rather monotonous agricultural landscape. In addition, it seems to begin nowhere and end at no particular place either, so it was disappointing in that manner. Future plans include connecting the Chrysler Canada Greenway with the City of Windsor, where there is a wonderful trail along the shore of the Detroit River. Adding that new section substantially lengthens this route and should significantly increase the pleasure for trail users.

Route description: From the parking lot, the path immediately crosses Road 3 E and turns left at Peterson Lane. The pathway runs beside the road past Colasanti's massive greenhouses and connects to the main trail after 900 m/yd. The signage here is excellent, even mentioning the distance to the next community, Kingsville.

Turn right, cross Peterson Lane, and go through the narrow passage between gate and signpost. The trail is straight and lined by thick, leafy vegetation, which is quite dense but not very high, so there is no overhead shade. It almost appears as if the path is lined by hedges.

The area through which you are passing is almost entirely dedicated to agricultural production, and the lands adjacent to the trail are either cultivated or boast enormous greenhouses. Yet this development can only be dimly sensed in the protected natural corridor bisecting the county thanks to the thick vegetation.

The crushed-stone pathway is without potholes or deep ruts, and often a strip of grass runs down the middle, breaking it naturally into two narrow lanes. The next road crossing at 2.1 km (1.3 mi) and the following one 200 m/yd further on, both cross roads on a diagonal. The second crossing, Graham Side Road, has a small parking area, and both have excellent signposts with road names and distance to the next community. Some also have GPS coordinates.

The long, straight corridor continues, rich farmlands visible from time to time, but mostly hidden by the trail's verdant screen. Aside from a few farm equipment crossings, the next break occurs at the Katz Side Road at 4.5 km (2.8 mi). This is a quiet country lane, with only a few farm buildings nearby. In contrast, County Road 20, 500 m/yd later, is very busy and has a large shopping centre on the right. The signposts say that 1.4 km (0.9 mi) remains to Kingsville; it appears you have already arrived.

Wigle Avenue is crossed at 5.5 km (3.4 mi), after which the trail begins a gentle curve to the right. Many more businesses are near the trail as you approach the town of Kingsville, followed by more residences.

At 6.2 km (3.9 mi), the pathway reaches a set of gates at a junction where a side path leads left and continues almost to the shore of Lake Erie and the Pelee Island Ferry Terminal. The lake is less than 1 km (0.6 mi) from the Greenway and is worth visiting.

6.3 km (3.9 mi) The trail arrives at the Kingsville Railway Station, which has been restored and is now a restaurant. It sits in the middle of open, grass-covered parkland and just past it is a large trailhead parking area. The trail crosses Lansdowne Street 100 m/yd from the parking lot. The trail passes through the small community, with a short section on Stewart Street on the road.

At the end of Stewart Street at 7.1 km (4.4 mi), the off-road path resumes. Within 100 m/yd, it crosses over Mill Brook on a high embankment and then crosses Heritage Road (County Road 50) at 7.5 km (4.7 mi). A new subdivision lines the trail for another 350 m/yd before Kingsville is left behind and the path is once again bordered by farmlands.

There is a crosswalk at the busy County Road 20 (West) at 8.5 km (5.3 mi), but none of the many cars that passed yielded to me; be cautious when crossing. The trail continues behind some houses for another 300 m/yd before it encounters something unusual – a detour. The trail turns left, leaves the railbed, and returns

Kingsville Railway Station

One of Canada's most famous entrepreneurs of the 19th century — who happened to be an American — was Hiram Walker, the creator of Canadian Club whisky. He lived and worked most of his life in Essex County, Ontario, and he was instrumental in the construction of the railroad that extended south from Walkerville to Kingsville, called the Lake Erie, Essex, and Detroit River Railway.

Walker hired a famous architect to design and build the train station in Kingsville, completed in 1889. It was one of the few stations of the time built of stone and featured a slate roof. Designed as a showcase, it included separate gentlemen's and ladies' waiting areas and a ticket office, as well as freight and baggage areas. Far in advance of its time, it was equipped with gas heating and lighting.

To complement this well-appointed train station, Walker built the grand Mattawas Hotel, on the shore of Lake Erie. This elegant resort no longer exists, but the train station was rebuilt in 2008 as a fine-dining establishment, maintaining its tasteful historic exterior.

to County Road 20 where it turns right in 150 m/yd — immediately beside the entrance to the Kingsville Golf and Country Club, the reason for the odd detour. The pathway, now mostly grass covered and quite uneven, parallels the road beside the golf club and crosses the entrance to a condominium development.

At 9.4 km (5.8 mi), the path makes a sharp right turn and returns to the railbed trail 350 m/yd later, now bordered by a high, chain-link fence to protect against flying golf balls. A deep ravine is to the left with a fence to keep cyclists from disappearing into the vegetation-choked gorge. For 350 m/yd, the route actually twists and turns a few times and undulates over some low knolls, making it the section of this route I enjoyed most.

Once back on the former railbed, the straight path resumes, and soon cultivated fields again dominate the surrounding landscape. At 10.1 km (6.3 mi), there is a discovery panel on the snapping turtle, placed there for no apparent reason. McCain Side Road is crossed 300 m/yd afterwards. From this point, horseback riding is permitted on the Greenway. And so it continues, farmland and equipment crossings with only minor variations, for the next several kilometres.

📍**14.1 km (8.8 mi)** The trail reaches the parking area for the Schwab Farm Trailhead at County Road 23. This site contains a bench, a garbage can, and an outhouse. Schwab Farm, or at least its large feed silo, sits next to the pathway. The straight, level track continues across the road.

Only 850 m/yd from this trailhead is the largest stream that the trail crosses, Cedar Creek. I found this area fascinating because of the thick mats of vegetation bordering the creek and dipping into the murky, slow-moving water. The word "bayou" sprang to mind as I watched the varied bird and amphibian life that populated this little river. Because it is so far south, many of the plants and birds are found almost nowhere else in Canada. Spend a few minutes with your binoculars on this embankment; you might see something you haven't seen before.

This pastoral passage continues unabated, although the treadway now shows the effect of horse travel. Cyclists can find this section somewhat bumpy. At 17.9 km (11.1 mi), McCormick Road is crossed, after which it is an uneventful ride to Ferris Road, the end point for horseback riding on the trail at 19.8 km (12.3 mi). Extended views across the low countryside are possible throughout this stretch.

At Ferris Road, a rare crosswalk is provided, possibly because of the Essex County Public Works facility next door. Very quickly the countryside returns to farmland with the occasional orchard for variation. Less than 2 km (1.2 mi) remains to Harrow, and buildings become visible as you approach, in particular a large new structure at 21.4 km (13.3 mi).

📍**21.9 km (13.6 mi)** You arrive at the Harrow Trailhead, where there is a small park with benches, picnic tables, an information kiosk with a map, and an outhouse. In sight across the road is an ice-cream shop and restaurant to the right. To your left is a bar. Harrow is a pleasant place to stop for a break or meal.

After crossing Queen Street in Harrow, the trail makes its only major turn, curving right to switch from running east-west to north-south. There are still a number of businesses to pass, including one mammoth Atlas Tube factory, but after you cross Concession Road 3, the Greenway is back into agricultural land. After Concession Road 4 at 24.1 km (15 mi), there is another crosswalk, and horseback riding is once again permitted, this time for the remainder of this route.

This route is unexciting but quite relaxing; attention needs to be focused on the flora and avian life rather than the landscape. Cornfields border the pathway, and there is no overhead shade, but interesting flowering bushes frequently occur alongside the path.

At County Road 11, 25.2 km (15.7 mi), there is another crosswalk. There is a small metal bridge 600 m/yd further on, where the trail crosses the Richmond Drain. On the far side, the path angles slightly left, now aimed directly towards the city of Windsor.

The trail continues through the rural countryside, the kilometres unrolling gently. At each road crossing, the signposts count down the distance remaining to McGregor. On the left around 30.4 km (18.9 mi), nearly hidden by sumac branches, is a discovery panel about the butternut hickory, the only one of the pecan-hickory trees that is native to Canada.

Just past County Road 12 at 31.4 km (19.5 mi) is another bridge, this one crossing the slow-moving, muddy Canard River and its gully. A bench is on the far side of this bridge. Once again, bird lovers should observe the thick vegetation crowding the tiny brook for new sightings; I observed a bittern, a green heron, and a rose-breasted grosbeak in just a few minutes.

The trail continues straight for another 3.1 km (1.9 mi) to the next important junction. Along the way, it crosses two more paved roads and passes another interpretive panel, this one about red foxes. In the final 800 m/yd, there is a horse track and then a golf course on the right.

At 34.6 km (21.5 mi), the Greenway intersects a cross trail. The main trail continues straight, and signposts identify each branch. Turn left and follow the side trail in the direction of McGregor, along the slightly rougher track of another abandoned railway.

This final section is an equally uneventful ride through mostly a wooded area. After about 800 m/yd, the houses of McGregor come into view. After another 250 m/yd, the path reaches Grondin Avenue, where a small greenspace begins.

35.8 km (22.2 mi) You arrive at the end of the trail where it intersects Walker Road (County Road 11). A single bench faces the road, and the last signpost provides the GPS coordinates. To the left, less than 100 m/yd away, is a family restaurant. Stay and eat, then begin the ride back to Colasanti's.

Further Information:
Colasanti's Tropical Gardens: www.colasanti.com
Essex Region Conservation Authority: http://erca.org/conservation-areas-events/conservation-areas/chrysler-canada-greenway

29. Kissing Bridge Trailway

Opened in 1998, the Kissing Bridge Trailway extends more than 45 km (28 mi) from the outskirts of Guelph to the small community of Millbank. It is one section of a Canadian Pacific rail line, which originally extended to the town of Goderich on the shore of Lake Huron. Community groups there are attempting to complete the trail along the entire length of the abandoned railway.

Originally purchased by the province as a future utility corridor, the County of Wellington and the Regional Municipality of Waterloo leased the railbed in 1997 to develop as a recreational trail. As is so common in Canada, development and maintenance was largely undertaken by community groups, notably: Conestogo-Winterbourne Optimist Club, Elmira Lions Club, Golden Triangle Snowmobile Association, Guelph Hiking Trail Club, and Linwood Lions Club.

This is a peaceful and easy trek through some stunningly beautiful farmland. The section of the trailway that is registered as part of The Great Trail includes the full 27 km (17 mi) plus from Guelph to Wallenstein. I decided that the section from the covered Kissing Bridge to Wallenstein, between two large rivers where bridges have been removed, captured the essential elements of the entire route and minimized the amount of time travelling on roads. When you are finished this route, be sure to stop, as I did, in the Lost Acres Variety Store in West Montrose, run by Old Order Mennonites. Their selection of fresh baked pastries is sure to tempt almost anyone.

29. Kissing Bridge Trailway

TRUE
MAGNETIC

Contour Interval: 10M
4 KILOMETRES

P 16.4

P 12.3

Wallenstein

19

P S 9.6

Elmira

29

22

86

21

Canagagigue Creek

2.3

23

Conestoga River

West Montrose

0.0

P S

Grand River

Elevation

390

320

Metres

29. Kissing Bridge Trailway

Distance: 16.4 km (10.2 mi) – one way
Ascent: 89 m (292 ft)
Descent: 49 m (161 ft)

Trail conditions: asphalt, crushed stone
Cellphone coverage: yes
Hazards: poison ivy, road crossings, ticks

Permitted Uses							
Walking	Biking	Horseback Riding	Inline Skating	ATV	Snowshoeing	Cross-country Skiing	Snowmobiling
✔	✔	—	—	—	✔	✔	—

Finding the trailhead: This route begins at a small park in West Montrose at the junction of Letson Drive and Rivers Edge Drive. This cute little greenspace provides garbage cans, picnic tables, and an outhouse, and includes both an interpretive panel and a map of the trailway.

Trailhead: 43°35'07.6" N, 80°28'47.9" W (Start — West Montrose)
43°36'10.1" N, 80°37'57.1" W (Finish — Wallenstein)

Observations: This was another easy and delightful ride through an area of primarily agricultural land. I actually rode much more of the trail than I finally used in this trail description, but the section between the Grand and Conestogo Rivers seemed to adequately capture the spirit of the entire route, and with the rail bridges on these rivers having been removed, they seemed obvious places to stop.

Naturally, I had to include the eponymous span in West Montrose, and fortunately, there is a delightful little park alongside it. Because of the relatively short distance of this route, I decided to do a round trip, starting and ending at this span.

Route description: The bridge is in sight to the left, but no off-road path connects to it, so you must walk or cycle on the road initially. Within 100 m/yd you are on the one-lane bridge – with no dedicated walkway – and crossing the Grand River. On the far side is the Lost Acres Variety store run by Old Order Mennonites, worth mentioning twice as a "must visit."

At 300 m/yd, the road forks; keep right on Covered Bridge Drive. This is a quiet residential street but has no sidewalks, so be cautious. It climbs to busy Township

The Kissing Bridge

The last covered bridge in Ontario and the oldest in Canada, the West Montrose Covered Bridge — the Kissing Bridge — was first built in 1881. It earned its name as the Kissing Bridge because young couples allegedly could steal a quick kiss in the relative privacy inside the structure. Supposedly, some horses knew to stop once inside the bridge without a command from their driver.

There have been several reconstructions over the decades; it needed to be significantly strengthened to safely accommodate automobile traffic. However, even when metal elements were incorporated into the structure, they were carefully concealed by pine panels. Once the new Township Line 86 highway opened in 1959, vehicle traffic was substantially reduced. The bridge was designated as a Provincial Heritage Site in 1960; it was listed in the Canadian Register of Historic Places in 2007.

Line 86 at 950 m/yd. This is a dangerous crossing as the road speed is 80 kph (50 mph), and there is no crosswalk. Nor is there good trail signage while on the road. I discovered that you must cross and continue straight on Middlebrook Road for another 250 m/yd to reach the trail.

There is excellent signage at this road and trail junction, which has gates limiting vehicle access to the trailway. Turn right, and the trail immediately enters an area of rich farmland. Almost every scrap of land nearby is cultivated, and it would be difficult to imagine a more prosperous-looking pastoral tableau. The trail gradually climbs above the fields onto an earthen embankment.

2.3 km (1.4 mi) The trail ends on the banks of the Grand River, where the eroded concrete abutments of the former railway bridge stand in the shallow water like multi-storey stepping stones placed too far apart to be used. A barricade prevents you from launching over the end of the embankment, which towers more than 20 m (66 ft) above the western riverbank. It is because this bridge was removed that the railway follows roads and passes through West Montrose.

A single discovery panel about the blue heron stands next to the barricade, where there are excellent views of the river. There is also a marker for the Grand Valley Trail, a 275 km (171 mi) hiking footpath which runs from Lake Erie north to

connect to the Bruce Trail. It follows the Grand River for a considerable distance and intersects The Great Trail at this location.

Retrace the 1.1 km (0.7 mi) back to Middlebrook Road and continue along the pathway on its far side. Once past the gates, a rustic-looking, wooden sign indicates that it is 6.5 km (4 mi) to Elmira and 13 km (8 mi) to Wallenstein. The treadway is almost sandy, crackling beneath your bike tires. Once again, large, prosperous-looking farms line both sides of the straight pathway.

A bench nearly covered by vegetation sits 400 m/yd from Middlebrook Road; it is followed by the km 15 marker at about 4 km (2.5 mi). Almost immediately afterwards, the path enters an area where cedars grow on both sides of the path, providing it with a vegetative barrier. At 4.8 km (3 mi), another interpretive panel (the black-capped chickadee) is positioned just before a short bridge spanning a tiny brook.

Returning to the open, the trailway passes through cornfields and orchards. The km 16 marker is passed just before crossing Northfield Drive East, where gates force you to slow and where trail signs indicate you should come to a complete stop. At each of these road access points, there is excellent information signage about the trail and its permitted uses.

The remaining 4 km (2.5 mi) to Elmira is mostly a relaxing ride through vast cornfields. I would recommend this ride as a late summer experience, when the agricultural bounty of these farms is on full display. At 7.2 km (4.5 mi), the trail passes between very close farm buildings, and a track for its machinery crosses the pathway. It is almost as if the farm was located so close to the trail to be on display.

Soon afterwards, Elmira's water tower can be seen in the distance above the trees. At 8.7 km (5.4 mi), the path enters the first place where it is lower than the adjacent terrain. This is a lovely area, a sylvan laneway with flanking trees providing overhead shade and protection from the wind. An unnamed side trail branches left in 150 m/yd.

Houses are now visible through the trees to the left; you are in Elmira, though still on the edge of the community. Another interpretive panel, this one about fiddleheads, is found at 9.2 km (5.7 mi), where there are now buildings on both sides of the Trailway. The path curves right, passing next to the large Elmira Pet Products plant, then reaches busy Arthur Street North 400 m/yd further on.

9.6 km (6 mi) Once across Arthur Street, the trail is bordered by fence posts and snakes between adjoining parking lots. Businesses are located on either side of the pathway, and downtown Elmira is only 450 m/yd to the left. Another wooden signpost provides a list of distances to upcoming communities.

The next gate across the trail is more than 100 m/yd from Arthur Street after the parking lots. On the opposite side of it, there is a sparkling new bicycle repair station, a garbage can, and a trail map. These are situated just before the sturdy steel bridge crossing the modest Canagagigue (not a typo) Creek. On the opposite side of the bridge is an interpretive panel about the monarch butterfly.

After this brief moment in an urban milieu, the buildings are left behind. To the left is forest while on the right is a wetland. Fringing the trail are a number of young trees on the right, each of which has a small plaque with a name at its base. Within 200 m/yd, it appears that this is an arboretum as there are dozens of labelled saplings planted in rows.

In reality, this is a "memorial forest," created by the Elmira Lions Club. In it, there are hundreds of trees, each donated and named in memory of an individual. They continue along the trail as it crosses Snyder Avenue North at 10.3 km (6.4 mi) and Larch Creek 500 m/yd further. And about 100 m/yd after the brook, there is a side trail to the left into a large open field that is also covered in these memorial trees, as well as a Lions Club pavilion, benches, a gazebo, and walking paths through this fascinating area.

The memorial trees continue alongside the Trailway until it crosses Larch Creek a second time at 11.1 km (6.9 mi). After they end, there is a golf course on the left and farmland to the right. When the trail crosses Larch Creek a third time, 400 m/yd later, there are benches beside the bridge. In fact, there are several benches throughout this section of pathway that borders Elmira, and I saw many walkers.

📍**12.3 km (7.6 mi)** The Trailway crosses Floradale Road, the last major highway before Wallenstein. At this point, the community of Elmira is far behind and only cultivated fields border the trail. There is a small parking area beside the road gate, but no other facilities. A wooden signpost says that 4 km (2.5 mi) remains to Wallenstein.

The remainder of the ride is pleasant with the scenery alternating between rich farms and occasional groves of lush hardwoods. At 13.3 km (8.3 mi), signs warn of a shooting range to the right, and another tiny brook is crossed 500 m/yd later. The warning signs continue all the way to quiet Reid Woods Drive at 14 km (8.7 mi). Between Floradale Road and Wallenstein, there is an irregular smattering of benches, some well positioned beneath overhanging trees, others apparently randomly placed.

Few trees shelter the pathway after crossing Reid Woods Drive, but cornfields return. The frugal Mennonite farmers clear all the brush and plant by hand rather than with large machines, so they are able to grow their corn within one or two metres/yards of the edge of the trail. There are few trees until the next dirt road, Blind Lane, at 15.2 km (9.4 mi).

A gorgeous hardwood forest follows, but this quickly gives way again to farmland, and for the first time, several of the fields have horses running about. As the trailway approaches Wallenstein, several large agricultural buildings are located close to the trail.

The final gate across the pathway comes several hundred metres/yards before reaching the road, and the last 50 m/yd of trail are actually used as a parking lot. Ornamental trees and scrubs have been planted in a small park bordering the path, and at the head of the parking area, there is a trailhead kiosk with a map.

16.4 km (10.2 mi) You arrive at Yatton Side Road. The trail appears to continue on the far side, but this route actually ends in about 200 m/yd at the parking area of Wallenstein Feed and Supply. To the left is the Harness Supply and Tack Shop.

Quite a few beautiful horses are corralled next to the pathway, and you might be able to entice one of them to share an apple, should you have one. Do not be surprised to see one of the Mennonite community's horses and buggies go past. One of the interesting idiosyncrasies of this area is that horses are permitted on the highway but not on the trail.

The Great Trail turns left and follows the road towards the community of St. Jacobs. The trailway continues in a different direction and resumes on the opposite side of the Conestogo River.

Return to West Montrose from here; it is only 14.2 km (8.8 mi) back to the trailhead, unless you wish to return to the edge of the Grand River. Otherwise, turn right when you reach Middlebrook Road.

Further Information:
Grand Valley Trail: www.gvta.on.ca
Kissing Bridge Trailway: www.kissingbridgetrailway.ca
Region of Waterloo Tourism: www.explorewaterlooregion.com

Ruffed Grouse

At risk of a heart attack? Frighten easily? Then be careful while hiking on any wooded trail. If you encounter a ruffed grouse, it is likely to remain very still until you are almost upon it then explode into noisy flight away from you through the brush. It is questionable whether it or you will make the loudest squawk!

Conversely, should you appear to threaten her brood of chicks in the spring, a mother grouse might charge towards you, puffing her feathers to double her normal size and hissing menacingly. Since we are talking about a small bird that looks like a wild chicken, your risk of injury is small. (Looks scary though!) I have never had a charging grouse come close to making contact with me.

The ruffed grouse is not migratory, so may be sighted at any time of year. It is relatively abundant and a popular game bird. In fact, one of its Latin names, *Bonasa*, means "good when roasted."

30. Waubaushene to Midland

Midland was one of the earliest communities in Canada to acquire its abandoned rail lines. A busy port, most of this small community's lakeshore was used for industrial purposes. Beginning in 1994, Midland began acquiring many abandoned properties, including several sections of Canadian National branch lines, in order to reclaim their waterfront. The community's goal, now realized, was to create pedestrian connections with the neighbouring communities of Penetanguishene and Tay.

In 2004, Canadian Pacific donated its abandoned rail line on the southern shore of Severn Sound to the Trans Canada Trail Foundation. It, in turn, gave the land to neighbouring municipalities so that they could develop it as a recreational trail. Tay Township opened its section in 2007.

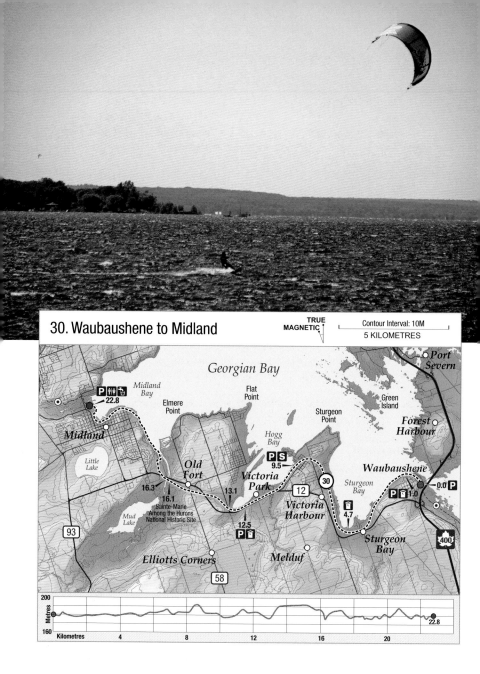

30. Waubaushene to Midland

TRUE
MAGNETIC

Contour Interval: 10M
5 KILOMETRES

Georgian Bay

Port
Severn

Midland
Bay

Flat
Point

Green
Island

Elmere
Point

Sturgeon
Point

Forest
Harbour

Hogg
Bay

Midland

Little
Lake

Old
Fort

Victoria
Park

P S
9.5

Waubaushene

30

Sturgeon
Bay

P
1.0

0.0 P

16.3

13.1

12

Victoria
Harbour

⚑
4.7

16.1
Sainte-Marie
Among the Hurons
National Historic Site

Mud
Lake

12.5
P

93

Elliotts Corners

Melduf

Sturgeon
Bay

400

58

200

Metres

160

Kilometres   4   8   12   16   20

22.8

30. Waubaushene to Midland

Distance: 22.8 km (14.2 mi) – one way
Ascent: 101 m (331 ft)
Descent: 102 m (335 ft)

Trail conditions: asphalt
Cellphone coverage: yes
Hazards: poison ivy, road crossings, ticks

					Permitted Uses		
Walking	Biking	Horseback Riding	Inline Skating	ATV	Snowshoeing	Cross-country Skiing	Snowmobiling
✔	✔	—	✔	—	✔	✔	✔*

Finding the trailhead: Begin your hike or bike at the Coldwater Road parkette in Waubaushene. There is a compact parking area — with room for only five cars — and a bench, picnic table, garbage can, interpretive panel, and very large trailhead kiosk featuring a map of the Tay Shore Trail.

Trailhead: 44°45'16.7"N, 79°42'15.3"W (Start — Waubaushene)
44°45'23.5"N, 79°53'50.5"W (Finish — Midland)

Observations: This was the final route that I hiked or biked in Ontario for this book, and I enjoyed it tremendously. Both the Tay and the Midland Rotary Trails were in excellent condition, with superb signage and first-rate facilities, and I particularly enjoyed the frequent views of Georgian Bay. It was also one of the busier rural trails that I encountered, with many walkers and cyclists.

I had intended to profile this route as far as the Penetanguishene waterfront but found automobile traffic and cycling conditions on Main Street to be just too challenging. I enjoyed this route until I reached the end of the off-road section at Murray Road in Penetanguishene, but I ultimately decided that ending it at Pete Pettersen Park in Midland, which – with its beach and picnic facilities – was more suitable.

Route description: The treadway is asphalt surfaced, wide, and smooth. It is rather noisy at the start because busy Highway 400 is only 150 m/yd away in the direction of Orillia. However, once you begin your ride through the quiet village, the traffic noise is soon left behind.

In the first few hundred metres/yards, the trail crosses several residential streets with unique gates blocking vehicle access to the pathway. Additional benches and several interpretive panels are found here as well, hinting at the large number of each on this route.

The trail curves left, reaching Pine Street at 950 m/yd. This is a lovely spot and your first view of the water. To the right is Waubaushene Beach and a pier extending out into Sturgeon Bay with wonderful views. Beside the trail sits a garbage can, an outhouse, and directional signs to local businesses.

Many yards, homes, and boathouses border the pathway. The shoreline of Severn Sound is a popular recreational destination as it is less than 200 km (124 mi) from downtown Toronto. Although a rural area, Tay Township is a busy place. Signs repeatedly warn trail users to respect private property because many people have unfenced yards and have placed flowering plants right to edge of the asphalt path. It is quite lovely here, almost like passing through an inhabited park.

At 1.6 km (1 mi) is a good lookout onto the water with two benches and an interpretive panel about Georgian Bay — almost as large as Lake Ontario. Not only is there a trash can here but, next to it, is a blue bin for recycling! The trail crosses Albin Road at 2.3 km (1.4 mi) and a parking and picnic area overlooking the water is on the right.

A few metres/yards later, the trail crosses Albin Road a second time, after which there is a short stretch where the cottages on the right are largely hidden by a buffering layer of vegetation. To the left is the undeveloped land of Waubaushene Beaches Provincial Park.

Tanners Road is crossed at 3 km (1.9 mi) after passing another bench, though with no view, and more information panels. About 600 m/yd beyond Tanners Road in an area of thick vegetation where no houses can be seen, another bench is set back from the trail on the left with a large, asphalted, pull-over area in front of it.

The trail reaches Duffy Drive in tiny Sturgeon Bay (population 95) at 4.2 km (2.6 mi), where busy Highway 12 and a service station are visible to the left. The first bridge on this route is in sight directly ahead, crossing Sturgeon River. The path makes a broad sweeping curve to the right as it works around the low, wet ground at the base of Sturgeon Bay. About 500 m/yd from the bridge is an outhouse, and 200 m/yd from that, there is another lookout with benches and several interpretive panels, overlooking the Sturgeon Bay Wetlands.

More benches and interpretive panels are situated in this stretch, which is bordered by swamp and wet ground on both sides. Yet another picnic table, garbage can, and recycling bin are found when the trail returns to higher ground and a forested area.

The next road crossing is at Caswell Road, at 6.2 km (3.9 mi). The trail's blue-and-white directional signs indicate that downtown Victoria Harbour is a further 3.2 km (2 mi) and has restaurants. From here, there are fewer wetlands, and consequently, adjacent houses are more frequent. The pathway still has a vegetated buffer, but cottages can often be sighted. Wildflowers grow in colourful profusion alongside the asphalt treadway.

The pathway continues straight, crossing the clearly signed Davis Drive and Bass Bay Road. There are additional benches and interpretive panels along the way, but since the Sturgeon Bay Wetlands, the water has not been visible. At 8.2 km (5.1 mi), the pathway begins curving to the left after crossing Industrial Road.

Oddly for a rail trail, there is a short climb before crossing Park Street 500 m/yd later. Once over the road, trees hug the trail more closely. At Ellen Street, 9.3 km (5.8 mi), the blue arrow indicates that a restaurant is 300 m/yd off the path to the right, and MacKenzie Park is 600 m/yd in the same direction and has washrooms.

📍**9.5 km (5.9 mi)** The trail reaches "downtown" Victoria Harbour at Albert Street. To the left is a large parking lot, with a grocery store and other businesses nearby. Houses, including large duplexes, are all around. Benches and picnic tables line the path, which is now bordered by mown lawn and newly planted trees.

On the right, Severn Sound is visible again and the small cove known as Hogg Bay. In sight from the trail and next to the water's edge, there is a small park with more tables and benches, where there is a boat launch. A marina is visible further away. This is a wonderful place to stop and have lunch.

The trail parallels a street for the next 500 m/yd until it reaches Eplett Park, where there are more picnic tables and fewer houses. However, in another 200 m/yd, the trail reaches more housing after crossing Winfield Drive. There are homes to either side now as the pathway makes its way towards busy – and noisy – Highway 12. At 10.9 km (6.8 mi), the trail reaches the bridge spanning Hogg River, where there is an access path from a parking area on the left.

A long, straight section follows, where the trail and Highway 12 run parallel to each other and quite close. This area is mostly wooded, often blocking the highway from view, but the traffic noise is a constant companion. Two more roads, Vents Beach and Reeves, are crossed before the trail arrives at Trestle Park, 12.5 km (7.8 mi).

> ### Sainte-Marie Among the Hurons Mission
>
> Barely twenty years after the founding of Québec City, Jesuit priests constructed a mission 1,200 km (746 mi) away in the heart of Wendat (Huron) territory. These zealous Jesuits were eager to spread Roman Catholicism to First Nations peoples and had already established themselves throughout the villages of the Wendat. However, they wished to create their own settlement, a place of refuge and retreat.
>
> It was not to be. By 1649, disease and constant Iroquois attacks forced the abandonment and destruction of the settlement, and within a year, the surviving priests and Christian Wendat fled to Québec City. Eight of Sainte-Marie's priests were martyred and were canonized in 1930. The nearby Martyr's Shrine commemorates their memory.
>
> Sainte-Marie Among the Hurons was designated a National Historic Site of Canada in 1920, and in 1964, it was rebuilt to be a living history museum. It remains a popular tourist attraction. (www.saintemarieamongthehurons.on.ca) (image pp. 308-09)

On the left is a large parking area, where there are outhouses. A bronze plaque describes how a very long, wooden trestle once crossed Hogg Bay at this point until it was dismantled in 1978; the trail passes one of the large, concrete pillars that had supported it. Interpretive panels, picnic tables, and benches are also found in this wooded parkette.

13.1 km (8.1 mi) The path arrives at the junction with the Trestle Trail, another rail trail, which branches right into the community of Port McNicoll. There is a large trailhead kiosk with a map on the main trail. You might also notice a marker for the Ganaraska Hiking Trail, which uses the Tay Shore Trail as part of its route. Watch for white-paint flashes on some of the trees; this is their directional signage.

Triple Bay Road is crossed 100 m/yd past the trail junction, after which forest closes in tightly to the pathway on both sides. At 14 km (8.7 mi), there is an interesting, picnic table location next to an interpretive panel for a short piece of rail with a handcart atop it. Just 500 m/yd later, the trail passes through a very short tunnel with Highway 12 crossing overhead. At 15.1 km (9.4 mi), Old Fort Road also crosses but is just an overhead bridge.

Thick forest is to the left through the Wye Marsh National Wildlife Area. The next bench is positioned next to a bridge 200 m/yd from Old Fort Road, where there is a parallel track for motorized use. The Wye Marsh Road is crossed at 15.9 km (9.9 mi). Once over this road, a vast parking area becomes visible to the left and large buildings after that.

Two hundred m/yd from the road, you come to a large trailhead map sign and an access path to the Sainte-Marie Among the Hurons Mission National Historic Site. The palisade of the rebuilt mission abuts the trail for the next 100 m/yd until the bridge crosses the broad Wye River. Interpretive panels provide a brief history of the former Jesuit Mission.

16.3 km (10.1 mi) Once across the Wye River, you are travelling on the Midland Rotary Trail, and actually entering a short section where snowmobiles are permitted. The trail crosses over four-lane Highway 12 in 250 m/yd and then passes a number of large industrial buildings. For the first time, the treadway sports a painted, yellow centre line.

After initially following the abandoned rail line, the pathway makes a sharp 90° right turn off the railbed at 17.3 km (10.8 mi); snowmobiles continue straight. The path drops down towards the Wye River, intersecting another pathway in 200 m/yd where you turn left. Almost immediately, the trail runs behind a row of houses, separated from their backyards by only a chain-link fence.

At 17.8 km (11 mi), the trail reaches Tiffin Basin at the base of Midland Bay. The pathway makes a left turn and begins to follow the shoreline, quite close to the water's edge. A huge marina comes into view to the right.

The treadway is now concrete, and for a considerable distance, the trail is nothing more than a narrow passage between houses and the water, tightly bounded by fences on both sides. The path even needs to make a detour around a multi-storey apartment building, which is almost on the lakeshore. Yet this is a lovely area, a typical municipal recreation space with many benches, connecting paths, gazebos, interpretive panels, and other amenities. The fences tightly edging the pathway might make it feel a bit claustrophobic, especially when there are oncoming cyclists, but the view is splendid.

The trail continues to be wedged between houses and their boat docks until it passes a trail gate at 19.6 km (12.2 mi) and enters a wider greenspace with a large inukshuk. From here, the trail climbs up to Aberdeen Street then resumes alongside the road. At the junction of Bayshore and William Streets, where it crosses the entrance to Midland Bay Landing Park, the path begins to follow alongside the road like a sidewalk. The concrete treadway ends here, returning to asphalt.

The trail climbs up Bayshore Drive, and at 20.7 km (12.9 mi) – the highest point – there is a lookout with a parking area, a flag pole, benches, and several interpretive panels. An easy downhill ride follows with the greenspace widening and the pathway moving further away from Bayshore Drive as you descend.

The path passes a large playground and crosses the entrance to Central Marina, but when it reaches King Street at 21.4 km (13.3 mi), the off-road section ends, leaving you to traverse an extremely busy parking area on a painted track. Fortunately, this on-road component lasts barely 200 m/yd until the off-road pathway resumes opposite First Street. (There is a coffee shop there if you need to fortify yourself.)

The path continues passing through the Midland waterfront beside some grain silos. After following a rail trail for 600 m/yd, your route turns sharply right, bringing you to a wooded area right on the water's edge. Multiple footpaths connect and cross here, and teens perch on the rocks, swimming and playing on the remains of concrete docks.

22.8 km (14.2 mi) The trail emerges from the forest into an open space at Pete Pettersen Park. To the left is a baseball diamond, and on the right is a beach. The off-road path ends at its parking lot, where there is a small building with washrooms and a trail map. Benches and picnic tables are scattered throughout the greenspace. End your hike or bike here and maybe have a swim. When ready, retrace your route back to Waubaushene.

Further Information:

Ganaraska Hiking Trail: http://ganaraska-hiking-trail.org
Midland Recreational Trails: http://www.midland.ca/Pages/Recreational-Trails. aspx
Tay Township (Trail page): www.tay.ca/en/living-here/Tay-Shore-Trail.asp
Tourism Simcoe County: https://experience.simcoe.ca

Red Pine

Also known as the Norway pine, this tree was favoured for use as wharf and bridge pilings, power poles, and other purposes requiring a sturdy wood that could be easily treated with tar or pitch for resistance to rot. Red pine was also used for ship masts, and its heartwood was popular for ship decks. Because of its commercial value, almost all the old-growth red pines in the province have been harvested.

A red pine adds one row of spreading branches each year during its up to 350-year lifespan and grows to a height of 24 m (79 ft). Its bark is reddish brown with broad, flat, scaly plates. The needles come in bundles of two that are slender, whorled, and dark green year round. Red pines prefer well-drained soils, particularly sand plains, and usually grow in mixed forests rather than pure stands.

Acknowledgements

So many people have assisted with this book that it makes for an imposing list. Nevertheless, I have attempted to mention every person who helped me – at least, all those whose names I recorded. After all, without their participation and knowledge, I could not have written this book.

However, in addition to these people, there were dozens of others that I met and spoke to as I walked and cycled these many trails, "ordinary Canadians," who were themselves enjoying the pathways. From them I heard personal stories of how much the trails meant to them and how much the concept of The Great Trail (Trans Canada Trail) excited their imagination. I appreciated their candour and enthusiasm.

In order to choose those sections of The Great Trail that could be characterized as "the best," I contacted the various provincial organizations that are developing the trail. The following individuals are those who suggested what I might select as their provinces' finest:

Dan Andrews, (former) General Manager, Trans Canada Trail Ontario
Ruth Delong, Trails Community Relations Coordinator, Confederation Trail
Vanda Jackson, Executive Director, Nova Scotia Trails Federation
Poul Jorgensen, Sentiers NB Trails
Blaise MacEachern, Nova Scotia Trails Federation
Al MacPherson, General Manager, Trans Canada Trail Ontario
Kevin Maillet, Marketing and Communications Coordinator, Sentiers NB Trails
Terry Morrison, Newfoundland T'Railway
Jane Murphy, National Director of Trail/Directrice nationale du Sentier, Trans Canada Trail/Sentier Transcanadien
Melissa Pomeroy, (former) General Manager, Trans Canada Trail Ontario
Richard Senécal, Directeur exécutif, Conseil québécois du sentier Transcanadien
Adrian Tanner, Director, East Coast Trails Association
Holly Woodill, President, Nova Scotia Trails Federation

After I had completed hiking and/or biking the various pathways, I contacted various trail management authorities to determine whether my facts were accurate and to obtain additional information. The following list includes those who provided the route suggestions and also a number of helpful community trail managers. I know that there were more; I greatly apologize if I missed mentioning you.

Bryan Anderson, Manager of Parks, Recreation & Facilities, Township of Tay
Mike Bender, Associate Director, Master Planning and Greenspace Conservation, Toronto and Region Conservation Authority
Corey Burant, Niagara River Pathway

Don Cook, Trails Coordinator, Township of Uxbridge
Bruce Devine, National Capital Commission
Amanda Ferraro, Manager of Recreation, Culture & Tourism, Township of Uxbridge
Michael Goodyear, Trail Development Eastern Canada, Trans Canada Trail
Robert Gould, volunteer, Butter Trail, Tatamagouche
Jack Griffin, Grand River Conservation Authority
Jim Hazen, volunteer, Cataraqui Trail
Jason Hynes, Lands Planner, Cataraqui Region Conservation Authority
Marlaine Koehler, Executive Director, Waterfront Regeneration Trust
Nancy Lockerbie, Fundy Trail Parkway
Kevin Money, Chrysler Canada Greenway
Randy Murphy, President, East Coast Trail Association
Mark Schmidt, Trails Analyst/Analyste des Sentiers, Parks Canada/Parcs Canada

I also want to thank Paul Smith and Catherine Chandler, who permitted me to live in their guest house, so I could write this book. I needed a private space, and they made it available – and fed me too! A number of people generously provided me with a comfortable bed and meals for one or more evenings of my trek as I travelled through eastern Canada. This was appreciated more than they probably realized, so thanks to the following:

Kay Haynes, Toronto
Robert Hingley, Montréal
Ron Hunt and Ruth Oswald, Ottawa
Claire MacNeil, Creignish
Terry Morrison, Gander
Charles Stuart, Kitchener
Adrian Tanner, Petty Harbour

Perhaps most importantly, I wish to thank the thousands of volunteers in hundreds of communities who laboured for so many years to make The Great Trail/Trans Canada Trail a reality in their neighbourhoods. Without their enthusiasm and dedication, there would be no Great Trail today to hike and bike.

As Executive Director of the Nova Scotia Trails Federation from 1993 to 2003, I attended countless meetings of community trail associations throughout the province, and always marvelled at the ardour and fierce pride with which they tackled their projects. It was never easy, particularly in the first years when so many of the concepts were new and being attempted for the first time. Their perseverance in the face of so many challenges and such frequent disappointments was amazing. I could not do what they did; credit for the successful fulfillment of The Trans Canada Trail / Great Trail dream belongs to them.

Index

Michael Haynes is one of the leading authorities on trail development in Canada and the author of numerous trail guides covering Nova Scotia, Prince Edward Island, the National Capital Region, and Western Quebec. He is also a travel writer and regular commentator for CBC Radio. His travel articles have appeared in *Ottawa Magazine*, *Saltscapes*, and *Explore*.